The Poetry
of Melville's Late Years

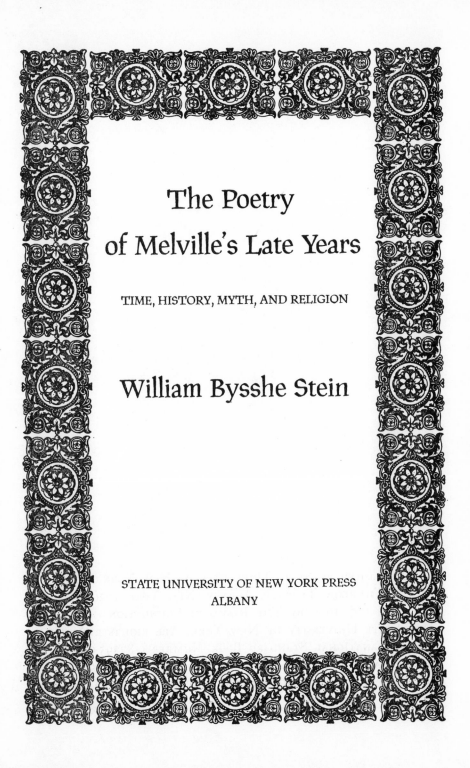

The Poetry
of Melville's Late Years

TIME, HISTORY, MYTH, AND RELIGION

William Bysshe Stein

STATE UNIVERSITY OF NEW YORK PRESS
ALBANY

Published by State University of New York Press
Thurlow Terrace, Albany, New York 12201
© 1970 by The Research Foundation
of State University of New York. All rights reserved
International Standard Book Number 0-87395-056-9
Library of Congress Catalog Card Number 73-91203
Printed in the United States of America

For my brother Charlie

*No murderer can still
the stormy symphonies
of your conviviality.
The innocent rage
of your thunderclapping voice
and laughter
will always echo
in the high mountains of memory.*

Table of Contents

Acknowledgments

PARTS OR THE WHOLE of several chapters of this study have appeared earlier in various college journals. I am grateful to the following editors for their permission to reprint the articles in the revisions necessitated by the perspective of a book: Leonard Manheim, *Literature and Psychology*, for "Melville's Poetry: Its Symbols of Individuation"; Albert Frank Gegenheimer, *The Arizona Quarterly*, for "Time, History, and Religion: A Glimpse of Melville's Late Poetry"; Paul Bernstein, *The Lock Haven Review*, for "Melville and the Creative Eros." I am likewise obliged to The Johns Hopkins Press for the permission on "The Old Man and the Triple Goddess: Melville's 'The Haglets'" which was published in *Journal of English Literary History*. For the permission to quote freely from *Collected Poems of Herman Melville* (ed. Howard P. Vincent) and to use a passage from *Clarel* (ed. Walter E. Bezanson), I am indebted to the publisher, Hendricks House, Inc.

The initial research on this study was subsidized by a fellowship from the Bollingen Foundation, and I cannot conceive of a patron of arts and letters that could be more generous and considerate to a grantee.

Every undertaking of this sort leaves one indebted to countless individuals. There are the students in my seminars on Melville's poetry at Washington and Jefferson College who sharpened my insights into the originality of his craftsmanship. There are old friends like Howard and Sally Goldfarb whose intellectual stimulation contributed immensely to my relish for the project. There are those two anonymous readers who approved publication of the manuscript and who helped to remedy certain inconsistencies in the presentation of my arguments. There is Harry R. Warfel, the graduate professor whose encouragement launched my career in critical writing. Then there are two of my present colleagues in the English Department at the State University of

ACKNOWLEDGMENTS

New York at Binghamton: Bernard Rosenthal whose perceptive reading of the manuscript led to innumerable stylistic changes and Bernard F. Huppé whose counsel at crucial times was always available. Finally, there is my wife Gertrude, the inspiration for all my adventures in the academic world.

Introduction

I Introduction

EVERY SIGNIFICANT NEW POET (and so I deem Melville) changes the definition of poetry, and his innovations, whatever they are, preclude impartial evaluation by the old and familiar standards of craftsmanship. The contemporary critics and scholars (the historical arbiters of artistic talent) are too prone to view the search for originality with suspicion, and they are reluctant to admit that appreciation often lags behind creation, sometimes for centuries. On the American scene Emily Dickinson was a victim of such conservatism, and yet today she is cherished as one of the greatest poets of all times. I do not predict a similar requital for Melville's poetry, though eventually it is bound to be read with more pleasure and understanding.

A flippant observation by Randall Jarrell, "Melville is a great poet only in the prose of *Moby-Dick*,"[1] helps to place the neglect of the latter's poetic achievement in perspective. Not living up to the lyrical expectations heralded by the language of the novel, it is looked upon as the labored output of an exhausted talent. This opinion is perfectly appropriate if the technical qualities are appraised in accordance with the virtuosity of the great nineteenth-century poets. Then Melville's verse has to be adjudged crude and unpolished. Its hobbled metrics, its stumbling rimes, its contorted language: none of these would make sense to an ear conditioned by the cadences of Shelley, Byron, Keats, Tennyson, Arnold, or even Longfellow (underrated though he is). But since we are concerned with the reaction to Melville's poetry after the revival of his literary reputation in the 1920's, it would seem that his critics have been strangely delinquent. Whereas they have been able to culti-

[1] *Poetry and the Age* (New York, 1953), p. 112.

3

vate the kind of awareness necessary to engage the originality of *The Confidence-Man*, they have not done so with the poetry—at least, not without apologizing for Melville's recalcitrance in renouncing inherited traditions. Yet there is no reason for this attitude. It is common knowledge that Melville chose to write as he did. As any cursory examination of his holograph manuscripts indicates, he was a painstaking reviser, finicky in his choice of diction and in his strategy of prosody, of course, as these were dictated by his own theory of poetry. As illustrated by his practices, its touchstone was earthbound factuality. Very consciously he set out to give embodiment to unmitigated experience, to events and emotions consistent with the nature of existence. Or put another way, he undertook to de-romanticize the idealistic view of human destiny that colors the traditions of English and American poetry during the nineteenth century. Thus he exalted the temporal over the eternal, the empirical over the mystical, the flesh over the spirit. The more he wrote poetry the more he became convinced that the measured euphony of verse belied experiental reality, and as a consequence he finally settled upon ugly discordance and incongruity—in meter, rime, image, symbol, and language—as the indices of truth in the finite world. Thus his poetry has to be judged in terms of his realization of a revolutionary method: no other standard has valid application.

During the last thirty-five years of his life Melville wrote mostly poetry, and that published at the beginning, *Battle-Pieces* (1866) and *Clarel* (1876), differs radically in execution from the late work, *John Marr and Other Sailors* (1888), *Timoleon* (1891), and the collection that he was assembling just before his death (1891). During the interim he resolved a tormenting psychological and spiritual crisis, learning that metaphysics and theology were intellectual poison for his volatile temperament. And this is the wisdom that he seeks to articulate in his old age. Nevertheless in *Battle-Pieces* he first realizes that orthodox poetics cannot be accommodated to his vision of life.[2] Extremely disturbed by the ir-

[2] Hennig Cohen's edition (New York, 1963) contains an informative introduction and some interesting notes.

rational animosities awakened by the Civil War, he sets out to etch a verbal picture of the conflict that will objectively display the impact of the warfare upon individuals from both sides, the military participants and the civilians. While forced by convention to pay tribute to loyalist patriotism, he equally lauds the bravery and fortitude of the contending forces—his gesture of justice and pity for all. But only the latter two sentiments really have meaning for Melville. The former virtues are tainted by the circumstances of the struggle, by the conversion of man into a puppet of his own technological ingenuity, a thing controlled by the things of destruction, from cannons to ironclad ships. Once this aspect of Melville's outlook obtrudes, the historical moment loses its significance, for the horror of war evolves into the horror of human nature in war, as illustrated by this quotation from "At the Cannon's Mouth," a beautifully ironical title:

> Palely intent, he urged his keel
>   Full on the guns, and touched the spring;
> Himself involved in the bolt he drove
> Timed with armed hull's shot that stove
> His shallop—die or do!
> Into the flood his life he threw,
>   Yet lives—unscathed—a breathing thing
> To marvel at.
>   He has his fame;
> But that mad dash at death, how name?

Insidious disparagement of this sort continually works to undermine Melville's often excessive praise of heroism, and as a result one wonders about the interpretation of the last three lines of the poem:

> That scorn of life which earns life's crown;
> Earns, but not always wins; but he—
> The star ascended in his nativity.[3]

Does the above manic act so skillfully fused into the kinetic meter, the inverted syntax, and the crazy dropped half-line figure the mo-

[3] *Collected Poems of Herman Melville,* ed. Howard P. Vincent (Chicago, 1947), pp. 82–83. Hereafter all parenthetical page references are to this edition.

tivation behind all self-martyrdoms? Then next, is the "he" a surrogate of the Christ-child? Was *He* a man, not a God? Was He
too the prisoner of a compulsive passion? Is there any difference
between the belief that a single life can save a nation or all of mankind? Such are the questions that Melville raises in the body of the
poem. Used again and again though not always successfully, this
rhetorical tactic casts doubt upon those exegeses of *Battle-Pieces*
which take his biblical and Miltonic imagery seriously—that is, af-
firmatively. The hyperbolic fatuity of so many of Melville's analogies—the battlefield as a wilderness and an agonistic stage; God as
the avenging Jehovah of the Union cause; the Southern generals
as Lucifer, Moloch, Belial, Mammon, and Dagon; the Northern
leaders as Michael and Raphael; the bloodless head-cracking of the
War in Heaven as the equivalent of the carnage by rifle, cannon,
and bayonet—reduces the war to utter folly and madness wholly
without any moral justification. Though he does not withhold compassion for the dead, the maimed, or the bereaved, he nonetheless
insists that disillusion is the inevitable product of illusion and delusion for all who court the glory of Mars.

A stanza from "The Scout toward Aldie" objectifies this attitude in an incongruous mixture of idiom and meter:

> By the hospital-tent the cripples stand—
>   Bandage, and crutch, and cane, and sling,
> And palely eye the brave array;
> The froth of the cup is gone for them
>   (Caw! caw! the crows through the blueness wing):
> Yet these were late as bold, as gay;
> But Mosby—a clip, and grass is hay. (p. 119)

Unaccustomed to antipoetic verse, a reader may logically scorn this
effort as aborted doggerel, yet there is an unforgettable picture
evoked by the method. The sequence of metonyms in the second
line parades the horrors of war before the eye, and then the next
line reverses the perspective with the jarring romantic image of
"brave array." Centered in the midst of the disarrayed sound-pattern of the first five lines, the phrase likewise emphasizes the ma-
cabre humor of the rime, "sling" and "wing," for certainly Mel-

6

ville is aware of the definition of the latter word (wound). The final couplet, of course, looks back in an identical fashion, crystallizing the total irony of the situation in the bizarre analogy with grass and hay. Mosby, incidentally, is the name of a cunning rebel officer whose raids on Union positions were sudden and deadly, like those of the crows on their prey. The reference to the crows in their implicit connection with death is bitterly sardonic. The repetition of "caw" echoes a distinct hah, hah, the voice of the trailing "blueness," the heavens or, by extension, God. Structurally, then, the interlinked relations of this stanza exemplify the way Melville exploits a system of atonalities to ridicule the inherent absurdity of heroism.

"The Portent," the introductory poem of *Battle-Pieces*, is a parodic masterpiece that foreshadows the subtle techniques of Melville's late creative activity. Actually written in honor of the revolutionist John Brown, it is revolutionary in conception and execution, an exquisitely controlled mechanism of irony which dramatizes the stagnation of Christian love:

> Hanging from the beam,
>   Slowly swaying (such the law),
> Gaunt the shadow on your green,
>   Shenandoah!
> The cut is on the crown
>   (Lo, John Brown),
> And the stabs shall heal no more. (p. 3)

The casual "such the law" embodies a dismissive comment on the moral authority of the New Testament. No longer do the scriptures influence the conduct of human affairs. In the case of John Brown on the gallows, society has surrendered the covenant of love to the laws of physics and of statutes. This particular association inspires Melville to cloak his rhetoric in the imagery of Psalm XXIII, the traditional symbolic epitome of the sacraments of Baptism and Holy Communion. The Shenandoah Valley is an obvious inversion of the "green pastures": it is "the valley of the shadow of death" from which there is no deliverance, at least if the practice of Christianity is any criterion of the validity of religious faith.

7

As the scapegoat of hypocritical legalism, John Brown is a mock Christ. His crown of glory is a wound inflicted on the head by his captors, and the stabs of bayonets are the counterparts of the spikes that impaled Christ on the cross. In contradiction of the last verse in the Psalm, "Surely goodness and mercy shall follow me all the days of my life: and I will dwell in the house of the Lord for ever," John Brown is the victim of a mistaken belief in the brotherhood of man, the equality of all His children. To modulate this crucifixion of idealism Melville brings into play a fantastic assortment of rhythmical devices. The initial trochees in each of the first four lines, reenforced by alliterative stress and a combination of vowel and consonant rimes, generate the mournful cadence of a tolling bell. This effect operates to transform the swaying body into the knell of moral failure symbolized by the event at Shenandoah, the name assimilating the total weight of the sound-pattern. The last three lines, a spate of monosyllables, are deliberately shorn of the grim solemnity of the first part of the stanza because Melville wants to evoke the bloody horror of the scene. Thus "cut" and "crown" mutually stress one another, and the spondaic refrain, like the sonorous Shenandoah, absorbs the ironical implications of the alliteration. The last line with its anapest brakes the flow of the measure, accentuating the finality of "no more," the martyrdom without redress in heaven or on earth. Unquestionably, Melville here exhibits a great poetic talent, welding together form and thought with dazzling finesse.

The last stanza is no less supurb in its rendered disharmonies. Charged with reverberations of the crucifixion, it parodies the experience of Christ on the cross when, in a moment of inconsolable despair, he cried: "My God, my God, why hast thou forsaken me?" For what Melville attempts to recapture in these lines is John Brown's unutterable sense of alienation from all things:

> Hidden in the cap
>   Is the anguish none can draw;
> So your future veils its face,
>   Shenandoah!

> But the streaming beard is shown
> (Weird John Brown),
> The meteor of the war. (p. 3)

Melville's incongruous recourse to "cap" instead of hood evokes the absurdity and pathos of John Brown's condition. As a mocking extension of the earlier "crown," it reduces his appearance to that of a scarecrow; and as an implicit pun on head, it calls primary attention to his mental agony that "none can draw." Though the latter situation can be taken literally as hidden from view, actually the experience in question is the shock of incredulity—the parallel to the disillusionment of Christ. Confronting his failure on the scaffold, John Brown also confronts a crisis in faith—the doubt in the existence of God, even as suggested in the analogy with Shenandoah. The beard hanging out of the hood (the traditional mark of the biblical prophets) is the flag of despair and defeat. A double scapegoat, of the times and of his own fanaticism, he dies futilely, heralding the futile struggle of the Civil War. This experience is reflected in the antipoetic prosody of the stanza—the deceptive half rimes and the jarring meter, not to overlook the reciprocal discord of the two terminal phrases "no more" and "the war." Once again Melville evinces a rare ability to versify complex emotions.

The meagre sampling which I have presented exaggerates the creative achievement of *Battle-Pieces*. More often than not, Melville's experiments in rhythmical atonality do not succeed, probably as a consequence of his own uncertainty about the method. In the longer poems there are frequent lapses in figurative language, an addiction to the commonplace in image and analogy that is tasteless and trite. Such flaws occur mostly when Melville shackles his thought in rigid metrical forms which force compromises in acuity of expression. This is to say that he writes most cogently when he disregards conventional mechanics and allows his thought to find its own mold. Then his perceptions evolve with thorny sharpness, couched in a diction and rhythm pregnant with the immediate realities of the subject, not affected or strained, not wishy-washy or insincere. Nevertheless, given the climate of opinion when he composed *Battle-Pieces,* his performance is quite extraordinary, providing a glimpse of war that can be compared only to Goya's paintings of military carnage. No such candor nor integrity about war had ever before governed the composition of poetry—not excluding Walt Whitman's.

Unlike *Battle-Pieces,* Melville's *Clarel* is essentially a personal creation, a product of psychological necessity. It represents a deliberate attempt to face up to a crippling pessimism about the basic corruption of human nature—an outlook far darker than any articulated by the most fanatical Calvinist. The various personas in the poem think out, feel out, and act out all the problems inherent in this plight, providing him with an arsenal of defense mechanisms. Though nothing is finally resolved, Melville does empty himself of the most virulent emotional and spiritual poisons. An excerpt from one of his wife's letters in 1876 confirms the neurotic origins of the work: "If ever this dreadful *incubus* of a *book* (I call it so because it has undermined all our happiness) gets off Herman's shoulders I do hope he may be in better mental health." [4] The narrative of a pilgrimage to the Holy Land is based on the journey that his family forced him to take in 1856–57 when he was threatened with a nervous breakdown (the euphemism for impending madness so carefully employed by contemporary biographers and critics). Though the volume was not published until twenty years after the therapeutic holiday, its composition over a period of some six years was always freshened by observations and meditations from a journal that he had kept. What self-torture the reliving of the past involved is depicted in the opening lines of the poem. Anticipating Rodin's sculpture of *The Thinker,* Melville evokes the despair of a thinker undone by thinking:

> In chamber low and scored by time,
> Masonry old, late washed with lime—
> Much like a tomb new-cut in stone;
> Elbow on knee, and brow sustained

[4] Jay Ledya, *The Melville Log* (New York, 1951), 2, 747.

> All motionless on sidelong hand,
> A student sits, and broods alone.[5]

By no coincidence, the later poetry celebrates his emancipation from the illusion that human thought is the solution to unhappiness. Without Melville's conscious awareness, the poem argues that ideas per se have no permanent validity, especially as applied to human acts. In their impact upon the mind they take the coloring of an individual's complex conditioning, and as a consequence every expression or implementation of a belief assumes the form of an unconscious prejudice. In short, it is impossible to view reality objectively, except to the extent that the laws of nature are immutable. This knowledge shapes the philosophy of Melville's old age, providing him a belated reconciliation with the treacheries of existence.

The riming iambic tetrameter is the norm measure for the six hundred odd pages of *Clarel*, and not even the most beguiling sophistries can justify Melville's stubborn allegiance to this monotonous pattern of verse. Since it is not easily adaptable to the subtleties of metaphysical discourse, Melville is betrayed into countless infelicities of execution: grotesque inversions, tortured ellipses, banal rimes, expedient archaisms, distorted word forms, and limping rhythms. These flaws unite to convey the effect of a bewildering prosiness that defies categorization. Stiff, stuffy, and stultifying, the style is out of key with the subject of the poem. Of course, on occasions the octosyllables are extremely effective in descriptive passages and in exchanges of dialogue, but, generally speaking, they produce a crudeness of expression that undermines the sober and formal tone of the narration. If there is an explanation for this programmatic mode of versification, it has to be psychological. The prodigious effort involved in maintaining the meter and manipulating the rime of thousands of lines served to impose a semblance of order upon the disorder of his internal life, giving Melville the sense that his consciousness was the mediating agency of his emo-

[5] *Clarel: A Poem, and Pilgrimage in the Holy Land*, ed. Walter E. Bezanson (New York, 1960), p. 3.

tions. Actually *Clarel* is a psychograph of his warring spiritual beliefs.

The chief value of the poem is probably biographical. There are numerous allusions to books that profoundly influenced his thought, and they span a wide range of subject matter. But except for contemporary writings on science and religion, most of Melville's reading is just as easy to pinpoint in his fiction. His taste was both esoteric and exoteric all of his life, but from one period to another in his career he responded to the same ideas quite differently. What we miss in *Clarel* is the jocular seriousness of *Moby-Dick*, where the ideas of the great thinkers were convenient grist for the buoyant imagination. In the poem he is the protesting prisoner of too many protesting iconoclasts. As such, then, *Clarel* is a special book in the Melville canon, not the product of the emancipated creative activity of the 1850's.

Since both *Clarel* and *Battle-Pieces* are constricted expressions of his poetic talent, they do not figure at all in this critical study. Melville's late poetry flowers out of the rich soil of emotional and spiritual contentment. It is written in a mood of quiet exultation. Even though his recurrent subjects are still disaster, death, defeat, suffering, and frustration, they are treated with a resilient irony. The old bugaboo of dualism no longer haunts his mind, and he revels in the exposure of Manichean fancies and fantasies. While he is not at peace with the aspirations of his times, he is at peace with the wisdom of old age. Thus what he has to say, he says with candor, simplicity, and probity. Speaking through innumerable personas—old and young, male and female, ancient and modern, biblical and legendary, historical and mythological—Melville rarely distorts objective truth, even where subjective feeling is deeply rooted. For the most part he cultivates an ironic detachment from his subject matter, adapting his rhetoric to the peculiarities of individual situation and sensibility (especially in the handling of his own recollections of experience). However, on occasions there are clumsy, disconcerting lapses in imaginative expression, a seemingly inexplicable recourse to folksy archaisms, trite figures, and gushing colloquialisms. But these breaches of poetic decorum are consistent with his deceptive employment of grating literalities, and are an indication of his desire to underscore the crudeness of ordinary existence. And it is in this sense that Melville changes the definition of poetry, at least as understood by his contemporaries. He refuses to be governed by the traditional conventions of prosody, diction, form, and theme. Apparently he is convinced that his vision of reality, as strictly defined by personal interests, associations, and memories, has to be articulated in a harsh, forthright manner, without undue concern with sublime thoughts or idealistic fancies (a far cry from the great white whale of creative aspiration so familiar to most of his readers). Nevertheless Melville still retains an early habit of composition. He delights in the pleasure of ulteriority, of saying one thing and meaning another, of saying one thing in terms of another. In effect, his metaphors work deep beneath the surface of his poems, always requiring close analysis.

John Marr and Other Sailors invites precisely such an approach. The poems in this collection are all matter-of-fact in situation, with many of them characterized by sudden shifts in style and tone and by unexpected dislocations of syntax and meter. This sort of originality (or perverseness) is apt to stagger or poison the judgment of the critic. But if it is taken for granted that Melville is in rebellion against the romantic subjectivity of so much nineteenth-century verse, then his achievement has to be measured by other standards of appreciation or excellence. As even a cursory reading discloses, the poems are bizarre impressions of things-as-they-are in the contingent universe. Generally speaking, they project the radical limitations of finite existence, the pathos and bathos of the human condition when observed with disinterested eyes. The world of John Marr and the other sailors reflects the cold neutrality of nature, the setting of life in which the absence of God is as self-evident as the inevitability of suffering and death. This fact inspires literally hundreds of chortling blasphemies on the absurdity of belief in a supernatural power. A kind of Freudian in his old age, Melville also relates the basic insecurity of experience to unsuspected psychosexual anxieties and disturbances which are induced by the frustrations of hope and desire. Moreover, he couches

13

these insights in patterns of mythic imagery which embrace the now commonly recognized archetypes of the unconscious. In short, his relentless focus on the inherent disorder of things coincides with his antipoetic rhetorical practices.

Timoleon complements the vision of *John Marr and Other Sailors*. This volume of poems catalogues the human subterfuges which down through time have been employed to build up defenses for the ego against the marauding forces of historical contingency. According to Melville, the instinctual appetites provide escapes from reality no less delusory than infatuations with the importance of art, science, religion, philosophy, and politics. Surveying the rise and decline of the great civilizations of the past, he is unable to arrive at any significant distinction between the self-reliance and the self-deception of prideful cultural attainments, either material or intellectual. As Melville finally resolves this paradox in the terminal poem of the collection, he concludes that in the face of ultimate oblivion the grandest human aspirations are a waste of energy and ingenuity. For him there is nothing that can order the blundering course of history and of life. This outlook on the futility of existence determines the execution of the poems. Less startling and contorted in formal organization and more traditional in diction and imagery, though by no means without crusty innovations in perceptual detail, he relies chiefly upon the play of irony and wit in conveying his thought. Except in the few instances where he tacitly exalts the transcendent value of artistic creation, he invariably undercuts literal meaning through tonal incongruities produced by his analogies. Such discordances are his substitute for the wrenchings of form and language in *John Marr and Other Sailors*. From this point of view, then, *Timoleon* captures Melville in his conservative moments of poetic experimentation.

The manuscript collections, *Weeds and Wildings, with A Rose or Two* and *Marquis de Grandvin,* offer a reinterpretation of the terrors of time, and once again Melville's rhetoric is carefully molded into angular and twisted, if not grotesque, expressional forms. However, he tempers the cynicism and pessimism of the two previous collections. Now he posits a formula of reconciliation:

the revival of Dionysian worship. No longer dismayed by the defects of mortality, he insists that the unchanging cycle of the year in its rhythm of birth, death, and rebirth attests the continuity of existence, though not of individual organisms. Cosmic becoming is viewed as an eternal succession of rounds in which the same reality is made, unmade, and remade. On this basis Melville argues that the preoccupation of advanced civilizations with historical determinism obviates a genuine psychological adjustment to the contingent manifestations of time, to the inevitable disillusionments of finitude. In accordance with this logic he ridicules the nineteenth-century obsession with evolutionary political, economic, social, and moral progress—the delusion that human effort can transform the world into a paradise. He also finds the linear timetable of Christian salvation incompatible with the cyclical scheme of things. These negative attitudes culminate in his buoyant consecration of the fecund energies of nature and the sexual gustos of man. Needless to say, Melville has to resort to indirection in order to convey most of these iconoclastic sentiments. On the one hand, he affects all sorts of bumpkin poses so that he can slyly poke fun at the self-deceptions lurking behind the pompous ideals of Victorian culture. On the other, he masks his celebration of Dionysian freedom in a torrent of hilarious puns, euphemisms, and double entendres. In effect, both *Weeds and Wildings* and *Marquis de Grandvin* reveal that Melville has finally resolved the agonizing moral and emotional conflicts of his middle years. This fact is evident not only in the themes of the poems but also in the manner of their execution: what he has to say, he says the way he wants to—be damned tradition!

A similar independence has to be exercised in the judgment of the entire body of Melville's late poetry. Its originalities prohibit the arbitrary application of conventional standards of craftsmanship. Since the disharmonies of form and style are apparently programmatic, the critic cannot simply condemn Melville for artistic ineptitude. Every serious poet sets out to change the definition of poetry, and his means of doing so have to be tolerated, especially in this particular case where the complacent tastes of a closed socièty are being defiantly challenged. Thus my analyses of Melville's poetry take his manipulated clumsiness for granted, focussing primarily on his strategies of imagery and word-play. This approach, I think, succeeds in eliciting the complex themes that are shared behind even the crudest of metrical expressions. As in virtually every sustained creative effort, there are certain metaphors that Melville repeatedly employs to organize the activities of his sensibility, like the rose, the Great Mother, the redeemer figure, and the sea, to mention only a few. As such, they command a great deal of attention, but thankfully in many different contexts. And since Melville has a keen understanding of the archetypal symbols of the unconscious, I frequently undertake psychoanalytical interpretations, Freudian, Jungian, and sometimes plainly Steinian, and I believe that these probings often shed light on Melville's emotional and spiritual anxieties.

Ultimately, the varied perspectives of time, history, myth, and religion, directly and indirectly, mediate whatever interpretation that I broach, though I always try to respect the self-contained unity of the individual poem. In any event, I have steadfastly labored to chart some of the eccentric paths of Melville's imaginative thought. Perhaps on occasions I have not read wisely, but at least I have attempted to read well (closely and patiently)—that is, as well as anything as subjective as poetry (or the mind of a critic) permits. This is the code of integrity by which I abide and for which I do not apologize. Here I see eye to eye with Melville, the man and the artist.

John Marr and Other Sailors

II   The Sea of Time

MELVILLE's *John Marr and Other Sailors* (1888) is the product of an unclouded state of consciousness (or inspiration). Unlike *Battle-Pieces* (1866) and *Clarel* (1876), the collection of poetry is almost devoid of anxiety, melancholia, or spiritual unrest. Old age and retirement apparently reconcile Melville to his role of the eccentric patriarch—the incorrigible scribbler. But apart from his external social behavior, it is unwise to assume that he is even in aloof empathy with the Victorian Age. Here, I think, the factual record of biography is often misleading.[1] At any rate, the "guarded 'meliorism,' " for instance, that Robert Penn Warren finds in the Civil War poetry is not in evidence in *John Marr*. Nor is there any metaphysical effort made to resolve what Warren calls "the fundamental ironical dualities of existence."[2] Man, time, and destiny are liberated from the terrors of historical existence. For Melville finally decides to confront directly the nightmares of conscience unloosed in the agonizing confessions of *Clarel*. In one respect, however, his purpose still remains the same: he is relentlessly bent upon isolating "the Real" meaning of life (p. 194). But Melville no longer engages in theological and philosophical speculations on the origins of good and evil. Instead he renounces all modes of abstract thought with their temptation to intellectual self-deception. Where previously passion and polemic characterized his view of man's earthly lot, he now is serenely objective. He simply reports the incontestable facts of human finitude, and they do not admit of any kind of transfiguration under

[1] For such information Leon Howard's *Herman Melville* (Berkeley: University of California Press, 1952) and Leyda's *The Melville Log* are most useful.
[2] "Melville the Poet," *Kenyon Review*, 8 (Spring 1946), 219, 214.

divine will or universal necessity. In death man relapses into the unending darkness of his beginnings. Heaven and hell do not exist. In short, the universe of Melville's *John Marr* is a primal creation. It knows only the cycle of birth, life, death, and transient human affection; it is a bleak community of man and nature. This is the basis of Newton Arvin's remark that "the dominant symbol in *John Marr* is . . . the symbol of wreck and disaster." [3] But while the statement is true, it needs further elaboration. The forces symbolized operate to evoke a world at the mercy of contingency. Yet despite the constant menace to "the flower of life" (p. 161), Melville still correlates self-fulfillment with the bud that grows and blows, however brief or unnoted its particular career. In contrast with the fiction of his young manhood, he expresses no bitterness about such a fate. Accepting change and process as the basic rhythm of the universe, he revels in the grim truth.

These observations, for the most part, only define the obvious themes of *John Marr*. They do not take into account the main problem of Melville's late poetry—its bewildering discordance and unconventionality. Like the trope of unpredictable catastrophe, the practices are controlled artifices. They mediate and perpetuate a private joke, his utter scorn of the guiding values of his culture. This secret dissent is concealed behind a façade of brutal naturalism and, on occasions, of affected sentimentality. But the chief vehicle of his scathing irony is a submerged pattern of inverted biblical symbolism, a mixture of blasphemy and bawdiness that establishes the ultimate tone of the collection. The austere reconciliation enunciated in the terminal poem "Pebbles" illustrates his method of composition:

> Healed of my hurt, I laud the inhuman Sea—
> Yea, bless the Angels Four that there convene;
> For healed I am even by their pitiless breath
> Distilled in wholesome dew named rosmarine. (p. 206)

In the context of the Revelation the deliverance of "the sealed" is heralded by the appearance of "the four angels, to whom it was

[3] *Herman Melville* (New York, 1950), p. 279.

given to hurt the earth and the sea." But Melville shuns identity with the multitude "which came out of great tribulation, and . . . washed their robes, and made them white in the blood of the Lamb" (VII:2, 14). He elects to accept the suffering, regardless of its origin, as the pitiless condition of existence in the realm of nature:

> Implacable I, the old implacable Sea:
> Implacable most when most I smile serene—
> Pleased, not appeased, by myriad wrecks in me. (p. 206)

By the same token, he does not fear death. It terminates the ordained cycle of his tenure on earth. In fine, he prefers to uphold the wisdom of experience as opposed to the solace of mystical prophecy.

A similar dialectic is the organizing principle of "Far Off-Shore." The predominance of monosyllabic words in the first stanza produces an effect of clipped breathlessness that adds a note of urgency to the silent question in the last line:

> Look, the raft, a signal flying,
> Thin—a shred;
> None upon the lashed spars lying,
> Quick or dead. (p. 197)

The situation, of course, is a burlesque of the authority assigned to the scriptures by Paul: "I charge *thee* therefore before God, and the Lord Jesus Christ, who shall judge the quick and the dead at his appearing and his kingdom; preach the word; be instant in season, out of season; reprove, rebuke, exhort with all long-suffering and doctrine" (2 Tim. IV:1–2). By changing "the quick and the dead" to "quick or dead," Melville impugns the Christian dogma of salvation. While "the quick" literally means the living, in the biblical sense it denotes spiritual expectancy of resurrection. Therefore the verse in the poem can be read as a query: "resurrected or dead." At least so the apparent answer of the second stanza implies:

> Cries the sea-fowl, hovering over,
> "Crew, the crew?"

> And the billow, reckless, rover,
> Sweeps anew! (p. 197)

The weighted sound of "e" throughout discourages the extension of curiosity beyond the naked scene, for, climactically, the rushing sea rolls its shroud of waters over the unresurrected dead. With diction and rhythm delicately sustaining the evolution of theme, Melville conjugates the future tense of human fate—the silent void.

This method of controlling shades of meaning provides the clue to the understanding of the other poems in *John Marr*. Regardless of whether the poetic voice speaks through the agent of a character or the mask behind a specific experience, he always seeks to illuminate the knowable destiny of man. As exemplified in "Far Off-Shore," the knowledge is not easily abstracted from the direct statement of the poem. Melville constantly plays with words, setting up contradictions in thought consistent with the dubieties of fate. Hence he resorts to tricks of syntax, buried allusions, double entendres, and other devices of inversion. Ultimately, the image of "The implacable sea" governs the thematic content of the poems. As embodied in "Pebbles," it always operates to glorify the most abject individual doom above the "sealed" promises of the Apocalypse.

The title poem "John Marr" clearly reflects this intention. Melville's prose introduction briefly outlines the history of a sailor who, as a result of "a crippling wound" (p. 159), is compelled to become a landsman. His unhappiness ashore leads him to turn within himself and to live on memories of his past at sea which have a reality more substantial than his present circumstances. But in the course of his incantatory revery he inadvertently isolates a meaning for life and records the circumstances which tend to destroy or enhance the meaning. To begin with, he is another of Melville's Isolatos. Even his name is an accidental irony (a brand of Cain). In his infancy he is deserted, "born in America of a mother unknown" (p. 159). "A sailor under divers flags" (p. 159), he at last ventures to carve out a destiny on the "frontier-prairie" (p. 159), but he is deprived of the chance by a fever which "carries off his young wife and son" (p. 159) and by his neighbors who, "through moral bias" (p. 161), are not cordial to outsiders. When John Marr in his loneliness attempts to talk about the past, they are wont to say as did one of them, "a blacksmith, and at Sunday gatherings an earnest exhorter. . . . 'Friend, we know nothing of that here' " (p. 161). In this turn of events Melville ascribes John Marr's disillusionment to a group of "narrowly religious" Christians who refuse to assimilate him into their community (p. 161). Melville's historical perspective is at this point scrupulously accurate. In the course of American history clannish racial-religious groups populated the entire Middle West. But if in their intercourse with strangers of loose faith they did nothing to store up riches in heaven, their offspring eventually reaped the rewards of the earth: "Throughout these plains, now in places overpopulous with towns *overopulent;* sweeping plains, elsewhere *fenced off* in every direction into flourishing farms—pale townsmen and hale farmers alike, in part, descendants of the first sallow settlers . . ." (p. 163; italics mine). In a further turn of irony John Marr thinks of the prairies as "the bed of a dried-up sea" (p. 163). Thus Melville equates the undulating prairie and its pitiless settlers with the wormwood element of the Apocalypse.

When John Marr "invokes . . . the visionary ones" of his "retrospective musings" (p. 164), his former companions at sea, Melville clearly indicates that what the old man deplores in his landsman's role is not physical pain or suffering but rather the lack of fellowship and community in the common struggle against the impersonal forces of nature:

> Once, for all the darkling sea [4]
> You your voices raised how clearly,
> Striking in when tempest sung;
> Hoisting up the storm-sail cheerly,
> *Life is storm—let storm!* you rung.
> Taking things as fated merely,
> Child-like though the world ye spanned. (p. 165)

[4] This line echoes Matthew Arnold's "Dover Beach" and a spark kindled by Melville's own discontent with Christian faith. Certainly the poetic voice of the poem pines for a meaningful human relationship in the manner of John Marr. A marked volume of Arnold's *Poems . . . A New and Complete Edition,* which included the above poem, was owned by Melville; see Merton

In contrast with the prairie ascetics morosely pondering the strange justice of God in their dreary struggle to till the soil, the sailors before the mast accept natural evil, the dangers of "roaring gales" and "the wilds of midnight waters" (p. 166). Nor does their courage blink before "foemen looming through the spray" (p. 166); they discharge their duties with responsibility, dignity, and honor. Therefore Melville distills the meaning of their lives from the commission of acts jointly undertaken to preserve the right to live, their thoughts distant from the profit or the politics which their bravery underwrites. Their loyalty is to each other; they abide by a human code, "to music haughtier strung" than driving selfish desire (p. 165). Though constantly separated, they are one:

> Twined we were, entwined, then riven,
> Ever to new embracements driven,
> Shifting gulf-weed of the main! (p. 165)

In this contradiction Melville crystallizes the intention of the poem. In self-renunciation they enter, in the words of William E. Sedgwick, "into the destiny which binds all human beings in one great spiritual and emotional organism." In this "umbilical relation to live" they assert their fidelity to the feminine principle of the heart: [5]

> A beat, a heart-beat musters all,
> One heart-beat at heart-core. (p. 166)

Quite obviously in this position Melville openly renounces allegiance to the code of nihilistic individualism developed in *Moby Dick*, *Mardi*, and *Pierre*. But in addition he also repudiates constrictive Protestant Christianity with its fear of the unholy flesh. Almost in Whitman's terms he conceives of man as a great receptive agent in whom relative good and evil seek a balance of salutary well-being. Consequently he glorifies all maritime "larks ashore" (p. 165). The primal innocence of man is inviolable, at least in the nostalgic perspective of boredom and old age:

M. Sealts, *Melville's Reading* (Madison: University of Wisconsin Press, 1967), No. 20.
[5] *Herman Melville: The Tragedy of the Mind* (Cambridge: University of Harvard Press, 1945), p. 221.

> Tattooings, ear-rings, love-locks curled;
> Barbarians of man's simpler nature,
> Unworldly servers of the world. (p. 166)

This conviction is also incorporated into "Bridegroom Dick" where he expresses uninhibited contempt for the social mores that are intolerant of these amusements:

> Very jolly, very wicked, both sea and crew,
> Nor heaven looks sour on either, I guess,
> Nor Pecksniff he bosses the gods' high mess. (p. 174)

He finds precedents for such behavior in both nature and human nature. Only a canting hypocrite would condemn self-righteously what he himself would enjoy secretly. The same gusto for life emerges in "Jack Roy":

> Ashore on liberty he flashed in escapade,
> Vaulting over life in its levelness of grade,
> Like the dolphin off Africa in rainbow a-sweeping—
> Arch iridescent shot from seas languid sleeping. (p. 185)

Even in the face of death, Tom Deadlight says his last farewell with jovial allegiance to his expiring body:

> But give me my *tot*, Matt, before I roll over;
> Jock, let's have your flipper, it's good for to feel;
> And don't sew me up without *baccy* in mouth, boys,
> And don't blubber like lubbers when I turn up my keel. (p. 184)

And, of course, in *Billy Budd*, a novel of this same period, Melville excuses the hero's irrepressible animal exuberance:

> Habitually living with the elements and knowing little more of the land than as a beach, or, rather, that portion of the terraqueous globe providentially set apart for dance-houses, doxies, and tapsters, in short what sailors call a 'fiddler's green,' his simple nature remained unsophisticated by those moral obliquities which are not in every case incompatible with that manufacturable thing known as respectability. But are sailors, frequenters of 'fiddlers' greens,' without vices? No; but less often than with landsmen do their vices, so-called, partake of crookedness of heart. . . .[6]

[6] ed. Harrison Hayford and Merton M. Sealts, Jr. (Chicago: University of Chicago Press, 1962), p. 52.

As long as physical impulses stem from an affirmation of joy in human existence, without deceit or malice, man is incapable of sin against himself, regardless of the edicts of conventional morality. The recurrent motif of natural goodness shows Melville's deep concern with psychosomatic balance. The asceticism imposed upon the instincts by authoritarian creeds leads, as in "John Marr," to a moral rigorism out of harmony with the impulses of mankind. In the cleavage set up between the body and the soul, the emotional resources of humanity are reduced to parched desolation. As we have seen in the prose preface to "John Marr," self-aggrandizement compensates for self-denial. The virtues of industriousness and thrift are introduced into the framework of morality, and this perversion sanctions the development of ruthless economic competition and religious mummery. Gone is all the childlike faith which Paul exhorts; surviving is only the wisdom of the serpent. Such, Melville observes in one of his letters, is "that prudential worldly element, wherewithall Mr. Arnold has conciliated the conventionalists. . . ." [7] A similar contempt for humanity also informs those wars supposedly fought for the noblest ideals:

> Of all these thrills thrilled at keelson, and throes,
> Little felt the shoddyites a-toasting o' their toes;
> In mart and bazar Lucre chuckled the huzza,
> Coining the dollars in the bloody mint of war. (p. 171)

According to this quotation from "Bridegroom Dick," patriotism is nothing more than an amusing joke. Of course, here Melville has in mind the holocaust of the Civil War, the most striking example of the breakdown of cultural unity:

> But better, wife, I like to booze on the days
> Ere the Old Order foundered in these very frays,
> And tradition was lost and we learned strange ways.
> Often I think on the brave cruises then. (p. 174)

As the ballad-narrative unfolds, it traces the disintegration of human values directly to the decline of brotherly love. And the

[7] *The Letters of Herman Melville,* ed. Merrell R. Davis and William H. Gilman (New Haven: Yale University Press, 1960), p. 280.

choice of poetic form helps to dramatize the presentation. Like a typical sea chantey, it enables Melville to achieve a naked concreteness through the use of maritime vernacular and vivid colloquialism. Eschewing subtlety, it permits him to speak of "the Real" without sentimentality. There is no need to speculate about the codes of men; their actions eloquently speak for themselves.

But "Bridegroom Dick" cultivates a new credo in default of the old. It combines a testimony of acceptance that stems on the one hand from the recognition of man's aloneness in the "wormwood sea" of "John Marr," on the other from the obstreperous obstinacy of Job:

> . . . . (and I speak o' what I know),
> Wormwood the trial and the Uzzite's black shard. (p. 171)

Again the terms of acceptance are not Christian, certainly not the conditions of salvation set down in Revelation. Fortitude enables man to endure on earth, not faith. Perhaps in writing these lines Melville had in mind the passage which he had underscored in Balzac: "It is the weak who live with grief, and who, instead of changing it into apothegms of existence, toy and saturate themselves therewith, and retrograde each day consummated misfortunes." [8] The poem, however, is not overburdened with stoical pronouncements on the conduct of life. To the contrary, the tone is genial, humorous, tolerant. Even though nostalgic in point of view, the narrator, as much as he wonders about the whereabouts of his former shipmates, does not long to resurrect the past. If anything, he takes the present for what it is, calling attention to the heritage disowned—"giving truth her due" (p. 173).

In the materialization of this poetic method, the sinewy diction is adapted to the pervasive mood. Melville gayly scoffs at the gods while extolling the heady wine of life quaffed by his old comrades:

> But talk o' fellows' hearts in the wine's genial cup:—
> Trap them in the fate, jamb them in the strait,
> Guns speak their hearts then, and speak right up. (p. 173)

[8] Leyda, *The Melville Log*, 2: 791.

Here the imagery is oriented along the lines of the familiar symbol of the heart and its natural oscillations of love and hate. Its ways are contrasted with the egregious pettiness of the moralists, an attitude contemptuously dismissed by the pun on intestine and the allusion to the spinning top:

> The troublous colic o' intestine war
> It sets the bowels o' affection ajar.
> But, lord, old dame, so spins the whizzing world,
> A humming-top, ay, for the little boy-gods
> Flogging it well with their smart little rods,
> Tittering at time and the coil uncurled. (p. 173)

There is no repining note in this reminiscence. Instead Melville's impolite scatological play affirms life on its own terms, even to "the coil uncurled" as the bowels come ajar.

The ridicule is also carried on in a much more oblique fashion, especially when the narrator speculates on his survival in battle: "It irks me now, as it troubled me then" (p. 173). Now Bridegroom Dick has a mature understanding of his good fortune:

> In the *Battle for the Bay* too if Dick had a share,
> And saw one aloft a-piloting the war—
> Trumpet in the whirlwind, a Providence in place—
> Our Admiral old whom the captains huzza,
> Dick joys in the man nor brags about the race. (p. 173)

No God ordained his fate. It rested in the hands of the Admiral whose skill and bravery in maneuvering the ship assured the safety of the crew. On the surface, perhaps, the passage is self-evident in meaning. But the second and third lines conceal a shocking heresy based on a parody of Job in a context of heaven's inscrutable decrees: "Then the Lord answered Job out of the whirlwind and said, Who is this that darkeneth counsel by words without knowledge? Gird up thy loins like a man; for I will demand of thee, and answer thou me" (XXXVIII:1–4). Melville's answer, I believe, needs no further comment. It represents another statement of his conviction that the meaning of life emerges within the human community in the midst of sorrow and death, of fear and hope, of love and hate.

The remainder of the poem is devoted to the exaltation of the qualities of benevolent fellowship. And the first tribute takes its cogency from a parody of the God of the Revelation. In this case the blasphemy is even more outrageous, for Melville apotheosizes Tom Tight, an alcoholic naval officer:

> A cutwater-nose, ay, a spirited soul;
> But, boozing away at the well-brewed bowl,
> He never bowled back from the voyage to China. (p. 174)

In these lines Melville's punning is us nimble as lightning. In the nose epithet he plays on the unerring olfactory sense of alcohol belonging to the hero, and out of it he develops the double meaning of spirited. He also uses the sailor's name in the same way, preparing for the transformation of the drinking bowl into the sailing vessel. Then Tom Tight in the midst of storm and danger enacts the role of "the Spirit on the Lord's day" when it spoke in a "great voice, as of a Trumpet" (Rev. I:10):

> Trumpet at mouth, thrown up all amain,
> An elephant's bugle, vociferous demanding
> Of topmen aloft in the hurricane of rain,
> "Letting that sail there your faces flog?
> Manhandle it, men, and you'll get the good grog."
> O Tom, but he knew a blue-jacket's ways,
> And how a lieutenant may genially haze;
> Only a sailor sailors heartily praise. (p. 175)

Melville once again employs the resurrection motif to show that human fate hinges on the joint action of men, not the intercession of God:

> *Muster to the Scourge!*—Dawn of doom and its blast!
> As from cemeteries raised, sailors swarm before the mast,
> Tumbling up the ladders from the ship's nether shade. (p. 176)

Here is a neat paraphrase in sea lingo of St. John the Divine's vision of the Day of Judgment, and it allows Melville to vent his wrath upon Christianity. Whereas the common sailor is touched to the quick at the prospect of lashing,

> But ah for the sickening and strange heart-benumbing,
> Compassionate abasement in shipmates that view;
> Such a grand champion shamed there succumbing! (p. 178)

29

a proxy of God stands among the officers "disciplined and dumb" (p. 177). And at first glance the captain of the ship is another Vere: "In the martinet-mien/Read the *Articles of War*, heed the naval routine" (p. 177). In the pose of the crucifixion, before him hangs the counterpart of Billy Budd:

> . . . cut to the heart a dishonor there to win,
> Restored to his senses, stood the Anak Finn;
> In racked self-control the squeezed tears peeping,
> Scalding the eye with repressed inkeeping.
> Discipline must be; the scourge is deemed due. (pp. 177–78)

But just as the lash is about to fall, brotherhood asserts itself. With compassionate heart Captain Turret steps forward, saying

> "Untie him—so!
> Submission is enough, Man, you may go."
> Then promenading aft, brushing fat Purser Smart,
> "Flog? Never meant it—hadn't any heart.
> Degrade that tall fellow?" Such, wife, was he,
> Old Captain Turret, who the brave wine could stow. (p. 178)

Thus, on this day of judgment, man forgives man. Tempering justice with sweetness and light, a magnanimous sea-god pardons the rebel, Anak Finn. Fittingly Melville names the latter after the giants of the Old Testament who challenged the Jews and their wrathful God. He is well aware that under similar circumstances in Revelation sinners are judged "according to their works. And death and hell were cast into the lake of fire. This is the second death. And whosoever was not found written in the book of life was cast into the lake of fire" (XX:13–15). There seems little doubt that throughout this poem Melville insists that MAN qua man is superior to the individual whose attitudes and values have been conditioned by the perfunctory morality of a Chaplain Le Fan (take note of the pejorative):

> Who blessed us at morn, and at night yet again,
> D—ning us only in decorous strain. (p. 175)

In effect, the poet argues that man's salvation lies within the province of fate over which man has some control; beyond this realm, in the vast domain of nature, the law of chance operates with inexorable blindness; further beyond, in the incomprehensible infinite of heaven, silence is poised over the unanswerable question.

Nor can the recurrent imagery of wine in the poem be scanted in considering Melville's wit and blasphemy. Each of the men idealized is familiar with the brimming cup. Even though indulgence sometimes leads to physical incapacitation, it more often than not helps to maintain the cordial balance of the heart. Therefore, as in *Marquis de Grandvin*, it evolves into a symbol of human communion. It commemorates man's capacity for love in the visible sense, becoming for Melville the only knowable Eucharistic principle.

Obviously, the movement of thought and action in "Bridegroom Dick" smacks, if not of radical heresy, then of plain, unmitigated blasphemy. And what fun Melville was having with his Victorian readers—his wife and the close friends among whom the edition of twenty-five copies were distributed! While apparently respecting all the proprieties of the day (the ellipsis of the innocuous "damn" is a good example), he was perpetrating a private joke of the most unholy proportions—much like the one in his short stories.[9] Unquestionably he was convinced that the literature of the day, and poetry in particular, was in need of a healthy infusion of life, "as a counterpoise to the exorbitant hopefulness, juvenile and shallow, that makes such a bluster these days—at least, in some quarters." [10]

But he was not only manipulating profane ideas in the poem, he was also yielding to his uncontrollable predisposition towards Rabelaisian bawdry. In the narration of the poem, frequent asides are directed at the listening wife, and these come, usually, at the end of some sacrilegious observation, as if to apologize for neglecting her chief interest in life. The double-entendres are wholly obvious:

> Now, now, sweetheart, you sidle away,
> No, never you like *that* kind o' *gay*;

[9] See my "Melville's Comedy of Faith," *ELH*, 27 (December 1960), 315–33.
[10] In context Melville contrasts Thomson's "City of the Dreadful Night" with the optimism of other contemporary poets, Leyda, *The Melville Log*, 2: 788–89.

> But sour if I get, giving truth her due,
> Honey-sweet forever, wife, will Dick be to *you!* (p. 173)

If "gay" is taken in its sense of wantonness, then the last line of the passage is self-explanatory. In the next example there is an obvious phallic pun on head:

> Wistful ye peer, wife, concerned for my head,
> And how best go get me betimes to my bed. (p. 174)

The third illustration validates the two previous explications. Melville is quite explicit about the context of reference, at least insofar as an equivoque can be:

> Don't fidget so, wife; an old man's passion
> Amounts to no more than this smoke that I puff;
> There, there, now, buss me in good old fashion:
> A died-down candle will flicker in the snuff. (p. 182)

Moreover, at the beginning of the poem, he supplies a rubric for these interpretations when he refers to the virility of his heroes in overt sexual terms:

> Here mellowing myself, past sixty-five,
> To think o' the May-time o' pennoned young fellows. (p. 167)

Certainly this vein of thought helps to explain the title, "Bridegroom Dick." But Melville's inclusion of off-color materials also has a personal basis. Living in a prudish age and, for the most part, among conventional people, his coarse equivocations no doubt represented the only way in which he could give vent to his contempt for an age which, at least outwardly, refused to recognize biological truths. Mainly, however, this emphasis fortifies his desire to evoke the meaning of "the Real."

He refuses to gloss facts. He acknowledges the disappearance of the old values fostered by the naval fleet in its flamboyant youth. He concedes that the fatality of death awaits all. Though as a result saddened,

> Hither and thither, blown wide asunder,
> Where's this fleet, I wonder and wonder.
> Slipt their cables, rattled their adieu,
> (Whereaway pointing? to what rendezvous?) (p. 180)

he does not relapse into pious sentimentality, as perhaps his use of a phrase from Thomas À Kempis suggests:

> Out of sight, out of mind, like the crack *Constitution*,
> And many a keel time never shall renew— (p. 180)

Thomas may argue that it is foolhardy to think only on the present, "O the stupidity and hardness of man's heart, which thinketh only upon the present, and doth not rather care for what is to come,"[11] but Melville's present-past meditations lead to the conclusion that the old order passes into the new as iron warships replace the beautiful heart-of-oak schooners:

> "Take in your flying-kites, for there comes a lubber's day
> When gallant things will go, and the three-deckers first." (p. 182)

But this does not necessarily precipitate a renunciation of life. Rather, "Nature teems, and the years are strong" (p. 181). Man, in short, must live in time under the conditions of existence defined by the world.

The conviction of the sacred meaning of immediate life is also expressed in the companion poems to "Bridegroom Dick." As Tom Deadlight lies in a hammock dying, he pledged the living, decrying the importance of his own demise:

> But what's this I feel that is fanning my cheek, Matt?
> The white goney's wing?—how she rolls!—'t is the Cape!
> Give my kit to the mess, Jock, for kin none is mine, none;
> And tell *Holy Joe* to avast with the crape. (p. 183)

Accepting death as a natural fact, he also ridicules the hypocritical last rites which will be his. Indeed he rejects all divine guidance on this last of journeys:

> Dead reckoning, says *Joe*, it won't do to go by;
> But they doused all the glims, Matt, in sky t' other night.
> Dead reckoning is good for to sail for the Deadman;
> And Tom Deadlight he thinks it may reckon near right. (p. 184)

[11] The phrase "out of sight, out of mind" occurs in the context of a meditation on death in which the monk disowns all connection with worldly things, especially with what Bridegroom Dick highly prizes. He is scornful in particular of comradeship: "Trust not friends and kindred, neither do thou put off care of thy soul's welfare hereafter; for men will forget thee

"Dead reckoning" is the crucial phrase in this passage. In the nomenclature of navigation, this means plotting a course without reference to any heavenly bodies. Symbolically, it indicates that man will achieve his destiny in terms of the human organism—in the cycle that concludes with death. And as noted earlier, the last stanza of this poem reiterates Tom's concern with his physical well-being; the soul is forgotten as he calls for his last tot of grog and a chew of tobacco.

The poetic strategy of "Tom Deadlight" is very devious. In a prose preface Melville discourages too much concern with the feverish incoherencies of the dying tar. By so doing, he invites consideration of the humor which pervades the scene of death. But when the reader focuses on this aspect of the poem, he loses sight of the undercurrent of blasphemy which the very method initiates. In other words, it is in the apparent wandering of Tom's mind that Melville plants his seeds of ridicule, continuing the private joke of "Bridegroom Dick."

"Jack Roy" concludes the glorification of the credo of the sea —full participation in life. The ditty sings the praises of the paragon of the foretop who never blinked "life's gay command" (p. 185). Thus the persistent note of the other three poems is modulated in another key, Melville's way of saying that ripeness is all. It is in the bitter waters of the wormwood sea that Jack Roy defines the meaning of life. His transcendence of the forces which destroy him is embodied in the legend which he perpetuates:

> Kept up by relays of generations young
> Never dies at halyards the blithe chorus sung;
> While in sands, sounds, and seas where the storm-petrels cry,
> Dropped mute around the globe, these halyard singers lie. (p. 184)

But this glorification of life is also accompanied by the profane implications of the previous poems. Jac Roy becomes a "manly king" who emulates the sacrifice of Christ: [12]

sooner, sooner than thou are aware of" (*Imitation of Christ*, Chicago, n.d., pp. 33–34).

[12] It is interesting to note that Melville accomplishes virtually the same kind of symbolic transformation in *Billy Budd*, by exploiting the double meaning

Only in a tussle for the starry flag high,
When 't is piety to do, and privilege to die.
Then, only then, would heaven think to lop
Such a cedar as the captain o' the *Splendid's* main-top. (p. 184)

He even descends into hell and rises again. Ironically, the ascent is deemed merely an act of gallantry:

"In Limbo our Jack he would chirrup up a cheer,
The martinet there find a chaffing mutineer;
From a thousand fathoms down under the hatches o' your Hades,
He'd ascend in love-ditty, kissing fingers to your ladies!" (p. 185)

Next Melville slyly couches his description of Jack Roy in the traditional Christian symbols of the resurrection:

Vaulting over life in its levelness of grade,
Like the dolphin off Africa in rainbow a-sweeping—
Arch iridescent shot from seas languid sleeping. (p. 185)

Yet the final couplet of the poem commemorates the sanctity of human existence in an apparent dismissal of all interest in immortality. Jack Roy's transfiguration attests this conclusion:

Larking with thy life, if a joy but a toy,
Heroic in thy levity wert thou, Jack Roy. (p. 185)

The mingling of solemnity and happiness in these lines is balanced by the rollicking rimes and the deferential quality of the archiac language, a homespun virtuosity that imbues the theme with a kind of transcendent ordinariness. And so Melville finds the meaning of life in life itself—in the inexhaustible spirit that enables man to preserve his basic dignity in the center of natural chaos.

of the " 'King's Bargain,' " the impressment of a merchant sailor by one of His Majesty's ships or the bargain of salvation from God contingent on the willing sacrifice of Christ. In the novel, as the *potential* captain of the mizzen-top, Billy Budd would have handled the sails most responsible for the steering of the ship, *Selected Writings*, p. 809. In "Benito Cereno" he uses an equivalent symbolic interplay to convert the captain of the ship into the commander of the dominical vessel of Christ; see my article, "The Moral Axis of Benito Cereno," *Accent*, 15 (Summer 1955), 21–33.

III The Triple Goddess

THE STATE OF CONSCIOUSNESS in his old age is perhaps nowhere more clearly evoked than in his composition of "The Haglets." The poem is a work of the *Billy Budd* period, say 1888 and shortly before, as opposed to 1888–1891. It is the final revision of the much earlier "The Admiral of the White." [1] A cursory reading of the first finished draft of "The Admiral of the White" immediately brings to light the poet's thematic focus. Unfolded is the ironical narrative of a victorious English admiral and his crew who, speeding homeward in anticipation of merited honor and acclaim, are wrecked and drowned. The catastrophe is ascribed to trophies of war collected from the enemy French—swords which deflect the compass of the ship. So Melville defines the problem of fate to be resolved. At any rate, his flat and interrogatory diction seems directly to reflect such a purpose:

> Why went the needle so trembling about,
> Why shook you, and trembled to-day?
> Was it, perchance, that those French Captains' swords
> In the arm-chest too near you lay?
> Was it to think that those French Captains' swords
> Sur[r]endered, might yet win the day?
> O woe for the brave no courage can save,
> Woe, woe for the ship led astray. (p. 406)

This explication is a condensed version of my article. The Old Man and the Triple Goddess: Melville's 'The Haglets,' "*ELH*, 25 (March 1958), 43–59, reprinted with the permission of The Johns Hopkins Press. © The Johns Hopkins Press.

[1] This latter poem was probably written on Melville's voyage to San Francisco aboard his brother Tom's ship in 1860. The piece was first revised about twenty-five years later; for in 1885 it appeared in both the New York *Daily Tribune* and the Boston *Herald*, still under the original title. The subsequent expansion, called "The Haglets," was included in *John Marr and Other Sailors* (1888).

However, the personified compass (the principle of rational design) of the ship (the traditional ship of life or ship of fools) does not offer an answer (because there is none?) to the mystery of the sword of destiny (the mythic shape-shifting symbol of life and death). If there is one, it lies in Melville's description of the event:

> High-beetling the rocks below which she shocks,
>   Her boats they are stove by her side,
> Fated seas lick her round, as in flames she were bound,
>   Roar, roar like a furnace the tide. (p. 406)

But what is one to make of this? In the implicit image of the holocaust there is a suggestion of sacrifice. But if so, for whom or what? Melville's silence on a divine transfiguration of the calamity and his emphasis on the indifferent cruelty of nature thus become rubrics of interpretation. So he declares that man is estranged from both God and His world.

This explication is confirmed in the next stanza by the shockingly unpoetic images. The similes are carefully chosen pejoratives. They degrade life into anarchy and meaninglessness:

> O jagged the rocks, repeated she knocks,
>   Splits the hull like a cracked filbert there,
> Her timbers are torn, and ground-up are thrown,
>   Float the small chips like filbert-bits there. (p. 406)

Here the rhythmical pattern of the quatrain makes a significant contribution to meaning. Its irregularity, bolstered by the prosaic matter-of-factness of the diction, evokes the disorder of the universe. As the internal rhyme charges irrationally upon the end rhyme of the first and third lines, the futility of human existence is proclaimed. Finally the rhyme of "there" in the second and final line, with its vagueness and imprecision, sounds the knell of death's despair.

The tone of the passage also carries over to the final stanza. Again the rhythm assaults the sensibilities, but, underlying the effect of dissonance, another purpose is manifest. The conjunction of "proud" with "loud" and "shroud" echoes a sardonic irony. As the

37

muffled allusion to the ballad of "Sir Patrick Spens" teases the ear, Melville deliberately surrenders his attempt to rationalize fate. He signals this collapse of conviction in a sentimental bromide:

> Pale, pale, but proud, 'neath the billows loud,
> The Admiral sleeps to night.
> Pale, pale, but proud, in his sea-weed shroud,—
> The Admiral of the White:
> And by their gun the dutiful ones,
> Who had fought, bravely fought the good fight. (p. 406)

This termination looks back at the prosy, unenthusiastic beginning, and the weary, awkward syntax sustains the abortive glorification of the last line. Under the influence of a melancholy inspiration, the poet mocks the illusory dreams of man.

Obviously, this is a testament of despair, a statement of the disillusionment of Melville's middle years. But why then did he return to the topic of the swords of doom in his old age? And why in these later revisions did he reverse his attitude toward the problem of fate? Probably because "The Admiral of the White" was an unforgettable personal vision of reality and had to be thus exorcized. "The Haglets" became the vehicle of the deliverance. The poem materializes in the form of a ritual, marking the evolution of a new state of consciousness. This inward experience is clearly projected in the structure and the meaning of the work (even the change in title indicates the ascendancy of a transpersonal inspiration). Contradicting the major premise of "The Admiral of the White," Melville celebrates the transfiguration of the malignant force of fate. Without any reservations he accepts the eternal cycle of birth, life, and death in nature. This outlook emerges in *all* of his later poetry, particularly in *Weeds and Wildings, with A Rose or Two* and in *Marquis de Grandvin*, the titles symbolic of the point of view. However, specific poems can be cited to advantage here. For instance, in "Trophies of Peace" the archetypal fertility Goddess Ceres reconciles war to the processes of nature.[2] In "Pontoosuce" the ancient Earth Goddess sanctifies her life-death func-

---

[2] See my "Time, History, and Religion: A Glimpse of Melville's Late Poetry," *Arizona Quarterly*, 22 (Summer 1966), 136–45.

tion. And finally, in a much subtler fashion, Aphrodite Urania emerges as the creator-preserver-destroyer in "After the Pleasure Party."

The dedication to the principle of the eternal feminine in nature is also characteristic of Melville's later years. It marks the rejection of the *logos* or masculine principle of the sea chanteys. This turn to primal *eros* denies the authority of light or the intellect, a moment of insight clearly embodied in "After the Pleasure Party." In this allegiance he expresses his belief that discursive reason is ego-bound. Writing poetry in his old age taught him that the permanent emotional values belong to the level of the instincts, to the dark side of consciousness (unconsciousness). This perception is negatively anticipated in *Mardi*, *Moby Dick*, and *Pierre*. The inability of the hero to come to terms with his own inward darkness deprives him of that transcendent superconsciousness acquired in the descent of Jonah into the belly of the whale. Taji, Ahab, and Pierre all deny that their egos float on a primitive Underworld. Because they value life too highly, they obsessively seek death and annihilation, surrendering to what they think is ultimate evil. Actually all are estranged from nature and a world of dynamic process. In "The Haglets" Melville shows that death is transformation, the outer reflex or manifestation of life energy in the compound of the individual. Hence it becomes, in the cosmic sense, a transfiguration, a drama of the reciprocal play of night and day, of decay and growth. With this perspective on bio-cosmic reality, the idea of fate is transmuted into a universal principle of chance and metamorphosis. It is no longer an inscrutable force of evil or a divine retributive agency. Instead it is the sacred law of nature administered by the Great Mother in her role of Triple Goddess, at once creator, preserver, and destroyer. This is the pattern of fate which defines itself in the final revision of "The Admiral of the White."

Before we examine the ritual configurations of "The Haglets," it is necessary to provide a view of the dramatic structure of the poem, the artifice which controls the emergence of meaning. For in this work, at least from the standpoint of form, Melville

exhibits the talents of an extremely skillful poet. This fact is immediately evident in the stanzaic architecture. Framed between the interrogatory induction and the terminal dirge or *requiescat* are
twelve expository stanzas in which he progressively traces his conception of human fate, that is, as he infers it from the experience of
the Admiral and the crew. The division of twelve, as later analysis
will indicate, prefigures the cycle of human destiny in the number
of the sacred year. Melville uses the induction to describe an imaginary cenotaph which, inexplicably, commemorates the tragedy of
the wreck in the secret depths of the sea. But in the next twelve
stanzas he proceeds to re-create the circumstances which govern his
erection of the poetic tomb. Finally in the dirge he defines the
transcendence which nature seems to provide for the apparent loss
of temporal fame.

Thus in the first stanza of the interior story Melville envisages the victorious ship in her proud, homeward voyage. He follows this with the Admiral's apprehensive introspection in regard
to the honors which, though merited, somehow lose their reality
in the midst of the ocean's infinite aloneness. In the next three
verse units we witness nature's unpredictable neutrality in this aspiration for fame as the ocean's waves and winds alternately hasten
and impede the movement of the ship. But in this truce of cosmic
disinterest a foreboding note asserts itself in the relentless pursuit
of the ship by a flight of haglets and a school of sharks. Their menacing import climaxes in the ensuing stanza as the moon contorts itself in the sky, and a huge sea momentarily engulfs the vessel.
This paraphrase of the first half of the interior narration, inade-
quate as it must inevitably be, is designed to suggest the manner in
which Melville conveys the unstable condition of human destiny in
the domain of nature and time. Indeed he implies that death, as
symbolized in the portentous images of the haglets, the sharks, and
the moon, will ultimately defeat all human purposes. Hence this
brute datum of earthly existence may be said to require urgent resolution if man is to make any sense out of the fact of life.

Assuming this vision of reality, Melville, in the second half of
the twelve-stanza section, posits the tragic consequences of a lack of

awareness of this alienation from the truths of nature. Using the ironic device of the seasonal turn of the year, the poet intimates that man disingenuously transforms the coming of the new year into an arbitrary symbol of hope and promise, disregarding the sacrifice of the old year which makes the latter phenomenon possible. And so as to reduce all human endeavor, as seen in the restrictive view of time, to sheer illusion, he introduces the element of chance into the pattern of human fate, the swords which pervert the direction of the ship's compass. For in the midst of wishful dreams and of drinking toasts to the future of a fellowship of honor, the Admiral and his men are plunged into a reef. In the scene of horrible annihilation that results, Melville callously strips such virtues as bravery, self-discipline, and piety of any significance. This courageous complement of seamen perishes ignominiously, its cherished fame annulled by indifferent nature. This catastrophe, in Melville's eyes, is the penalty of an egocentric perspective on the meaning of human fate. But, on the other hand, he recognizes that man will forever lay claim to the admiration and affection of posterity. Therefore in the *requiescat* he salvages the honor that appears to be lost.

Harmonizing his vision with the cyclical movements of nature, he transforms apparent defeat into transcendence. Life and death are joined in a sacred marriage under the authority of a pagan myth. The poem, in this alteration of perspective, becomes a statement of belief in the redemption of the Great Mother, directly contradicting the Christian conviction that death ends in irredeemable corruption and annihilation.

Though the Triple Goddess is first encountered in the surrogates of the Spinners or the *Moirai,* she gradually metamorphoses into her lunar identity of the Great Mother, becoming Hecate, the Moon-Goddess.[3] Interestingly enough, as Hesiod tells us,[4] the

---

[3] In his visit to the Capitoline Museum of Rome, Melville undoubtedly saw the impressive statue of Hectate *Triformis,* Howard C. Horsford, *Journal of a Visit to Europe and the Levant* (Princeton: Princeton University Press, 1955), pp. 190–1.

[4] See Leyda, *The Melville Log,* 2, 649, for Melville's familiarity with the *Theogony.*

great *Triformis* was the only goddess independent of the will of Zeus. Thus all the secret powers of nature were at her command. She had control over birth, life, and death. And her triform shape defined her influence in heaven, on earth, and in the Underworld. As such, of course, she incorporates all the attributes and powers of Melville's Triple Goddess of Fate. In the coda of the poem he also identifies Hecate with Artemis, Semele, Persephone. In this shape-shifting parallel as Artemis she superintends the movement of the seasons; as Semele she is the moon in its three phases; and as Persephone she is the Goddess of the Underworld, supervisor of procreation, birth, and death. None of this emerges in direct poetic statement; rather it is projected and symbolized in the three haglets, the controlling images of the poem. But even here, Melville merges her into another vegetation myth. In consideration of her dominion over nature—actually the annual pattern that figures the life, death, and resurrection of the Spirit of the Year, the Goddess's son and lover—Melville so invokes her:

> For now the midnight draws anear:
> Eight bells! and passing-bells they be—
>
> The Old year fades, the Old year dies at sea.
> He launched them well. But shall the New
> Redeem the pledge the Old Year made,
> Or prove a self-asserting heir? (p. 190)

Significantly, the ritual implications of this passage are entirely absent from its counterpart in the earlier poem:

> Tis Saturday night,—the last of the week,
> The last of the week, month, and year—
> On deck! shout it out, you forecastle-man,
> Shout "Sail ho, Sail ho—the New Year!" (p. 405)

These lines are local and immediate, with their associations confined to the routine of a mariner's life. They lack the intimations of life and death found in the cyclical pattern presided over by the Triple Goddess. Prosaic fact predominates, not the trembling reverberations of myth.

A similar transformation takes place in the course of another revision. In the original poem the moon is invoked to symbolize the imminence of death. But while the image is apt, it is limited in time and space, too close to the event:

> Catching at each little opening for life,
> The moon in her wane swims forlorn;
> Fades, fades mid the clouds her pinched paled face
> Like the foeman's in seas sinking down. (p. 405)

The Triple Goddess controls the alterations. The mystery of the waning moon is portentously related to the three haglets and to the destiny of man:

> Dim seen adrift through driving scud,
> The wan moon shows in plight forlorn;
> Then, pinched in visage, fades and fades
> Like to the faces drowned at morn,
> When deeps engulfed the flag-ship's crew,
> And, shrilling round, the inscrutable haglets flew. (p. 189)

"(D)rowned at morn" is an ingenious life-death image that, in a paradox, promises resurrection in the eternal return of the sun, even though annihilation is in momentary control. This idea unites with the circular movement of the haglets over the engulfing seas to create the illusion of a formal ceremony. In effect, the Triple Goddess Hecate, under the emblem of the moon, ritually reenacts the mystery of death while her avatars monotonously sing its inevitability.

Nor does the poet forget that the sea is at once the womb and the grave. As the ship scuds through the waters, the redemptive role of the *Triformis* is signaled. In an image unanticipated in the original poem, the ship of death is for a moment envisaged as a procreative agent, symbolically foreshadowing the birth of the Spirit of the Year:

> The eddying waters whirl astern,
> The prow, a seedsman, sows the spray;
> With bellying sails and buckling spars
> The black hull leaves a Milky Way;
> Her timbers thrill, her batteries roll,
> She revelling speeds exulting with pennon at pole. (p. 186)

The sexual ritual consecrates the divine power of the Triple Goddess, for the Milky Way conjures up Hecate in another of her incarnations as the eternal feminine. The image correlates with the myth of the Spirit of the Year in its twofold relationship with the father and the son. The Milky Way is formed when the milk of the great Mother Goddess spouts into the sky after the birth of the infant Zeus. Later the same miracle occurs when Alcmene gives birth to Hercules after her seduction by Zeus. In the latter instance, of course, the twelve labors of Hercules figure the birth and death of the Spirit of the Year. Nor is Zeus's fathering of the Seasons on Themis an irrelevant association.

Ultimately this complex web shapes the iconotropic significance of the three haglets as the Fates. This revision of the first poem provides the title of the final work, and charges it with primitive mystery and terror. In the incarnation of the Triple Goddess as the Spinners, the haglets preside over the violent death of the admiral and his crew. In accordance with their function in the scheme of human destiny, they sanctify the annihilation of the men. This would seem to negate the regenerative role of Hecate, but actually death is equated in importance with birth:

> There, peaked and gray, three haglets fly,
> And follow, follow fast in wake
> Where slides the cabin-lustre shy,
> And sharks from man a glamour take,
> Seething along the line of light
> In lane that endless rules the war-ship's flight.
>   The sea-fowl here, whose hearts none know,
> They followed late the flag-ship quelled,
> (As now the victor one) and long
> Above her gurgling grave, shrill held
> With screams their wheeling rites—then sped
> Direct in silence where the victor led. (p. 187)

These lines adumbrate the inevitability of death. The sharks symbolize the primitive forces of nature and human nature constantly bent upon destruction. Not until man recognizes that they possess a holiness transcending his egotistic will towards life can he reconcile himself to the idea of cosmic transformation. The problem maddened Melville as it did Ahab and Taji; not until he was able to live with the Gorgons of his institutions did he come to terms with the unalterable truth of this cycle. The poem thus exorcizes the demons of desire and fear long untamed in the poet's consciousness.

Even while the passage renders sacred the triumph of death, it anticipates the resurrection of the Spirit of the Year. This is made clear in another revision, the changing of the French enemy in the first poem to Spanish in "The Haglets." Melville here implies resurrection in recurrence (as in nature, the individual thing dies but its form is reborn). In other words, no event is unique, occurring once and for all (the condemnation and death of a Socrates or a Christ), but it has occurred, occurs, and will recur. Cosmic duration is repetition and *anakuklosis,* eternal return. In sum, as the French were destroyed in "The Admiral of the White," so were the Spanish along with the English in "The Haglets." The cycle will go on eternally. This vision of human destiny takes man out of time. He lives in a continuous present which is not history. Melville defines his new state of consciousness, his fealty to the muse of the Triple Goddess. No longer need he ponder the desolating antinomies of existence. By denying history, he testifies to his thirst for "the Real." The terror of losing himself in the meaninglessness of durative time—the profane life of ego desire—is forever alleviated. Change and metamorphosis explain everything; permanence and stability are illusions.[5]

Under the influence of this creative transformation, Melville in "The Haglets" undertakes to resolve the question of the ship's

[5] When Melville wrote *Mardi, Moby Dick, Pierre, The Confidence-Man,* and *Clarel,* he was entangled in the dilemma of linear time and history. Each of his heroes allowed himself to be annihilated by events. Did Billy Budd transcend time in the legend that his death perpetrated—and in no other way? It is the irony of history that man makes an effort to achieve the balance of eternity in the province of time, a prerogative subverted by nature at every turn. In short, no one can make his own fate. One's humanity precludes this. And this is the way Melville looks at life in his later poetry. Whether he was conscious of the precise details of this perspective is irrelevant. We only know that, as in "The Aeolian Harp," he designated "the Real" as a marriage of life and death. This change in the balance of his sensibilities marked his dedication to the muse of Hecate *Triformis.* We find this implied in all the poetry of the late period. See my *"Billy Budd:* The Nightmare of History," *Criticism,* 3 (Summer 1961), 237–50, for an analysis of this problem.

fate in a formula other than history, chance, or the malignant will
of the gods. At the beginning of the poem he poses the question to
be answered:

> I invoke thy ghost, neglected fane,
> Washed by the waters' long lament;
> I adjure the recumbent effigy
> To tell the cenotaph's intent—
> Reveal why fagotted swords are at feet,
> Why trophies appear and weeds are the winding-sheet. (p. 186)

But, in a paradox, the query answers itself. The figure of "weeds
and winding sheet" is another of his ambiguous life-death images.
Nature swathes her children in her green embrace, in death resum-
ing her maternal compassion and care. Yet, as the poet views life in
time, man is constantly under the threat of nature in the guise of
the three haglets—the Great Mother in busy attendance upon the
round of the eternal return:

> Unflagging pinions ply and ply,
> Abreast their course intent they take;
> Their silence marks a stable mood,
> They patient keep their eager neighborhood. (p. 189)

The temper of these lines captures the Triple Goddess in the shape
of the spinning Fates. The very repetition of "ply" depicts the relentless movement of the thread on the spindle of fate held in the
hands of Hecate *Triformis* as she weaves the tapestry of human
destiny in its precarious life-aspect. For whenever Melville contrasts the ambitious desires of the crew with the treacherous illusion
of historical time, he invokes the haglets in ironical counterpoint:

> And follow, follow fast in wake,
> Untiring wing and lidless eye—
> Abreast their course intent they take;
> Or sigh or sing, they hold for good
> The unvarying flight and fixed inveterate mood. (p. 191)

But however omnipresent these shadows of death, they exemplify
the paradox of the Great Mother as destroyer and creator. They
"sigh or sing" her sorrow and joy, but with a permanent lease on

life granted to no living thing they hasten on the cycle of the eternal return.

Even on the brink of death, man blinds himself to the unalterable character of his destiny. On the one hand, he proudly steers the ship of life along a course of death; on the other, he continually exhibits his utter helplessness before the wrath of nature:

> Plumed with a smoke, a confluent sea,
> Heaved in a combing pyramid full,
> Spent at its climax, in collapse
> Down headlong thundering stuns the hull:
> The trophy drops; but, reared again,
> Shows Mars' high-altar and contemns the main. (p. 189)

The image of "Mars' high-altar" resolves the divided purpose. In the lust and fury of war, man instinctively serves the ends of nature in her cyclical process. The altar-image, though couched in irony, is a sacrificial symbol. On the surface it betrays man's service to the god of war and death, but these blood-offerings are not, in the scheme of things, without meaning. The primitive logic behind them takes into account the new life promised by every sacrifice. Thus Mars loses his common identity, reclaiming his ancient role as an agricultural god. The metamorphosis returns us to the domain of the Triple Goddess, to the seasons and the Spirit of the Year whose life and death they exemplify.

Thereby Melville lays bare the grim point of view that he is defending. He wants to deprive death of its personal reference, for the ego always defines itself within narrow subjective limitations, as if a single human entity equalled biocosmic existence instead of merely reflecting it. For this reason the poet delineates the catastrophe with a detachment that verges on heartlessness. The treatment symbolizes the necessity of a disavowal of the importance of self in the total scheme of nature. Melville undertakes to initiate the reader into a fearless acceptance of his inevitable immolation —into the discernment that in the most humiliating and ignominious death there is transcendence. The next passage, which envisions the Triple Goddess in remorseless contemplation of such a scene, is proof of this intention:

47

The haglets spin, though now no more astern.
   Like shuttles hurrying in the looms
Aloft through rigging frayed they ply—
Cross and recross—weave and inweave,
Then lock the web with clinching cry
Over the seas on seas that clasp
The weltering wreck where gurgling ends the gasp. (p. 193)

The image of "the web" suggests that man is victimized by her pitiless will. Even more, the "gurgling" that "ends the gasp" reduces human life to ludicrous, unheroic strife with nature. Man is stripped of all his vain pretensions. The ritual of death leaves no illusion to cling to. None, at least, that reason has formulated. In ceremonial flight the haglets enunciate a vigilance over human fate without any personal concern with it.

Having degraded man in his dying, the poet now proceeds to show why such an ironic and ignoble event is also a transfiguration:

On nights when meteors play
And light the breakers dance,
The Oreads from the caves
With silvery elves advance;
And up from ocean stream,
And down from heaven far,
The rays that blend in dream
The abysm and the star. (p. 194)

The triple Goddess of Fate metamorphoses into the compassionate Great Mother. In the flaming "meteor" she rules the sky; in the "Oreads" and the "silvery elves," caught in the rays of the moon, she rules over the earth; and in the depths of the sea she is Queen of the Underworld. The last two lines bespeak the unity of her domain. In the rays of light converging from above and below, the meaning of life is defined. The middle plane is a composite of heaven and hell, of good and evil, of all the ambivalences and polarities of life. Though the admiral

Imbedded deep with shells
And drifted treasure deep,
Forever he sinks deeper in
Unfathomable sleep—

His cannon round him thrown,
His sailors at his feet,
The wizard sea enchanting them
Where never haglets beat. (pp. 193–94)

is deprived of the temporal glory of "flags and arms" hanging "in
Abbey old," he nevertheless is not "less content" (p. 193). Nor
should he be: "The wizard sea" is the womb and the grave. This is
the paradox of the Triple Goddess; the Spirit of the Year, her son
and lover, endlessly renews himself outside the framework of history. For as the graceful Oreads advance from the caves, maids
and brides-to-be, they symbolize the regeneration of the human desires which will perpetuate themselves in the recurrent acts of man.
No *one*, no thing, dies in vain. No virtue or energy is lost. There is
only transfiguration and transformation. Time and death are only
evil in the limited perspective of the selfish ego.

This interpretation of the poem charts an old man's sober, and
sometimes humorous, resolution of the troublesome polarities of
his young manhood. At least this is true of the thought embodied
in *John Marr and Other Sailors* and the proposed collections left
unpublished during his lifetime. "The Haglets," for instance,
sheds considerable light on the contradictory thematic tensions of
the other poems in the *John Marr* volume. In the title poem and
its companion pieces, Melville extols the virtues ostensibly annulled by the wreck of the Admiral's ship. Yet, as in the case of
John Marr, they live on; in Melville's desperate isolation from
the historical concerns of his neighbors, they provide an endless
fund of solace and spiritual fortitude. The old sailor does not deplore his individual existence; he merely laments the fragmentation of common human values. In "Bridegroom Dick," "Tom
Deadlight," and "Jack Roy," the same creed is affirmed. The opposing group of poems, like "The Maldive Shark" and "Far Off-
Shore," formulate the immitigable conditions of man's relations to .
apathetic nature. But, as we have seen in "The Haglets," Melville
does not surrender human integrity to any atheistic naturalism.
Nothing can victimize man. For, whether good or evil in the
human view, what has been, is, and will be, even as the Triple
Goddess ordains.

49

As observed earlier, other miscellaneous poems testify to Melville's preoccupation with this conception of natural salvation. For instance, in "Pontoosuce" or "The Lake" the Triple Goddess comes to woo his approval:

> "Since light and shade are equal set
> And all revolves, nor more ye know;
> Ah, why should tears the pale cheek fret
> For aught that waneth here below.
> Let go, let go!" (p. 398)

The abyss and star, she whispers, are one and the same. In the cycle of birth, life, and death, she urges him to find peace and to forsake concern with the naked flux of things. Thereupon she initiates him into her cult:

> With that, her warm lips thrilled me through,
> She kissed me, while her chaplet cold
> Its rootlets brushed against my brow,
> With all their humid clinging mould.
> She vanished, leaving fragrant breath
> And warmth and chill of wedded life and death. (p. 398)

The shocking dualities of existence do not merely appear—they are! And only death can resolve them. It annihilates all antitheses, dissolving them into the timelessness of cosmic processes. Yet, according to an excerpt from "Madam Mirror," they will re-emerge once more:

> But ah, what of all that is perished,
> Nor less shall again be, again! (p. 372)

There is resurrection in recurrence. Though a particular man dies, his destiny will repeat itself. This outlook on life clarifies the dilemma of reality and appearance explicit in the image of the mirror:

> Tho' lone in a loft I must languish
> Far from closet and parlor at strife,
> Content I escape from the anguish
> Of the Real and the Seeming in life. (p. 372)

Melville's metaphor of the closet and parlor in conflict further refines this ambiguity. Though private meditation in the closet can illuminate the discontinuities of parlor existence—that is, human communion in the ordinary sense—nevertheless it is in the latter sphere that the ritual of birth and life is preserved in disdain of the mirror which continually

> . . . , retrospecting thro' tunnels
> See[s] but widowers and widows on biers! (p. 373)

For life itself, as "The Wise Virgins to Madam Mirror" states in a paradox, receives transfiguration at the very moment of extinction. In the defloration of the virgin, an act of defilement and corruption in the Christian sense, there is a physical death. But nonetheless a sacramental fruition is promised:

> 'Tis we view the world thro' an arbor,
> The bride with the bridegroom appears. (p. 373)

The immortality prefigured in the "twilight inklings" of death is discarded as "worth scarce the Pope's old shoes" (p. 373). Instead "the wise virgins" transcend all thoughts of death, even death itself, in Dionysian revelry—ceremonial escape:

> Oh yes, we are giddy, we whirl in youth's waltz,
> But a fig for *Reflections* when crookedly false! (p. 374)

So once again the omnipresent Triple Goddess neutralizes all polarities. Life and death merge into one another, beyond all "Reflections," Melville's pun on the futility of attempting to resolve the problem of evil, the fig of the fall, through logic or faith.

IV The Gorgons of the Underworld

THE REMAINING POEMS of *John Marr* also bear witness to the apparently senseless reign of death, to catastrophe and tragedy which spring out of the unknown with impersonal finality.[1] On the one hand, they are a record of the poet's nightmarish memories, the unconscious terrors of his dreams. Or put in more explicit terms, they are dramatic externalizations of Melville's undefined inward fears.

In restricting these experiences to the locale of the sea, he discloses the shape of the creative inspiration at work. Along with the recurrent imagery, the physical setting suggests that he is trying to reconcile his ego to certain monstrous Gorgons of anxiety and insecurity—those deep-seated emotional and spiritual problems whose haunting insolubility, like the mystery of the fabled Medusa, paralyzes his will to think and to act. But as he evokes these horrors of memory and fantasy in the various poems, a remarkable change occurs; they metamorphose into different forms of self-understanding.

The imagery in "The Tuft of Kelp" clearly reveals such a transfiguration of experienced despair, even in the midst of remembered disillusionment:

> All dripping in tangles green,
> > Cast up by a lonely sea
> If purer for that, O Weed,
> > Bitterer, too, are ye? (p. 199)

[1] In a somewhat different form the rest of the chapter was the basis of my article, "Melville's Poetry: Its Symbols of Individuation," *Literature and Psychology*, 7 (May 1957), 21–26.

The unexpected question of the last line negates the explicit pessimism; at least the reversal of sentiment, seems to be supported by the imagery. Though called the ashes of seaweed, kelp is the source of iodine, a healing element. As the product of the ocean's tumultuous purgation, it symbolizes the power of natural transformation, of the attainment of an invincible fortitude through exposure to unavoidable adversities. For Melville it serves as the perfect analogy of his psychic adjustment to the ordeals of existence.

A similar transvaluation of experience is dramatized in "The Aeolian Harp." In the romantic sense, the musical box is a symbol of transcendental inspiration. Not for Melville, however. Instead its "mad crescendo" invites meditation on the ghastly tyranny of contingency:

> Listen: less a strain ideal
>   Than Ariel's rendering of the Real.
> What that Real is, let hint
>   A picture stamped in memory's mint. (p. 194)

While at first glance Melville appears to invoke the airy spirit of Shakespeare's *Tempest* in order to show his repugnance for life's dislocations, there is the possibility that he is alluding to Ariel, the Lion of God in the Old Testament, the vengeful, omnipotent deity of the prophets. If so, then Melville is slyly bent on exposing His limitations in controlling the movement of a derelict:

> Drifted, drifted, day by day,
>   Pilotless on pathless way.
> It has drifted till each plank
> Is cozy as the oyster-bank;
>   Drifted, drifted, night by night,
>   Craft that never shows a light. (p. 195)

At any rate, the floating menace is no respecter of human life or happiness. It strikes out of the silence with aimless malevolence:

> Fatal only to the *other!*
>   Deadlier than the sunken reef
> Since still the snare it shifteth
>   Torpid in dumb ambuscade
> Waylayingly it drifteth.

O, the sailors—O, the sails!
O, the lost crews never heard of!
Well the harp of Ariel wails
Thoughts that tongue can tell no word of! (p. 196)

Surely, Melville here images not only the plight of man on earth but also the hidden dangers of the unconscious. For concealed behind the symbol of the submerged wreck is the sinister shadow of the universal death urge, at one time "the Real" problem of his life. Now no longer intimidated by this inward and outward convulsion of personal destiny, he proceeds to conjure up those old suicidal thoughts and feelings "that tongue can tell no word of." Thus he is liberated from the burden of a haunting fear.

"The Maldive Shark" approaches his search for psychic balance from another direction, focusing on guilt-ridden sexual desire —an inevitable occurrence in polite Victorian circles like his own where the sensual appetite was linked with not only immorality but perversion. He therefore educes this monstrous impulse in the form of the Gorgons, traditional surrogates of the Triple Goddess. Logically, she is evoked in her role of the potential destroyer, the negative aspect of the feminine *eros*. As such, she is the doting, castrating mother of the Oedipus complex, the unwilling censor of the virility of her male children. All these associations cluster around Melville's description of the shark's head, a perfect symbol of the *vagina dentata*, the hierogram of the mystery of female sexuality in primitive mythology.[2] Reversing his past feelings of anxiety and dread, without shame the poet now reverses the taboo of female genitals in his culture:

> The sleek little pilot-fish, azure and slim,
> How alert in attendance be.
> From his saw-pit of mouth, from his charnel of maw
> They have nothing of harm to dread,
> But liquidly glide on his ghastly flank
> Or before his Gorgonian head;
> Or lurk in the port of serrated teeth
> In white triple tiers of glittering gates,

---

[2] Richard Payne Knight, *The Symbolical Language of Ancient Art and Mythology* (New York, 1876), p. 130.

And there find a haven when peril's abroad,
An asylum in jaws of the Fates! (p. 200)

Of course, it is not difficult to extrapolate the phallic connotations of the pilot-fish from context. Only then does its truce with the shark begin to make sense: the underworld of the instincts is in equipoise, even as Melville's.

The next turn of the poem validates the sexual interpretation, turning what seems to be a jarring digression into an integral extension of the earlier launched topic. If nothing else, the peaceful tone of the passage harmonizes with the armistice between the shark and the pilot-fish, between death and life:

Where is the world we roved, Ned Bunn?
Hollows thereof lay rich in shade
By voyagers old inviolate thrown
Ere Paul Pry cruised with Pelf and Trade.
To us old lads some thoughts come home
Who roamed a world young lads no more shall roam. (p. 200)

Harking back to "Bridegroom Dick" and "Jack Roy," these lines clearly refer to the guiltless satisfaction of sexuality. Obviously, the Paul Prys are the canting missionaries who combined with the ruthless forces of commerce to debase and to disease the idyllic, amoral physical pleasures of the South Pacific natives. Not only did the latter learn the meaning of sin from these conquering preceptors, but they also were taught the vice of prostitution, so enduringly the monopoly of civilized societies. Unquestionably, here Melville is thinking of the adventures that he fictionalizes in *Typee,* especially of his liaison with the lovely damsel Fayaway, the naked Aphrodite whose name is probably a pun fashioned on the idea of fay—that is, fate. This is to say that in his youth he was not troubled by the moral scruples of his culture. That was to come later when he became a respectable member of the middle class and a victim of its absurd obsession with good and evil.

The coda of "The Maldive Shark" sums up his immediate attitudes towards sex and sin:

Nor less the satiate year impends
When, wearying of routine-resorts,
The pleasure-hunter shall break loose. (p. 200)

The image of the wheeling movement of time is less a comment on the shark than a jocular evaluation of good and evil. "The satiate year" is a symbol of the climaxing seasonal cycle, a prevision of the resurrection in recurrence of the coming new year. Responding to this natural determinism, man's dormant sexual appetites awaken, and he too undertakes to promote the miracle of annual renewal. The rebellion against "routine-resorts" takes us back to the Garden of Eden, the archetypal setting of intolerable ennui. For even as Adam and Eve activated the dynamics of temporality in their fall (an event frequently looked upon as carnal in origin), so does each of their distant progeny extend the process in tasting the forbidden fruit of self-indulgence. But unfortunately morality operates to dam up this stream of life with its abstract condemnations of the flesh. Under the circumstances the individual incarnates the guilt of his disobedience into the Gorgons of the unconscious, the monstrous terrors of his anxiety dreams. Lacking the divine helpers of a Perseus, he has to harrow this personal hell with his own powers of self-understanding. But if, like Melville, he is a product of puritanical conditioning, he may not be equal to the task, and the sharkish creatures of the undergound will destroy him.

The validity of this interpretation is sustained by the overt prophecy of "The Berg." For as the subtitle of the poem "(A Dream)" enjoins, the submerged mass of ice has to be equated with the specter of a self-motivated death urge:

> I saw a ship of martial build
> (Her standards set, her brave apparel on)
> Directed as by madness mere
> Against a stolid iceberg steer. (p. 203)

In the light of Melville's persistent use of the ship as a microcosm of the world (or, perhaps more accurately, of his culture), the act of self-immolation probably symbolizes the total bankruptcy of the vital traditions of existence, the inward convictions that enable man to bear the unpredictable dislocations of experience. At any rate, the "standards" of the parenthetical statement is in context the equivalent of beliefs, just as "brave apparel" is of outward pretensions. These assumptions are supported by the obvious pejorative,

"the infatuate ship." Here the modifier projects the loss of judgment connected with moral blindness, and, like the Greek conception of *Ate*, emphasizes the presence of self-deception.

The image of the iceberg also gathers its meaning from these
overtones. Its unsubmerged parts figure the sudden invasion of the
conscious mind by those impulses towards self-destruction long hidden in the darkness of the unconscious. As Melville's elemental description of its appearance suggests, it is an inchoate, primitive
force, an immovable obstacle to any counterforce of energy:

> Hard berg (methought), so cold, so vast,
> With mortal damps self-overcast;
> Exhaling still thy dankish breath—
> Adrift dissolving, bound for death;
> Though lumpish thou, a lumbering one—
> A lumbering lubbard loitering slow,
> Impingers rue thee and go down,
> Sounding thy precipice below. (p. 204)

Certainly the personification is designed to portray the instincts
tightly folding in upon themselves, not permitted any kind of normal expression. Indeed, the word "lubbard" connotes dumbness,
lack of resiliency and direction, the very condition of healthy emotions when they are rigidly repressed. Out of this scorn of life, disguised in pride and bravado, springs the unconscious suicidal desire
—the gist of the earlier quotation.

Melville's uncanny insight into this state first emerges in his
conception of Moby-Dick. Psychologically, Ahab's obsession with
the vindictive evil of the white whale externalizes a self-loathing
that is a mask of the death urge. It is no coincidence that he is an
old man, that he has lost a limb, and that he is married to a young
maiden. These details add up to a depletion of erotic energy, to a
case of instinctual entropy in which the ego is sabotaged by its uncontrollable masculine willfulness. The more Ahab hates Moby-
Dick, the less he nurtures the love for life symbolized by this creature of the ocean depths, a domain presided over by the Triple
Goddess. Like the berg, then, the whale is an inverted projection
of the disoriented emotions.

57

Melville's "Old Counsel" provides a kind of footnote on the folly of seeking the answer to human destiny in aggressive outward activity:

> Come out of the Golden Gate,
> Go round the Horn with streamers,
> Carry royals early and late;
> But, brother, be not over-elate—
> *All hands save ship!* has startled dreamers. (p. 199)

The imperative call of the italicized clause echoes Melville's concern with the tragic course of economic endeavor. "The Golden Gate" and "the Horn" are not static geographical images. Rather they denote the routes of the mercantile clippers. The importance of this fact is enhanced by the allusions to "streamers" and "royals." The festive banners signal a voyage that promises rich profits, and the carrying of full sails at all times reveals the lack of judgment that avarice induces. In effect, the concrete language is also casually metaphorical, and works to disclose a blind infatuation with materialistic values. Thus the final two lines of the poem function to convey Melville's evaluation of this perverted and perverting view of self-fulfillment. Though the wakening of the sleepers commands literal attention immediately, it is more likely contrived to symbolize the nightmares of anxiety attendant upon the success of the voyage. With happiness and security based solely upon the acquisition of temporal rewards, the inward resources of being are depleted of their strength, and man is psychologically left to face the unpredictable future without any sustaining purpose for life. As a consequence he is always plagued by unacknowledged fears, haunted by the monsters of incertitude that he himself has created. And here the title of the piece takes on added significance. It is an ironical pun that flaunts Melville's awareness of the complete lack of any guiding traditions of wisdom in Western culture.

The vision of nature in "The Man-of-War Hawk" illuminates this predicament still further. The manipulated contrasts of black and white in the first stanza reflect the rigid balance of life and death in the universe:

Yon black man-of-war-hawk that wheels in the light
O'er the black ship's white sky-s'l, sunned cloud to the sight,
Have we low-flyers wings to ascend to his height? (p. 197)

The ensuing answer denies the possibility of man's attaining any
such prospect on reality. As Melville goes on to indicate, the
hawk's instinctual harmony with light and shade defies logical comprehension, even the powers of science subsumed in the analogy of
the arrow's flight:

No arrow can reach him; nor thought can attain
To the placid supreme in the sweep of his reign. (p. 197)

So once again instinctual knowledge is elevated above intellectual
cognition. Left alone, uninfluenced by the selfish ego, it establishes
an unprotesting harmony with the ground laws of existence laid
down by the Triple Goddess in her passionless custodianship of life
and death. Beyond good and evil, the cycle of nature runs the
course rehearsed in the alternate play of day and night, of spring
and winter, of birth and annihilation.

The same kind of deceptive explicitness characterizes "The
Good Craft 'Snow-Bird,' " for beneath the surface obviousness a
sinuous wit uncoils with a flourish of mockery. The dramatic situation literally exhibits Melville's scorn of commercialism, though
without any distinct bitterness:

Brigs that figs for market gather,
　　Homeward-bound upon the stretch,
Encounter oft this uglier weather,
　　Yet in end their port they fetch.

Mark yon craft from sunny Smyrna
　　Glazed with ice in Boston Bay;
Out they toss the fig-drums cheerly,
　　Livelier for the frosty ray. (p. 198)

Ostensibly these observations are purely factual, but the posture of
objectivity is belied by his deliberate internal rime of "brigs" and
"figs" at the outset. Its purpose is clarified in the second stanza by
the allusion to "sunny Smyrna," the location of one of the churches

addressed by John in Revelation. Melville is about to undertake an analysis of the "fig" (the Fall) in relation to the launching of the "brig" (the Christian ship of salvation or, by way of pun, the prison of the human spirit). In any event, he next proceeds to deride the antagonism of good and evil, the formula underlying the need for redemption:

> What if sleet off-shore assailed her,
> What though ice yet plate her yards;
> In wintry port not less she renders
> Summer's gift with warm regards! (p. 199)

In the opposition of the seasons Melville sets up the polarity of life and death as the unalterable condition of human existence in the realm of nature. But nowhere does he sound a protest about this fate, nowhere a complaint about the alleged estrangement precipitated by the Fall. Instead he remembers "Summer's gift," the ripened wisdom of assimilated experience.

The next stanza examines the unscrupulousness of the commercial mind against the backdrop of human and divine values, and by recourse to the anti-poetic metaphors of trade Melville discloses the inanity of the moral pretensions of his materialistic society:

> And, look, the underwriters' man,
> Timely, when the stevedore's done,
> Puts on his *specs* to pry and scan,
> And sets her down—*A, No.* 1. (p. 199)

The cleverness of the indictment stems from the double perspective provided on the judgment of the insurance inspector. The latter is pragmatically discerning but spiritually blind, absorbed in the character of things rather than of people. Oblivious to the religious connotations of the figs, he is also oblivious to the lesson of good and evil that brought the fruit into prominence in the Garden of Eden. He perpetuates the selfishness and ignorance of Eve in her moment of temptation. He does nothing to allay the curse of suffering and sorrow that she wrought with her disobedience. Thus from the standpoint of Melville he is a typical Christian, unaware of his divided loyalties towards God and Mammon. Under the circumstances the poet dismisses the import of "fig truth," turning to the incorruptible touchstone of knowledge—forthright acceptance of the world as it is:

> Bravo, master! Brava, brig!
>   For slanting snows out of the West
> Never the *Snow-Bird* cares one fig;
>   And foul winds steady her, though a pest. (p. 199)

Abandoning the goals of biblical prophecy and of civilized progress, he hails the dauntless exposure to the wintry winds of life.

An analogous situation is the subject of "The Figure-Head," though hardly one broached in the genteel circles of society. Half in pity and half in jest, Melville exercises an old man's prerogative to talk about a climacterical ordeal. As he so often does, he employs the figure of a bride to implement his sexual play:

> The *Charles-and-Emma* seaward sped,
> (Named from the carven pair at prow,)
> He so smart, and a curly head,
> She tricked forth as bride knows how;
>   Pretty stem for the port, I trow! (p. 197)

Remembering Melville's blatant conversion of a prow into a phallic symbol in "The Haglets," it is not illogical to endow the "pretty stem" with a similar meaning. At least then the yonic connotations of "port" explain the snickering archaism, "I trow," and prepare the reader for the vulgar untangling about to take place:

> But iron-rust and alum-spray
> And chafing gear, and sun and dew
> Vexed this lad and lassie gay,
> Tears in their eyes, salt tears nor few;
>   And the hug relaxed with the failing glue. (p. 198)

Unquestionably, the rendering of this broken embrace evokes the lugubrious experience of senile impotence. Of course, Melville consciously disguises his purpose in the most outrageous sentimentalities, but surely no genius is required to explicate the hilarious sequence of double-entendres. It is a fact of life: the "gay" (amorous) days are bound to unglue. But however rawly Melville turns the thought, it is done so deliberately in order to establish a dramatic contrast with the wrenching poignancy of the concluding stanza:

> But came in end a dismal night,
> With creaking beams and ribs that groan,
> A black lee-shore and waters white:
> Dropped on the reef, the pair lie prone:
> O, the breakers dance, but the winds they moan! (p. 198)

The desperate attempt to effect a consummation is transformed into an elegiac convulsion of death in the womb of life—the sea. After all, every experience of frustration is a rehearsal of dying, of energy entombed. Be that as it may, Melville knows that everyone has to live through the winter of frozen emotions; that too is a desolating aspect of "the Real."

"Crossing the Tropics" overtly substantiates Melville's preoccupation with the theme of sexual frustration. However, on this occasion he centers his attention on young love:

> While now the Pole Star sinks from sight
> The Southern Cross it climbs the sky;
> But losing thee, my love, my light,
> O bride but for one bridal night,
> The loss no rising joys supply. (p. 202)

Obviously, the cross figures the crucified feelings of the lonely sailor, but the symbol also has naturalistic overtones. It is the popular phallic emblem of the nineteenth-century mythographers, even as the witty euphemism "rising joys" clearly implies. And paralleling the baffled desires of "The Figure-Head," the refrain picks up the motif of the winds, an ironical allusion to the archetypal breath of life:

> Love, love, the Trade Winds urge abaft,
> And thee, from thee, they steadfast waft. (p. 202)

Next Melville proceeds to frame the despair in a perfect inversion of natural law, the reversal of the seasons that occurs upon the crossing of the equator. Thus he makes the point that the interplay of

62

contraries in the scheme of nature is devised to serve the ends of life larger than the desires of any individual. Consequently, the anguish of frustration is the inescapable lot of mankind:

> My heart it streams in wake astern.
> When, cut by slanting sleet, we swoop
>   Where raves the world's inverted year,
> If roses all your porch shall loop,
> Not less your heart for me will droop
>   Doubling the world's last outpost drear. (p. 202)

The echoing consonance of the third line, one of Melville's flawless unions of sound and sense, perfectly objectifies man's experience of the discontinuities of subjective time. Yet by invoking the rose the sailor unthinkingly affirms the unquenchable vitality of the erotic impulse in the perpetuation of temporal existence.

The glorifications of the Golden Age in "To Ned" and "The Enviable Isles" still take note of "the Real"—the rhythm of joy and sorrow underlying human existence. In the first poem Melville nostalgically recalls his first impression of the South Seas; "Authentic Edens in a Pagan sea" where "man, if lost to Saturn's Age,/Yet feel[s] life no Syrian pilgrimage" (p. 201). Essentially autobiographical in content, these musings bind together two different phases of his life: the amoral adventures of his youthful whaling days and the spiritual dilemmas of his middle years. Neither is really now viewed through the glass of reality, for subjectivity and sensibility change from one stage of growth to another. Melville's recollection simply takes into account the different periods of his search for self-fulfillment under the moral prescriptions of his Protestant-Christian conditioning. Belatedly he realizes that inherited habits of thought do not function to reconcile thought and instinct:

> Well, Adam advances, smart in pace,
> But scarce by violets that advance you trace. (p. 201)

Glancing around his present world, he sees no signs of spiritual progress. The accursed progeny of Christianity's ancestral father are still divided in their fealty to good and evil. As the concluding stanza resolves this predicament, it seems that Melville looks upon all Edens as fantasies of wish-fulfillment, the idle mind toying with expedients to neutralize the unavoidable travails of life:

> But we, in anchor-watches calm,
> The Indian Psyche's languor won,
> And, musing, breathed primeval balm
> From Edens ere yet overrun;
> Marvelling mild if mortal twice,
> Here and hereafter, touch a Paradise. (p. 201)

The Indian dispassion described is the mood of the moment, an ethnic affectation. Melville knows too well that Western introspection and Eastern meditation touch opposing shores of ecstasy.

Appropriately enough, in "The Enviable Isles" the poet sadly admits that his cultural identity forbids the cultivation of nirvanic bliss. He has been reared in an atmosphere of activist aspiration. Struggle not quietude insures the attainment of happiness. As a consequence, his vision of the Fortunate Isles now is tinged with negation. He does not want a lotus-eater's contentment. Such an existence is a state of death-in-life:

> But, inland, where the sleep that folds the hills
> A dreamier sleep, the trance of God, instills—
> On uplands hazed, in wandering airs aswoon,
> Slow-swaying palms salute love's cypress tree
> Adown in vale where pebbly runlets croon
> A song to lull all sorrow and all glee. (p. 204)

Or perhaps Melville has reached the stage in internal development where he desires no truce with God or His creation. Having indurated his character to the naturalistic tensions of reality, he will not stoop to any kind of compromise with fate. His sea is a purgative element, not a cradle of soothing lullabies:

> Sweet-fern and moss in many a glade are here,
> Where, strown in flocks, what cheek-flushed myriads lie
> Dimpling in dream—unconscious slumberers mere,
> While billows endless round the beaches die. (p. 204)

Disowning the attraction of an Eden and its inertia of love, he implicitly consecrates a universe of dynamic antitheses. The sentiment is fitting at this point. It marks his rejection of all abstract ideals, in particular the idle dreams of his youth and the metaphysical placebos of his Jerusalem pilgrimage.

The articulation of this code anticipates the terminal epiphany of the "Pebbles." Once and for all, Melville attests his faith in the grim modes of reconciliation defined in the other poems of *John Marr and Other Sailors*. Thereby he establishes the foundations of "the Real" on which he has erected the meaning of life. Consistent with this intention, the first stanza opens up with a parody of a familiar passage from the Gospel of St. John:

> Marvel not that I said unto thee, Ye must be born again. The wind bloweth where it listeth, and thou hearest the sound thereof, but canst not tell whence it cometh, and whither it goeth: so is every one that is born of the Spirit. (III: 7–8)

This is the answer that Jesus gives to Nicodemus's question: "How can a man be born when he is old? can he enter the second time into his mother's womb, and be born (III:4)?" The poet's surrogate, however, does not heed the Redeemer's pronouncement. Instead he turns to the sound of the sea for his solution to the riddle of rebirth:

I

Though the Clerk of the Weather insist,
    And lay down the weather-law,
Pintado and gannet they wist
That the winds blow whither they list
    In tempest or flaw.

II

Old are the creeds, but stale the schools,
    Revamped as the mode may veer,
But Orm from the schools to the beaches strays,

> And, finding a Conch hoar with time, he delays
>   And reverent lifts it to ear.
> That Voice, pitched in far monotone,
>   Shall it swerve? shall it deviate ever?
> The Seas have inspired it, and Truth—
>   Truth, varying from sameness never. (p. 205)

"The weather-law" in the opening verse is probably a pun on "whether-law," a not so subtle projection of the alternative modes of truth in conflict during the latter part of the nineteenth century —biblical revelation and scientific knowledge. But Melville subscribes to neither point of view. Like the sea fowl, he simply adjusts his existence to the prevailing natural disorder or the imperfect creation, not especially concerned with the solace of a rational or supernatural explanation of things as they are. The same attitude is rehearsed in Orm's rejection of the glib platitudes of all the theological and philosophical systems. He too is an uncomplaining, unintellectual existentialist. He is free in his knowledge of his freedomless plight.

The next stanza develops the implications of this code in direct relation to the passage from St. John, mocking its apocalyptic message:

> In hollows of the liquid hills
>   Where the long Blue Ridges run,
> The flattery of no echo thrills,
>   For echo the seas have none;
> Nor aught that gives man back man's strain—
> The hope of his heart, the dream of his brain. (p. 205)

There is no question in Melville's mind about the actuality of the sounding waves, or of the subsequent silence. By the same token, he does not protest the necessity of steeling the nerves to this fate. For to cling to the illusion of an invisible Providence is to engage in self-deception, as the following couplet also implies:

> On ocean where the embattled fleets repair,
> Man, suffering inflictor, sails on sufferance there. (p. 206)

Man is his own worst enemy, according to the equivocation of "inflictor," both the agent and victim of his suffering. In order to emphasize the advisability of a truce in the war with self and with other men, Melville reiterates the indifference of nature:

> Implacable I, the old implacable Sea:
>   Implacable most when most I smile serene—
> Pleased, not appeased, by myriad wrecks in me. (p. 206)

Though perhaps the personification in this stanza is not organically evolved (just like the subject of the isolated couplet), it nevertheless appears to be a conscious tactic, specifically devised to enhance the corrosive blasphemy of the next development of thought.

In any event, the succeeding lines clear up the purpose of the personification in the conversion of the sea into a mixture of the Devil and Christ:

> Curled in the comb of yon billow Andean,
>   Is it the Dragon's heaven-challenging crest?
> Elemental mad ramping of ravening waters—
> Yet Christ on the Mount, and the dove in her nest! (p. 206)

While startling enough literally, the hypothesis of the question and the declaration of the exclamation point are designed to reintroduce the motif of an anti-biblical revelation. Obviously, the combined images derive from the story of the war in heaven described in the Book of Revelation, the drama of "the great dragon," the "old serpent, called the Devil," whose legions are overcome "by the blood of the Lamb (XII:8–11)." In uniting the traits of the Dragon and Christ in the savagery and serenity of the sea, Melville seems to imply that the two are indistinguishable, at least to judge by the lot of man on earth under the so-called new dispensation. The logic of this interpretation is dictated primarily by the name of Melville's mask in the poem. Orm, the Teutonic for serpent, is the root of worm (German *wurm*), and in Hebrew *orm* means wise, prudent, and ready-witted.[3] Since the poet obliquely connects Orm with seeking for the wisdom of the serpent, he apparently is still fascinated by the Ophite heresy. The Jewish sect in

---

[3] Harold Bayley, *The Lost Language of Symbolism*, 2 vols. (New York, 1952), 2: 219. Most of the sources of this study are nineteenth-century texts of the sort congenial to Melville's imagination.

question revered the serpent in early Christian times, holding that
the post-exilic Jehovah was a mere demon who had usurped the
Kingdom of the Wise Serpent.[4] Under the circumstances, Orm
prefers the direct epiphany of the conch simply because the doctrines of traditional Christianity are, if not a tissue of lies, then a
fable grafted on the true myth of the Saviour.

Following logically, the last stanza of "Pebbles" contains a
blanket repudiation of supernatural truth:

> Healed of my hurt, I laud the inhuman Sea—
> Yea, bless the Angels Four that there convene;
> For healed I am even by their pitiless breath
> Distilled in wholesome dew named rosmarine. (p. 206)

As indicated in the opening pages of this study, "the Angels Four"
are heralds of John's vision of "the sealed," those worshipers of
Christ insured of resurrection. But healed and hurt as he has been,
Melville experiences his rebirth in time through an acceptance of
the unchangeable polarities of existence. There is nothing that he
can gain by believing in the vicarious atonement of Christ. The
"pitiless breath" of the four angels is the searing wind that endlessly blows over the sea of life; it is the voice of "the Real," of
the contingent universe, not of any Spirit. Such is the meaning that
inheres in the purifying "dew named rosmarine." Etymologically,
it is a combination of the Latin *ros* (dew) and *marinus* (marine),
that is, sea-dew. However, Melville uses the word as a pun on
rosemary or rose of the sea, a symbol of Mary and of Christ, the
dew of Mary. The alchemists applied the latter meaning to the
word, equating it with the universal solvent employed to produce
the philosopher's stone, the source of the elixir of life. In effecting
the various transmutations of rosmarine through distillation, they
of course set out to attain salvation or immortality through physical means. By a similar sacrilegious procedure Melville attains a
transformation of consciousness. The bitter saline sea evolves into a
rose of redemption, an unprotesting vision of the cruel, contingent

---

[4] See Lawrance Thompson, *Melville's Quarrel with God* (Princeton: Princeton University Press, 1952), pp. 430–2, for a discussion of Melville's familiarity with the Ophite heresy.

nature of human destiny, and the implicit parody of Dante's mystical experience in *Paradiso* crystallizes the chief revelation of *John Marr and Other Sailors*.

The preceding explication does not take into account the symbolic function of the sea shell, the oracular voice of Melville's temporal salvation. In Greek myth it is the *concha veneris,* the hierogram of the Greek Goddess of Love, Aphrodite, who is the supreme incarnation of the Triple Goddess. As a result of her birth from the seed of Uranus (heaven) when he is emasculated and cast into the sea by Chronos (time), she is designated the oldest of the Fates, the daughter of the Goddess Necessity who initiates and controls the principle of life in the universe. All these associations—sea, life, death, sexuality, impotence, and time—are implicit metaphors in Melville's collection of poetry,[5] and, consonant with his attitudes towards Christianity, they likewise focus on the dethronement of the archetypal Greek God Uranus. As his powers were assimilated by Aphrodite in her role as the supreme Fate—the preserver, creator, and destroyer—so those of the Christian trinity are taken over by Melville's Triple Goddess.

[5] Charles Anthon's *A Classical Dictionary* (New York, 1841)—incidentally the source of Hawthorne's *The Tanglewood Tales* and *The Wonder Book*—is the key to this facet of Melville's knowledge of myth.

Timoleon

V   History and Man

Timoleon (1891) takes Melville full circle in his contemplation of the human condition.[1] Each separate work postulates a different formula of self-fulfillment, and these various alternatives are all carefully evaluated. In the title poem, for instance, Melville hands the palm of glory to the self-transcendence which man achieves despite the taboos of conventional morality:

> O, crowned with laurel twined with thorn,
> Not rash thy life's cross-tide I stem,
> But reck the problem rolled in pang
> And reach and dare to touch th[y] garment's hem. (p. 209)

Only in this poem and in "L'Envoi," does the poet enter into a passionate vicarious identification with his subject. Though the treatment of the personal plight in the other poems betrays his insight into complex emotions, his sympathies are those of sensibility, not of conviction. He wants his readers to view these trepidations of the spirit as the counterpoints to the fate of Timoleon, modulations of man's eternal desire to elicit a purpose from life, and as in *John Marr*, he employs a dazzling irony, quickened by pun, paradox, parody, and equivocation, to illuminate the ambiguous questions raised by the experiences. In the poetry of *Timoleon* he is not trying to exorcise the demons of doubt and despair. He no longer needs to explain himself to himself. What once tortured his soul, provoking gloom and pessimism, he now slyly derides.

[1] For an interpretation of the poetry in almost the exclusive framework of biography see Howard, *Herman Melville*, pp. 332–36. Arvin is somewhat noncommittal or perhaps aesthetically reserved. He finds the work "weaker, tamer, and more conventional than . . . *John Marr*," ascribing its general quality to the earlier writing of some of the poems, *Herman Melville*, pp. 279–80.

This attitude is manifest in "Timoleon." The historical meta-phor of the poem is the subtle vehicle of revelation, the interpreta-tion of whose function cannot be ascribed to an underscored line or two in Balzac[2] or to Melville's familiarity with Plutarch and Bayle. What he is attempting to convey turns on the ambiguity of language and situation. Because Plutarch is the source of certain facts or Bayle the inspiration of an insidious method of satire, these facts do not change the poem into a historical document. It is the organizing trope of the military deliverer that underscores the crushing irony of Melville's deification of Timoleon:

> A peace he won whose *rainbow* spanned
> The isle *redeemed*; and he was hailed
> *Deliverer* of that fair colonial land.
>   And Corinth clapt; *Absolved*, and more!
> Justice in long arrears is thine:
> Not slayer of thy brother, no.
> But *savior* of the state, Jove's soldier, *man divine*.
>   (p. 215; italics mine)

Obviously the vocabulary of this apotheosis is predominantly Christian. By implication it takes note of the failure of Christ to fulfill his sacred role as redeemer in Melville's culture. And even more heretically, it refutes one of the truisms of Scripture: "all they that take the sword shall perish with the sword" (Matt. XXVI:52). This, however, is only one edge of the poet's sword of irony. Not only is the power of redemption snatched from the reli-gious saviour, but it is also taken from the philosopher whose ethic has molded the speculative morality of Western civilization. In a malicious aside Melville notes that "The time was Plato's" (p. 213). The latter is directly connected with the history of Sicily and Syracuse in the period shortly before Timoleon. As a philosopher-saviour Plato was summoned to Syracuse by Dion, the idealistic ad-viser to the tyrant Dionysius. But all his attempts to stabilize the government failed, and he was compelled to flee for his life.[3] Whether this story is apocryphal or not, it suits the theme of the

---

[2] Leyda, *The Melville Log*, 2: 829.
[3] F. M. Cornford, *The Republic of Plato* (London, 1941), pp. xxiii–xxiv.

poem, impugning any abstract plan of human salvation. According to Bayle, Timoleon professed only a prudential belief in God, yet he overthrew the despot Dionysius and brought peace and prosperity to Sicily.[4] There seems little doubt that Melville had this observation in mind when he was writing the poem, for he focuses on the problem of divine influence in human affairs as the dialectical center of his theme:

> Or, put it, where dread stress inspires
> A virtue beyond man's standard rate,
> Seems virtue there a strain forbid—
> Transcendence such as shares transgression's fate?
>   If so, and wan eclipse ensue,
> Yet glory await emergence won,
> Is that high Providence, or Chance?
> And proved it which with thee, Timoleon? (p. 209)

In answering this question Melville resorts to a flank attack on the whole conception of Platonic virtue, a logical continuation of his implicit ridicule of the philosopher-saviour. The renown achieved by Timoleon through the heroic rescue of his brother exemplifies a negative exercise of virtue. As Timoleon's mother asserts, he acted under the discipline of instinct and military habits:

> He saved my darling, gossips tell;
> If so, 'twas service, yea, and fair;
> But instinct ruled and duty bade,
> In service such, a henchman e'en might share. (p. 211)

Here she rehearses a basic assumption of Platonism. Man's nature in the ideal shares nothing with the instincts of the animals below him. In the practice of virtue he shares the divine intelligence of the gods above.[5] But, according to Melville, Timoleon's later effort to abide by absolute morality occasions only indecision. His "just and humane heart" (p. 212), in Platonic doctrine so crucial to the life of the soul,[6] is haunted by the threat of nemesis. If he

---

[4] *The Historical and Critical Dictionary of Mr. Peter Bayle,* trans. Mr. des Maizeau (London, 1735–38), 5: 365.
[5] F. M. Cornford, *Greek Religious Thought* (Boston, 1950), p. xxiv.
[6] Cornford, *Greek Religious Thought,* p. xxvi.

75

acts to promote the cause of universal equity by slaying his despotic brother, he will arouse the vengeance of the Furies by his *hubris*. Nothing in the poem or in historical fact supports the charge of pride against the Greek hero. Indeed, Melville carefully points out that Timoleon determines to slay his tyrant brother even after taking cognizance of the possible consequences:

> But undeterred he wills to act,
> Resolved thereon though Ate rise;
> He heeds the voice whose mandate calls,
> *Or seems to call*, peremptory from the skies. (p. 212; italics mine)

But what of Melville's reservation in the last line? Is it not a reminder that religious codes are conditioned habits of response to good and evil, not necessarily injunctions of the gods?

At any rate the hero's fratricide is judged by the reigning standards of right and wrong which do not take into account his high motive of justice:

> Wandering lights
> Confirmed the atheist's standing star;
> As now, no sanction Virtue knew
> For deeds that on prescriptive morals jar. (p. 213)

Under the impact of this disillusionment, the substance of Timoleon's belief in divine order crumbles, and he is led to conclude that moral imperatives are the products of intellectual self-deception and that, by extension, the gods are either impostors or illusions:

> If conscience doubt, she'll next recant.
> What basis then? O, tell at last,
> Are earnest natures staggering here
> But fatherless shadows from no substance cast?
> Yea, *are* ye gods? Then ye, 'tis ye
> Should show what touch of tie ye may,
> Since ye, too, if not wrung are wronged
> By grievous misconceptions of your sway. (p. 215)

When finally he does achieve his destiny in Syracuse, it is a matter of chance. Historically, the Corinthian officials summon Timoleon in their hour of need when an idle voice of a commoner in the audience counsels his recall. Because this relieves them of their responsibility to a Sicilian peace delegation, they willingly consent.[7] By preserving the island's freedom, Timoleon becomes a military deliverer, succeeding where the philosopher-saviour failed. But what Melville leaves unsaid is crucial to the interpretation of the poem: God is dead.

In "Night-March" Melville again probes the distance of God from man. In the militaristic imagery of an army marching inexorably into darkness, he symbolizes the disciplined mass of Christian soldiery:

> With banners furled, and clarions mute,
>   An army passes in the night;
> And beaming spears and helms salute
>   The dark with bright. (p. 222)

Armed with the strength of faith, they seek to penetrate the darkness surrounding their deity. But as the second stanza makes clear, the endless army never catches sight of its leader:

> In silence deep the legions stream,
>   With open ranks, in order true;
> Over boundless plains they stream and gleam—
>   No chief in view! (p. 222)

The second line is almost certainly a metaphor of the various Christian sects and of their common belief in the Saviour. Therefore the third line figuratively establishes the persistence of the quest through the innumerable centuries of the Christian tradition —though without the inspiration of a theophany! Accordingly, in the third stanza Melville impeaches the validity of the sustaining myth:

> Afar, in twinkling distance lost,
>   (So legends tell) he lonely wends
> And back through all that shining host
>   His mandate sends. (p. 222)

The unity of belief in the Saviour, he willingly admits, has been perpetuated through the generations. But, he queries, are the dumb

[7] Thomas North, *Plutarch's Lives* (London, 1898), p. 137.

longings of man proof of the existence of an infinite God? Or is it that man believes only to believe?

Other interpretations of the poem are possible, but only if Melville's parody of a familiar Christian hymn is ignored. A favorite in all Protestant services, "Fling Out the Banner! Let it Float," was unquestionably known to Melville; and, by a curious coincidence, its music accommodates the words of his poem. In contrast with the atmosphere of uncertainty which envelops Melville's musing on the Saviour, the hymn exultantly proclaims His eternal presence:

> Fling out the banner! let it float
> Skyward and seaward, high and wide;
> The sun that lights its shining folds,
> The cross on which the saviour died.
>
> Fling out the banner! distant lands
> Shall see from far the glorious sight,
> And nations crowding to be born,
> Baptize their spirits in its light.[8]

Its blind assumption of faith coupled with its revivalistic tone may well have inspired the subversive overtones of "The Night-March." In any event, the execution of the poem does shed palpable light on Melville's methods of irony.

In "The Margrave's Birthnight," the poet attributes the vitiation of Christianity to the common Protestant degradation of the rite into a memorial or symbolic communion. Of course, here he merely reasserts his interest in a subject travestied in his short stories many years before.[9] On the level the poem can be read as a comment on the perfunctory ritual of a meal given to commemorate the birthday of a deceased host. But this approach ignores the axis of puns on which meaning turns. The title, for example, is an equivoque. "Margrave" is another name for prince and hence "the prince's birthnight," now a marred grave, a desecrated memory. Since the season is unquestionably Christmas,

---

[8] *The Student Hymnary* (New York, 1937), p. 332. The hymn was composed in 1842.
[9] See my article, "Melville's Eros," *Texas Studies in Language and Literature*, 3 (Autumn 1961), 297–308.

O the hall, and O the holly!
Tables line each wall;
Guests as holly-berries plenty,
But—no host withal! (p. 223)

the prince is of course Christ. Then holly, traditionally, is the tree of the cross.[10] But the ambiguity operates on a much subtler level of reference. In the stanza which follows, "throne" and "cover" are surrogates respectively of the monstrance, the vessel in which the host is carried, and the corporal, the cloth on which the Eucharistic vessels are laid:

May his people feast contented
While at head of board
Empty throne and vacant cover
Speak the absent lord? (p. 223)

In the rhetorical question posed in the passage, Melville asks whether Christianity can endure without the New Testament vision of the living Christ. This inference follows from his play on "host" earlier and from the performance next of a meaningless ritual:

. . . ; and when,
Passing there the vacant cover,
Functionally then

Old observance grave they offer;
But no Margrave fair,
In his living aspect gracious,
Sits responsive there. (p. 244; italics mine)

Finally Melville virtually asserts that empty forms and phrases have been substituted for spiritual communion with the Real Presence:

No, and never guest once marvels,
None the good lord name,
Scarce they mark void throne and cover—
Dust upon the same. (p. 224)

With usage fallen into this state of mechanical observance, the bread and the wine have become physical facts. Forgotten are the

[10] George Ferguson, *Signs & Symbols in Christian Art* (New York, 1954), p. 37.

79

miracle of Cana and the selfless love at the Last Supper. Remembered only is the present moment of carnal gratification:

> Ah, enough for toil and travail,
> If but for a night
> Into wine is turned the water,
> Black bread into white. (p. 224)

And so, as Melville would have it, Christ the son of God is also dead! And his age sanctions the view—its religion, its science, its morality.

Eucharistic imagery again controls the emergence of meaning in "Magian Wine," but Melville's thought is cloaked in the darkest of figurative equivocations. Wine, in the Christian sense, is a heady drink of transcendental bliss, and this is the logic of the title of the work. The magian allusion, however, refers to the occult power of the three priests of an alien religion who come to worship the Christ Child (Matt. II:3–11). For the faith the miraculous birth induces in them becomes the property of the communion wine. An ineffable mystery, it cannot be understood rationally; its intimations must be intuited from the symbols which have crystallized around it:

> Amulets gemmed, to Miriam dear,
>   Adown in liquid mirage gleam;
> Solomon's Syrian charms appear
>   Opal and ring supreme.
> The rays that light this Magian Wine
> Thrill up from semblances divine. (p. 225)

In this context Miriam refers to the mother of Christ as a variant of Mary, and Melville, in surrounding the name with pejoratives like "amulets" and "mirage," simultaneously argues for and against the promise of salvation which the birth of Christ heralds: "But I say unto you, I will not drink henceforth of this fruit of the wine, until that day when I drink it new with you in my Father's kingdom" (Matt. XXVI:29). Similarly, the allusion to the Seal of Solomon is another depreciative phrase, referring to the latter's wisdom and its potent talisman, the opal ring with its pentagonal star.[11] With this implication of magic and its direct connection with Christ as "the rose of Sharon" in the Song of Solomon (II:1), Melville leads the reader directly into the ambiguity of "semblances divine" (p. 225). Does he mean here that the symbol of the wine is only mummery, a disguise for a mystery that doesn't exist? Or does he mean that Christ is to be seen under this aspect of ritual incantation? Or does the phrase simply underline priestly wizardry?

It seems to me that these obscurities are all resolved in the next passage:

> And, seething through the rapturous wave,
> What low Elysian anthems rise:
> Syblline inklings blending rave,
>   Then lap the verge with sighs.
> Delirious here the oracles swim
> Ambiguous in the beading hymn. (p. 225)

Negation attends the introduction of classical imagery. The intrusion of the Greek heaven suggests that each different culture has its own peculiar conception of salvation. Moreover, the Sibylline image extends this interpretation. Though the Sibyllae were in origin oracles whose prophetic powers foretold the fall of Troy, they were also the reputed heralds of the triumph of Christianity, at least so the early fathers of the Church claimed. But the irony of this claim lies in the fraud that it harbors: "What we have remaining under the title of the Sibylline Oracles were evidently fabricated by . . . early Christians, ever anxious to discover traces of their faith in pagan mythology." And since these books of prophecies contain a mixture of borrowings from the Old and New Testament and pagan sources,[12] "blending and rave" and "delirious" are obviously derisive in connotation. There is no question that "Magian Wine" can be read as a treatment of mystical experience. But, unfortunately, the interrelated image patterns are the main vehicle of theme. Centering on the prophetic statements of Christ, on the messianic content of so-called Wisdom Books, and on Solo-

[11] Bayley, *The Lost Language of Symbolism*, 1: 256.
[12] Anthon, *A Classical Dictionary*, p. 1230.

mon's injunctions to love the rose of Sharon, Melville reduces the
Christian hope of salvation to a dubious mass of confusion. Thus
religion promises to give less insight into human destiny than the
disenchanting tribulations of Timoleon.

In "Herba Santa" Melville ironically recapitulates the ludicrous history of Eucharistic controversy,

> Shall code or creed a lure afford
> To win all selves to Love's accord?
> When Love ordained a supper divine
>   For the wide world of man,
> What bickerings o'er his gracious wine!
>   Then strange new feuds began. (p. 236)

and then proposes an alternative conciliatory ritual, the American
Indian ceremony of the peace pipe. To establish the logic of the
substitution, he glibly argues that the act of smoking eases the
tensions of temporal adversities:

> After long wars when comes release
> Not olive wands proclaiming peace
>   An import dearer share
> Than stems of Herba Santa hazed
>   In autumn's Indian air.
> Of moods they breathe that care disarm,
> They pledge us lenitive and calm. (p. 236)

In effect, like religion, it generates a feeling of divine serenity. An indrawn breath of smoke, like the spirit of God, passes into
the smoker, and in exhalation rises into the air and disappears into
heaven. Thus the inner world and the outer world are miracu-
lously fused. And as the ego surrenders all its desires, a state of
selflessness akin to Eucharistic communion arises, and the celebrant
is lulled into what Melville calls "the *Truce of God*":

> Insinuous thou that through the nerve
>   Windest the soul, and so canst win
>   Some from repinings, some from sin,
> The Church's aim thou dost subserve.
>
> The ruffled fag fordone with care
>   And brooding, Gold would ease this pain:

> Him soothest thou and smoothest down
> Till some content return again. (p. 237)

This comic seriousness, however, can also sting. For the next quatrain implies that the wiser saints have accommodated religion to common human nature using material sedations, not unlike tobacco:

> Even ruffians feel thy influence breed
> Saint Martin's summer in the mind,
> They feel this last evangel plead,
> As did the first, apart from creed,
> Be peaceful, man—be kind! (p. 238)

So, at least, one can infer from the reference to Saint Martin who was the patron saint of ruffians—that is, drunkards. Traditionally, on his feast day the consumption of wine helped to alleviate the dread of winter. According to a proverb of Martinmas, mortality is the lot of man as it is of the hog, the animal slaughtered during the holiday.[13] By extension, then, the body's desires are not to be flouted.

This irreverence also informs the next passage, for the tobacco is broached as an appropriate incarnation for the Second Coming. The logic of this proposal is based on Melville's argument that the willing sacrifice was an empty gesture:

> Rejected once on higher plain,
> O Love supreme, to come again
> Can this be thine?
> Again to come, and win us too
> In likeness of a weed
> That as a god didst vainly woo,
> As man more vainly bleed? (p. 238)

This sentiment leads inevitably to the conclusion of the poem. Salvation through Christ is no longer a pregnant issue. In a Saint-

---

[13] E. Cobham Brewer, *Dictionary of Fact and Fable* (Philadelphia, 1886), p. 558. This was an extremely popular volume during the nineteenth century. Its publication date marks the appearance of the seventeenth edition. With our knowledge of Melville's intellectual curiosity there is a good possibility that he might have known it quite well.

Martin's-tide mood Melville looks forward to the release from
cares of death. "The passive Pipe of Peace" drugs any intense concern with Eucharistic potencies. Since the church has encouraged
the soul to repress its vision of the Christ within, he joyfully accepts the verdict of his culture:

> Forbear, my soul! and in thine Eastern chamber
>   Rehearse the dream that brings the long release;
> Through jasmine sweet and talismanic amber
>   Inhaling Herba Santa in the passive Pipe of Peace. (p. 238)

But if the saviour ideal promises no deliverance from sorrow,
perhaps there is an alternate scheme of salvation. In Christian tradition we know it as the Jobian epiphany: the voice of God who
spoke to the suffering man "out of the whirlwind" (XXXVIII:
1). The poet explores its implications in "The Enthusiast." In
structure the first two stanzas of the poem are explicitly dialectical.
A series of questions is posed, based on the causes of man's default
from faith. The last stanza contains an affirmative resolution, at
least on the surface. Melville's epigraph to the poem establishes
the context of Job, for he quotes the familiar verse: "Though he
slay me yet will I trust him." But the remainder of this passage
does not permit the simple exegesis of which the first statement is
susceptible: there is a ring of stubborn human pride in "but I will
maintain mine own ways before him" (XIII:15). Not until the
theophany does Job recant the belief in his personal integrity and
virtue. But does Melville wish his reader to anticipate the change
in attitude, or does he wish him to limit his associations? As I see
it, the title of the poem negates the resolution of the Book. When
organically related to the epigraph, "The Enthusiast" becomes
highly derogatory, an epithet derisive of zealous and fanatical devotion:

> Shall hearts that beat no base retreat
>   In youth's magnanimous years—
> Ignoble hold it, if discreet
>   When interest tames to fears;
> Shall spirits that worship light
>   Perfidious deem its sacred glow,

> Recant, and trudge where worldings go,
> Conform and own them right? (p. 230)

Is not the condition of belief in this stanza the unwisdom of youth? This is the age of ignorance, of service to dream and wishful thinking. This is the world of Pierre who cannot cope with the implacable truth that where there is light there is also shadow—that we know good only because we know evil. In this plight man does not need to conform; he must recognize life for what it is. Though the second stanza also pleads, even in its questions, for integrity of convictions,

> Shall faith abjure her skies,
>   Or pale probation blench her down
>   To shrink from Truth so still, so lone
> Mid loud gregarious lies? (p. 231)

there is a diabolic flicker of verbal equivocation in the third line. Whose truth is "still" and "lone?" Is it the voice from the whirlwind which speaks in Sunday sermons? Questions, of course, are not answers. But they do succeed in objectifying the doubts that Melville raises in the mind of the reader of his poetry. He virtually *dares* one to believe in "The Enthusiast."

The last stanza, in particular, increases apprehension about the choice to be made. In a sudden allusion to history the poet warns that mundane philosophy is a design of self-will and ambition. The domains of Caesar and of God stand in radical opposition:

> Each burning boat in Caesar's rear,
>   Flames—No return through me!
> So put the torch to ties though dear,
>   If ties but tempters be. (p. 231)

But even as the dictator callously subordinates friendship to self-interest, so does the fanatic. His heavenly aspirations are not coordinated with the goals of the human community; his quest for divine favor reveals the hidden side of self-obsessed piety. However righteous his aims, however steadfast his soul, he is still motivated by egocentricity:

Nor cringe if come the night:
  Walk through the cloud to meet the pall,
  Though light forsake thee, never fall
From fealty to light. (p. 231)

In fine, the enthusiast is as sinful as his tempter. The poet's paradox in the last two lines discloses the spurious credo of the zealot. If in order to achieve grace he is willing to disown the Christian brotherhood of love, then, unwittingly, he is a Caesar in the moral world.

The poem reveals the subtlety of Melville's speculations on the meaning of life. Both the title and the epigraph generate a rhetorical ambiguity that must be resolved before any understanding of the poet's purpose is disclosed. By the same token, these initial obscurities anticipate the paradoxes which emerge in the body of the poem. Since, in essence, this composition is religious, it illustrates Melville's premise in this collection of poetry that the design of life cannot be reduced to an unequivocal and consistent mode of morality.

The idea also inheres in the gnomic form of "Buddha." Alone the poem simply enunciates the Buddhist's scorn for the physical. For in freeing himself from bondage to the flesh, his soul dissolves into the divine void in which all dualities are reconciled:

Swooning swim to less and less,
  Aspirants to nothingness!
Sobs of the worlds, and dole of kinds
  That dumb endurers be—
Nirvana! absorb us in your skies,
  Annul us into thee. (p. 232)

But again this interpretation does not take into consideration the epigraph beneath the title; " 'For what *is* your life? It is even a vapor, that appeareth for a little time, and then vanisheth away' " (James IV:14). In context James also berates the obsession of so-called Christians with their physical lusts, exhorting them to humility and purity, deploring the temptations of the devil, warning them that God will only extend his salvation to the righteous. Obviously he advocates the same contempt for the flesh and the world found in Buddhist thought, but here all similarities end. Whereas the heavenly destiny of man in Christian eschatology depends upon the final judgment of God, the Buddhist, conversely, believes that by an exercise of the moral will he can achieve union with the absolute. In other words, Melville implies that there are spiritual incentives in other religions far superior to those of Christianity. They allow man to preserve a dignity of the moral being unsullied by servile piety. Thus the extra-poetic device directs the reader to interpret the poem against a definite and understandable background of religious contradictions. By indicating his awareness of these similarities and differences, Melville tacitly questions the vaunted sovereignty of the Christian church.

This view is also embodied in "The Weaver." On this occasion Melville evaluates the practice of abstinence in Moslemism. The poet's cancellations of words like "Mecca" and "Allah" in the original manuscript establish the religious identification beyond question.[14] The asceticism of the disciple of Mohammed, of course, offers a contrast with the spiritual ideals in the other two poems. Even more intensely conscious of sin and of fear of hell than either the Christian or the Buddhist, the penitent literally seeks to die to himself and to live in God:

> The face is pinched, the form is bent,
> No pastime knows he nor the wine,
> Recluse he lives and abstinent
> Who weaves for Arva's shrine. (p. 227)

Beyond pleasure and pain, he patiently weaves his garment of the spirit on the thread of hope which ties him to his God,[15] and in this ritual he works out the pattern of his faith:

> For years within a mud-built room
> For Arva's shrine he weaves the shawl,

[14] From my personal examination of the manuscript in the Houghton Library of Harvard University.

[15] The thread at issue is the golden thread that ends in heaven, a recurrent symbol in mystical poetry. See Amanda Coomaraswamy's provocative discussion of this image in Joseph T. Shipley's *Dictionary of World Literature* (New York, 1953), pp. 405–406.

Lone wight, and at a lonely loom,
His busy shadow on the wall. (p. 227)

The ceremonial intent of the weaving is evident in both quatrains, and the shadow image in the second emphasizes the phenomenal insubstantiality of earthly existence. Thus this poem, like "The Enthusiast" and "Buddha," recognizes still another variation of longing for divine transcendence.

However, there are some men who bluntly assert that the material world is the only reality. Of this "Fragments of a Lost Gnostic Poem of the 12th Century" takes note:

Found a family, build a state,
The pledged event is still the same:
Matter in end will never abate
His ancient brutal claim. (p. 234)

No concern with future life or the soul is apparent here. Though man does not survive, the material world does. The operation of this law obviates metaphysical speculation. But, in the event the impulse to believe persists, the results are still inevitable—bitter and frustrate ignorance:

Indolence is heaven's ally here,
And energy the child of hell:
The Good Man pouring from his pitcher clear,
But brims the poisoned well. (p. 234)

Matter endures, providing no answer to the mystery of its timelessness. Even though the moral man may seek to resolve the problem of good and evil, this aspiration is doomed to expire in the bitterness of empty endeavor.

Melville next turns from empirical philosophy to the phenomenon of solar mythology, the universal attempt of man to interpret the mystery of his destiny in the struggle between the forces of darkness and light. In "The New Zealot to the Sun" he charts the career of man's worship of the sun—immemorially the visible theophany of God. But in a twist of ironical circumstance, what primitive man once deemed a personification of God has in its most recent development been reduced to an observable and calculable scientific fact, and the new cult of light holds to this faith with the same fanatic devotion of its despised predecessor. The poem, then, is a blind hymn to the sun—the modern scientist caught in a mood of self-exaltation. Like any priest who has access to supernatural power, he proudly declares the transcendence of his extra-divine knowledge, scornfully mocking the barbarism of the Persians who stood at the fountainhead of sun-worship:

> Persian, you rise
> Aflame from climes of sacrifice
>   Where adulators sue,
> And prostrate man, with brow abased,
> Adheres to rites whose tenor traced
>   All worship hitherto. (p. 226)

Indirectly, of course, this contempt reflects the attitudes of scientific rationalism: its arrogance, its dogmatism, its spiritual emptiness. And as a result, there is little sympathy with or understanding of the manner in which solar myths eased man's terror of nature. Instead religion is treated as a conspiracy of the priesthood to perpetuate ignorance, "of night their purple wove" (p. 226), and to exploit superstition:

> Chemist, you breed
> In orient climes each sorcerous weed
>   That energizes dream—
> Transmitted, spread in myths and creeds,
> Houris and hells, delirious screeds
>   And Calvin's last extreme. (p. 226)

On this assumption, the creation story, common to all faiths, is summarily dismissed as a hoax:

> What though your light
> In time's first dawn compelled the flight
>   Of Chaos' startled clan,
> Shall never all your darted spears
> Disperse worse Anarchs, frauds and fears,
>   Sprung from these weeds to man? (p. 227)

And as the rhetorical question sarcastically implies, the alleged divine conquest of darkness has served to promote still worse forms

of tyranny. Therefore it follows that science alone can rescue mankind from the devil in the pulpit:

> But Science yet
> An effluence ampler shall beget,
> And power beyond your play—
> Shall quell the shades you fail to rout,
> Yea, searching every secret out
> Elucidate your ray. (p. 227)

Melville, of course, does not subscribe to these megalomaniacal
pretensions. They are the counterparts of the religious fanatic's insights into the hidden design of the universe. The poem, rather,
evinces his amusement in all doctrinaire enthusiasms. As the pejorative title indicates, he disclaims any sympathy with the self-extol-
ling priest-scientist.[16]

But for all his contempt of cultism, in "Lone Founts" Melville appears to pay homage to the imperishable wisdom of *gnosis*.
In line with his desire to expose the delusion of every closed formula of human salvation, he cannot ignore an interest which, even

---

[16] The philosophy of "The New Zealot to the Sun" may well be Melville's
careful burlesque of the unrestrained scientism of John William Draper who
undertook its defense with religious fervor. Melville was acquainted with at
least one of his books (Sealts, *Melville's Reading*, No. 190), and he probably
knew the volume in question:

That world is not to be discovered through the vain traditions that have
brought down to us the opinions of men who lived in the morning of civilization, nor in the dreams of mystics who thought that they were inspired.
It is to be discovered by the investigations of geometry, and by the practical interrogation of Nature. These confer on humanity solid, and innumerable, and inestimable blessings.

The day will never come when any one of the propositions of Euclid,
will be denied; no one henceforth will call into question the globular shape of
the earth, as recognized by Erathosthenes; the world will not permit the
great physical inventions and discoveries made in Alexandria and Syracuse
to be forgotten.

Moreover, in Draper's opinion "the traditions of European mythology,
the revelations of Asia, the time-consecrated dogmas of Egypt, all had passed
away or were passing away," *History of the Conflict between Religion and
Science* (New York, 1877), pp. 32–33. As in the poem, there was no question
in Draper's mind that the new religion would elucidate all the darkness in
which previous religions had shrouded the truths of the ages.

90

today, flourishes in numerous theosophical movements. The emphasis in this work contrasts with the previous one. The tone is hortatory and affirmative:

> Though fast youth's glorious fable flies,
> View not the world with worldling's eyes;
> Nor turn with weather of the time.
> Foreclose the coming of surprise:
> Stand where Posterity shall stand;
> Stand where the Ancients stood before,
> And, dipping in lone founts thy hand,
> Drink of the never-varying lore:
> Wise once, and wise thence evermore. (p. 229)

The fable in question is, of course, the *philosophia perennis*, what Augustine denotes the "wisdom that was not made; but is at this present, as it hath ever been and so shall ever be." [17] This ideal is the one most quickly surrendered to contemporary aspirations. The continuity of eternal truth has no appeal in a world dedicated to the pursuit of temporal values.[18] In the poem Melville is appalled by the degradation of the *philosophia perennis*. Its custodianship no longer rests in the hands of the sages; it has become a commodity to be purchased at a convenient fee. Though this interpretation may seem to be extra-poetic, it does take cognizance of the climate of thought in the latter part of the nineteenth century. As "The New Zealot to the Sun" objectifies Melville's awareness of the role of science in his day, so does "Lone Founts," even with its wistfulness, bespeak the alertness of his mind.

A less controlled sentimentality pervades "C——'s Lament," though the lack of emotional restraint may be an artifice, a deliberate parody of the romantic school of poets. Melville's revisions of

[17] *Confessions*, 9: 10.
[18] But however attractive the pursuit of *gnosis*, however credible its existence, during Melville's lifetime, right in New York City, he probably was acquainted with it as a fad competing with spirit-rapping. An extremely popular importation of supernaturalism, its most sensational exponent was Helena P. Blavatsky, "Immensely corpulent, slovenly, reckless, [and] romantically hysterical," who in 1875 founded the Theosophy Society, "its platform fus[ing] spiritualism with the Brahminic and Vedic teachings of India," Merle Curti, *The Growth of American Thought* (New York, 1951), p. 536.

91

the title indicate such a tactic. One after another, he deletes the names of Simonides, Anacreon, and Coleridge, finally preferring the anonymity of an ellipsis.[19] In the adult nostalgia for the innocent happiness of youth, not for the ideal of wisdom of "Lone Founts," Melville obliquely attacks the pastoral tradition in poetry, in particular its juvenile denial of the richness of ordinary experience. The choice of imagery in the first stanza, with its emphasis on affected piety, reflects this intention:

> How lovely was the light of heaven,
> What angels leaned from out the sky
> In years when youth was more than wine
> And man and nature seemed divine
> Ere yet I felt that youth must die. (p. 232)

Certainly regression underlies the expression of these sentiments. The adult poetic voice refuses to grow up into the responsibilities of maturity and to recognize the natural phenomenon of dynamic growth and change. As Melville further argues in the poem, the fixation on the past is not unlike a narcissistic fantasy:

> Ere yet I felt that youth must die
> How insubstantial looked the earth,
> Alladin-land! in each advance,
> Or here or there, a new romance;
> I never dreamed would come a dearth. (p. 232)

After all, Alladin's experience is a classic paradigm of autoeroticism. It is an improbable wish come true—a denial of reality. It radically contrasts with the idea of *gnosis* in "Lone Founts," with the acquisition of a knowledge capable of bearing the disillusionments of human existence. In effect, the yearning for Eden is a sin against life and nature. As the next stanza illustrates, in such a state even suffering degenerates into mawkish exhibitionism:

> And nothing then but had its worth,
> Even pain. Yes, pleasure still and pain
> In quick reaction made of life
> A lover's quarrel, happy strife
> In youth that never comes again. (p. 232)

[19] From an examination of the original manuscripts in the Houghton Library of Harvard University.

The hysterical alternation of emotions is a syndrome of infantilism. Anyhow, the stubborn self-pity shapes the conclusion of the poem. The dialectical ambivalence in regard to the inevitable passage of youth posits not merely the death of an illusion but also that of an immature adult:

> But will youth never come again?
> Even to his grave-bed has he gone,
> And left me lone to wake by night
> With heavy heart that erst was light?
> O, lay it at his head—a stone! (p. 233)

Self-love is also the subject of "Shelley's Vision," and once again Melville derides romantic attitudinizing. Shelley's rationalization of his personal disgrace is tied to the irony of his vicarious identity with St. Stephen. Unlike his supposed counterpart, he is an unwilling martyr: moreover, he is persecuted for renouncing rather than imitating the exemplary life of Christ. And he resents his blackened reputation only because of the tarnishing of his self-image:

> Wandering late by morning seas
> When my heart with pain was low—
> Hate the censor pelted me—
> Deject I saw my shadow go. (p. 233)

Conversely, St. Stephen, the first martyr, is hated because he will not renounce his faith in the Saviour. He discards all thought of self in order to love Christ more.[20] But Shelley loathes himself because he is himself, and he proceeds to crucify himself on the cross of this hate:

> In elf-caprice of bitter tone
> I too would pelt the pelted one:
> At my shadow I cast a stone. (p. 233)

The Saint, of course, is also stoned, and on the brink of death he beseeches forgiveness for his enemies, repeating the words of Christ: " 'Father, forgive them, for they know not what they

[20] Jacobus de Voraigne, *The Golden Legend*, trans. G. Ryan and H. Ripperger (New York, 1941), 2: 409.

do.' " [21] Shelley's self-persecution has the opposite effect: it induces self-love:

> When lo, upon that sun-lit ground
> I saw the quivering phantom take
> The likeness of St. Stephen crowned:
> Then did self-reverence awake. (p. 233)

Obviously, the meaning of the religious metaphor is distorted. Shelley's self-transcendence comes at the expense, not at the behest, of conscience. Melville's shadow image projects Shelley's awareness of his shortcomings, but its transmutation into a symbol of triumph is sheer vanity. It represents the ego's dismissal of traditional morality. Consistent with Melville's sardonic wit, the melodramatic situation of the poem is contrived to arouse the pity of the gullible reader, thus exposing his shocking ignorance of Christian spiritual beliefs.

[21] *Ibid.*, 2: 55.

VI Art and Time

IN PLACE OF cultivated egocentricity, "The Bench of Boors" treats the subject of the tyrannical instincts. Inspired by one of Tenier's tavern scenes,[1] it probes the wisdom of escaping the harassments of life in bestial oblivion:

> In bed I muse on Tenier's boors,
> Embrowned and beery losels all:
> A wakeful brain
> Elaborates pain:
> Within low doors the slugs of boors
> Laze and yawn and doze again. (p. 229)

But this is an expedient without any attraction for Melville, and so the imagery of the poem attests. For example, "slugs," the most undeveloped form of animal life, reduce the drinkers' willful denial of consciousness to an ignoble surrender of human dignity. And as the next stanza argues, they are no more than animals, responsive only to the basic sensations:

> In dreams they doze, the drowsy boors,
> Their hazy hovel warm and small:
> Thought's ampler bound
> But chill is found:
> Within low doors the basking boors
> Snugly hug the ember-mound. (p. 230)

[1] See Horsford, *Journal*, p. 241, for an earlier reaction to the painter. This poem might have been written in association with the journal entry of April 10, 1857, but it has nothing in common with Melville's epithet of "charming" of that time. To the contrary, the poem argues for composition late in life when he was less prone to the stereotyped responses of the Baedeker variety.

Yet the antiphonal refrain to this scene concedes that unrestrained thinking is analogous to physical dissipation, an abuse of a specialized organ:

> Sleepless, I see the slumberous boors
> Their blurred eyes blink, their eyelids fall:
>   Thought's eager sight
>   Aches—overbright!
> Within low doors the boozy boors
> Cat-naps take in pipe-bowl light. (p. 230)

While still not inclined to emulate the brutish boors, Melville nevertheless implies that his negative impression is not necessarily valid. It is too intellectual. His refusal to accept the habits of the boors does not destroy them: they are. Indirectly, therefore, Melville decries abstract judgment and its dehumanizing tendency. It also is voracious, even self-cannibalistic. If such is the case, then neither an excess of sensual indulgence nor an excess of intellectual ardor represents the true rhythm of life. Thus "The Bench of Boors" terminates in a neutral resolution of its tensions.

"Lamia's Song" explores still another human physical drive, and, not unexpectedly, Melville focuses on sex, in Western culture perhaps the most exalted and most misunderstood of creatural pleasures. He is quite aware that in a puritanical environment such a preoccupation polarizes into extreme self-consciousness and repression. Here the poem subtly outlines the essence of this emotional discord in image, rhythm, and situation. Lamia, of course, figures the dread of sexuality. Mythically, she is a vampire who, while lying with young men, sucks out their blood as they sleep. Like Eve, she is the irresistible temptress:

> Descend, descend!
>   Pleasant the downward way—
> From your lonely Alp
> With the wintry scalp
> To our myrtles in valleys of May. (p. 228)

She lures her victim downward—into hell or heaven, depending upon his outlook. Her myrtled retreat is the garden of love, the sanctum of Maytide orgies. Or put crudely, the myrtle is an immemorial symbol of the pudendum, the hierogram of Aphrodite, the great Goddess of Love, and, in her own right, the supreme Triple Goddess of Fate. Lamia's task is to overcome conventional inhibitions, to discourage studied poses of icy aloofness. Consequently, she intones a mating song:

> Wend then, wend:
> Mountaineer, descend!
> And more than a wreath shall repay.
> Come, ah come!
> With the cataracts come,
> That hymn as they roam
> How pleasant the downward way! (p. 228)

She invites the mountaineer to mount—to engage in the act of coition and share the climax of passion—*la petite mort.*

The expertness of Melville's composition resides not alone in the double meaning. He perfectly accommodates the rhythm to the thought. Intermingling a basic iambic meter with a lilting anapest, he traces the rise of uncontrollable desire to its culmination in the spondaic "come." He juxtaposes this foot with the sighing iamb, "ah, come," and end-stops the line with an exclamation point, the orgastic release. The last three lines are extremely irregular in meter, marking the tremulous surrender of body and soul to the experience. This poetic *double-entendre* of enslaving sexuality thus conveys the "Lamia" quality of woman, her power to overcome the vaunted rationality of man. In Melville's personification she is *la femme fatale* of the morbid Victorian imagination, the omnipresent figure of fantasy and dream.

In "After the Pleasure Party," which has so fascinated and perplexed the readers, Melville subjects another aspect of sexual repression to scrutiny, exploring the function of the rational and the intuitive in creative endeavor.[2] Therefore, in this perspective, what is revealed cannot logically be discussed without reference to the decline of his own artistic activity. Biographically, the time setting coincides with the period of his pilgrimage to the

---

[2] A version of the following explication appears in my article, "Melville and the Creative Eros," *Lock Haven Bulletin,* 1 (No. 2. 1960), 13–26.

Holy Land in a desperate search to resolve a nagging spiritual quarrel with himself, earlier the vital inspiration of his writing. When he began to reason out this inward unrest, he harnessed the play of his imagination: he supplanted introspective perception with the arid intellectualism of the philosopher and the theologian. Hitherto he had sublimated the neurotic, and at times even psychotic, tensions of his morbid sensibilities, enabling his ego to bear the burden of the conflict. However, when he lost the power to externalize the inner discord, his emotions began to prey on his intellect; and he apparently seriously contemplated suicide.[3] The poem vividly objectifies this plight. It is a symbolic disclosure of a compulsive desire to write and the inability to do so. It describes how studied intellection frustrates intuition. In this state *eros*, the feminine principle of instinct, comes under the domination of *logos*, the masculine principle of reason. In order to project the stasis of his creative impulses, Melville therefore depicts Urania, his symbolic Muse, as estranged from her natural womanhood.

It was, curiously enough, Melville's inward need to reconcile this psychic polarity that led to his greatest literary achievements. As did Hawthorne, he had to counteract his hereditary Protestant ethos. When his imagination rebelled against the taboo of sexuality, it acquired a passionate vitality from the liberated unconscious energy, and this inward drive, in turn, was sublimated in exuberant literary activity. Or articulated in terms of the poem's imagery, his instinctive identity developed the strength to neutralize the tyranny of conscience. When his ego renounced this fructifying feminine principle, it relapsed into creative paralysis. The struggle between outward shame and inward desire reduced him to the impotent condition of the narrator in "The Tartarus of Maids," a prisoner of his inhibitions. Rendered emotionally sterile, he was alienated from the roots of his natural being—the *prima materia* out of whose darkness the world and his consciousness had come.

[3] See Leyda, *The Melville Log*, 2: 521, for his father-in-law's response (Sept. 1, 1856) to Elizabeth's letters on Melville's "severe nervous affections." Hawthorne reports this condition more baldly in the former's own words (Nov., 1856): "[He] informed me that he had 'pretty much made up his mind to be annihilated,' " *ibid.*, 2, 529.

A glance at Melville's novels divulges the constant transformation of primal *eros*. Directly or indirectly, the resolutions of action pivot on sexuality. The protagonists, of *Typee* and *Omoo*, for instance, flee in self-conscious bewilderment from the temptations of various Polynesian Eves. Yet, paradoxically, both works openly attack the unrelatedness of sexual experience fostered by the bigotry of missionaries. Though the hero of *Mardi* ostensibly remains loyal to the idealized virginity of Yillah, his suicide in the maternal womb of the sea signals the vengeance of Hautia, the incarnation of lust. After an avulsive separation from a doting mother, the young adventurer of *Redburn* is troubled by homosexual inclinations. In *White-Jacket* the re-creation of a world of men without women also takes note of the prevalence of sexual abnormalities. In quite another fashion but still in accord with the taboo on eroticism, the unfortunate hero of *Pierre* rationalizes his fear of women in fantasies of incest guilt. A victim of paternal tyranny, the principal of *Israel Potter* wanders about aimlessly, estranged from his instincts. Though admittedly somewhat oversimplified, these generalizations nevertheless still categorize the tensions of *eros* that Melville externalized in his earlier creative endeavors. Through the decorum of art and symbolism he contained the inward doubts and anxieties unloosed by his rigid moral conditioning.

The opposite is true of the execution of "After the Pleasure Party." The poem is compounded out of an apparently insoluble conflict between *logos* and *eros*. Consequently it unfolds like the plot of a tormenting dream, and its content clearly bares the nature of an internal predicament only partly apprehended by the mind. The mode of poetic revelation supports this assumption, unfolding as a disorganized flow of associations from the past and the present of the time setting. The discontinuities of desire and fear are characteristic of a traumatic split of personality. Melville's equation of direct statement and subsumed feeling encompasses, on the one hand, an intellectual effort to refine the implications of the experience, on the other, an uncontrolled confession of his creative frustration. He desperately probes literature, philosophy, myth, and religion, seeking parallels to his emotional plight, and then, suddenly losing sight of this goal, relapses into sexual reveries. Thus the form of the poem is a blend of thought and feeling, of conscious and unconscious expression. Ultimately it embodies the conflict between the rational and the intuitive in the poet's search for the lost Muse of his inspiration.

The attainment of this goal hinges on the establishment of a sense of true "relatedness" with woman as symbolized by Urania. The latter is not to be mistaken for the personification of a historical person. She is Melville's shifting correlative of the creative *eros* that he has betrayed. In the execution of the poem he seeks to identify her. For, from one part to another, she changes shape according to the dictates of the power behind his pen at the moment —the rational or the intuitive. Therefore this polyvalent image of woman *is* the poem. Like the chaos preceding creation, she first appears as a blind, rampant force. Appropriately, she titillates the poet's consciousness in a garden into which he has wandered "after long revery's discontent":

> Tired of the homeless deep,
> Look how their flight yon hurrying billows urge,
> Hitherward but to reap
> Passive repulse from the iron-bound verge!
> Insensate, can they never know
> 'Tis mad to wreck the impulsion so? (p. 216)

As the first line implies, undirected *eros* is disorder, a convulsion of the creative unconscious, "the homeless deep." But the artist mentally erects a barrier to its free expression, "the iron-bound verge." His ego disdains any relationship with the instincts, and therefore his imagination cannot initiate the magic of sublimation. The *eros* remains formless—repressed sexual energy in the obvious imagery. Melville leaves no doubt that he is concerned with artistic motivation. Resisting intuitive insight, he construes creative activity as a recollection of past experiences, but this Wordsworthian formula of shaping perceptions is an obvious rationalization of personal lassitude: "An art of memory is, they tell" (p. 217). He loses in his own talents, and seeks a sanction for inspiration outside himself. But even as he affects this outlook, his emotions rebel, and the dissociation is objectified in an image of perversion, of a perpetual virgin turned Lesbian:

> 'Tis Vesta struck with Sappho's smart.
> No fable her delirious leap. (p. 217)

The equation of suicide and warped sexuality captures the confusion in the ego wrought by the conflict between fear and desire. Indeed, a traumatic revulsion ensues with the manifestation of a death wish concealed in the quotation from *Hamlet:* "but to sleep" (p. 217). Symbolically, this situation reflects the virtual extinction of creative ardor. As in the case of Hamlet, volition and aspiration are out of harmony. *Eros* is in the process of being stifled by *logos,* and as a result it cannot be transduced into the order of art. Rather it blindly struggles for survival, producing uncontrolled sexual hallucinations.

Perhaps haunted by this ferment of unconscious fantasy demanding transmutation into the formal patterns of literature, Melville takes cognizance of the mental torture generated by the impounded energy:

> Hence the winged blaze that sweeps my soul
> Like prairie fires that spurn control,
> Where withering weeds incense the flame. (p. 217)

Here "winged blaze" is a metaphor of his compulsion to write, and "withering weeds" figure his earlier works, intensifying his passionate desire to create. In turn, "incense" discloses the raging hopelessness of the ambition. The reminiscence of the next passage continues in the same vein, but now the poet begins to consider the significance of his renunciation of *eros* in the pursuit of self-fulfillment:

> And kept I long heaven's watch for this,
> Contemning love, for this, even this?
> O terrace chill in Northern air,
> O reaching ranging tube I placed
> Against yon skies, and fable chased
> Till, fool, I hailed for sister there
> Starred Cassiopea in Golden Chair.
> In dream I throned me, nor I saw
> In cell the idiot crowned with straw. (p. 217)

The mode of study depicts his attempt to apprehend the meaning of life in terms of reason, and directly explains his rejection of instinctual experience. Of course, this outlook has to be taken metaphorically, for the telescope, perhaps a disguised phallic symbol, brings into focus an ironical allusion to the Muse of Astronomy, Urania. Instead of inspiring heavenly wisdom as she does for Milton in *Paradise Lost,* she reduces Melville to a fool, the counterpart of the presumptuous Cassiopea comically tumbling in the sky—mutual victims of self-deception. Further on he traces the estrange· ment between *eros* and *logos* to the drama in the Garden of Eden:

> What Cosmic jest or Anarch blunder
> The human integral clove asunder
> And shied the fractions through life's gate? (p. 219)

As he envisages the creation of man, it is an inexcusable joke. Even as the Fall of Adam and Eve proves, from the beginning the human personality is cursed by the opposing impulses of the masculine and feminine principles. Though impelled to think otherwise, he now finds himself the dupe of a preposterous article of faith:

> And yet, ah yet scarce ill I reigned,
> Through self-illusion self-sustained,
> When now—enlightened, undeceived—
> What gain I barrenly bereaved! (p. 218)

Under the circumstances, his life is empty of meaning and purpose, and he lacks the initiative to seek a reconciliation of the divergent inclinations of human nature.

Yet the awareness of his cloven state activates a rehabilitation of his instincts, as subsequently he begins to long for erotic freedom:

> How glad with all my starry lore,
> I'd buy the veriest wanton's rose
> Would but my bee therein repose. (p. 219)

In context "starry lore" is a symbol of Melville's subservience to Urania, the Muse of Reason and of Protestant prudery. With the dismissal of her importance, the poet intuits the healing strength of sexual forgetfulness and emotional wholeness. The euphemisms of "rose" and "bee" exalt the simple and basic reality of *eros*. The universal feminine knows neither modesty nor dissimulation. If she has been endowed with these traits, they are the impositions of *logos*. By accepting her crude purity, he indicates the need to worship at the altar of eternal creation. For behind the glorification of sexuality resides the influence of the greatest of goddesses, Aphrodite Urania, the archetypal mother who wields the power to alleviate individual and cosmic discord. This fleeting recognition of her unifying grace contrasts with Melville's initial impression of her terrifying strength under the aspect of the tumultuous sea—the element out of which she was born. Regardless of her incarnation at any given moment, she is always bent upon supporting emotional holism, and so the epigraph to the poem argues:

> *Fear me, virgin whosoever*
> *Taking pride, from love exempt,*
> *Fear me, slighted. Never, never*
> *Brave me, nor my fury tempt:*
> *Downy wings, but wroth they beat*
> *Tempest even in reason's seat.* (p. 216)

But to arrive at an unconditional acceptance of Aphrodite Urania is no easy matter for the poet's conscience. It is a decision that must be introspectively debated in the spirit of his Protestant predecessors. Behind the reluctance to surrender this heritage lies the biblical deification of a creative *logos*—the Word. Hence in a wholly unconscious revelation of the fear of woman ingrained in his mind, he degrades *eros* into ignoble lust:

> The peasant girl demure that trod
> Beside our wheels that climbed the way,
> And bore along a blossoming rod
> That looked the sceptre of May-day—
> On her—to fire this petty hell,
> His softened glance how moistly fell!
> The cheat! on briars her buds were strung;
> The wiles peeped forth from mien how meek.
> The innocent bare-foot! young, so young!
> To girls, strong man's a novice weak.
> To tell such beads! And more remain,
> Sad rosary of belittling pain. (p. 218)

The striking feature of this passage is Melville's incongruous use of pagan and Roman Catholic symbols. Almost spitefully, he equates the icons of the Virgin Mary, the "beads" and the "rosary," with the phallic emblem of Dionysus. Still the incorrigible Puritan, he tries to convince himself that virginal beauty is a disguise of diabolic sexuality. In short, his sense of sin throttles the efforts of *eros* to undermine the domination of conscious reason.

Even though the most excruciating mental agony attends this repression, he still searches for a metaphysical explanation of his alienation from emotional reality. Rejecting belief in Christianity, he invokes a familiar Gnostic heresy to prove that God is responsible for his personal plight:

> Why hast thou made us but in halves—
> Co-relatives? This makes us slaves.
> If these co-relatives never meet
> Self-hood itself seems incomplete.
> And such the dicing of blind fate
> Few matching halves here meet and mate. (p. 219)

Here Melville alludes to the ancient belief that Adam was an androgyne until God fashioned Eve out of one of his ribs. In thus splitting the sexes God hastened the Fall. Presumably Adam in his hermaphroditic state typified the balance and unity of the Garden of Eden. However, after Adam was put to sleep to accommodate the creation of his mate, he momentarily forgot his Maker, and viewed woman as an entity apart from himself. Ironically, this was the thought divinely translated into the formation of Eve, and eventually the subjective disunity of self led to the Temptation and the Fall. Therefore Melville in a frenzy of bitterness traces the fragmentation of his creative psyche to God's failure to foresee Adam's lapse. In other words, he assumes that the male is predestined always to be at variance with the female. Unfortunately, such a rationalization continues to perpetuate his estrangement from *eros*.

Related to this angry outburst is his awareness that the Gnostic heresy is related to the subject of Plato's *Symposium*, a discourse on the nature of love. Aristophanes, one of the interlocutors, argues that the division of the sexes is a penalty imposed upon androgynous man for his disavowal of divine authority. Melville, of course, takes the opposite position, claiming that man fell because he was divided. This disagreement takes into account the role assigned to the Aphrodite Urania in the dialogue by Socrates. Much like Milton, he makes her the custodian of spiritual love and beauty, not the supreme instrument of *eros*. Like Aristophanes, he also contradicts the poet on a sore point. As a consequence, then, Melville's vehemence in defending the Gnostic heresy can be understood. He wants neither the solace of religion nor of philosophy.

Having abandoned his reliance upon abstract resolutions of his fate, the poet further rejuvenates his torpid *eros*. At least he tacitly concedes that the feminine is not entirely evil, though still unsexual. This subterfuge of unconscious desire marks a radical deviation from his Protestant heritage, especially since he turns for succor to the Virgin:

> Languid in frame for me,
> To-day by Mary's convent shrine,
> Touched by her picture's moving plea
> In that poor nerveless hour of mine,
> I mused—A wanderer still must grieve.
> Half I resolved to kneel and believe,
> Believe and submit, the veil take on. (pp. 220–21)

The appeal of the Virgin at this time manifests Melville's wish to ease the sexual fantasies generated by his creative frustration. Thus the image of "the veil" is not denotative; it is a metaphor of concealment that discloses his neurotic fear of instinctual reality. He still insists upon damming up the emotions. Unwittingly, he actually conjures up the prototype of the rejected Urania. Under the aspect of Sophia (the creative power of the Word), the Virgin is also the instrument of heavenly wisdom. Yet by invoking her he intuitively acknowledges the power of *eros*. She brings him nearer to the real source of inspiration than Urania, for in her mythic antecedents she is *prima materia*, the elemental substance out of which everything was formed. She is, as she was in life, the immaculate womb out of which in the past, as primordial Earth Mother, she gave birth to the world; and, when it fell, she conceived again to redeem it. But though he concedes her redemptive powers, the *logos* influence on his conscious and conscience will not allow him to depend upon her.

Regressing again, he invokes the Greek goddess who has an affinity with his Protestant sensibility—Athena Parthenos:

> But thee, armed Virgin! less benign,
> Thee now I invoke, thou mightier one.
> Helmeted woman—if such term
> Befit thee, far from strife
> Of that which makes the sexual feud
> And clogs the aspirant life—
> O self-reliant, strong and free,
> Thou in whom power and peace unite,
> Transcender! raise me up to thee,
> Raise me and arm me! (p. 221)

These lines prove that Melville is really preoccupied in the poem with the frustrate carnal desire that renders him incapable of creative effort. The "sexual feud" symbolizes the strife between the chthonic instincts and the intellect, an antagonism which "clogs the aspirant life," clearly defined earlier in terms of literary achievement—"great thoughts" and "high themes" (p. 219). His invocation of the invincible Virgin signals his desire to end this psychic war. The miracle of her birth, of course, indicates the manner. In springing full born from the head of Zeus, she manifests the power and the wisdom of her father: the transcendence of his thought over all. Without being tainted by sex, she epitomizes the perfection and purity of creation. Correspondingly, this is the miracle that Melville seeks to emulate in the realm of literature. Unfortunately, when he dissociates creativity and sexuality, he resorts to a blind edification of his ego. In so exalting *logos,* he denies his own humanity.

The realization of this self-deception leads to the poet's epiphany. Finally he acknowledges that the repression of *eros* devitalizes consciousness. Thus he recognizes that the "quarrel with himself" has to be externalized and ordered in the protective containment of art:

> Fond appeal.
> For never passion peace shall bring,
> Nor Art inanimate for long
> Inspire. Nothing may help or heal
> While Amor incensed remembers wrong.
> Vindictive, not himself he'll spare;
> For scope to give his vengeance play
> Himself he'll blaspheme and betray. (p. 221)

In these sentiments Melville unveils the basic psychological meaning of *eros* (or Amor): it is the enemy of narcissism. Like the arrows of Amor, it aims for outward relatedness. As in a mutually fulfilling union of love, the creative act presupposes the harmonious fusion of instinctual and intellectual impulses; only then are the tensions of unconscious sexuality eased. Thus in the coda of the poem, Melville gives sacral recognition to *eros* in her primal manifestation, and once again Aphrodite Urania is restored to her ancient role as the eldest of the Fates—the Triple Goddess. Now the poet's intuitions are in balance with the Protestant bias of his intellect.

The note of exhortation notwithstanding, the closing couplet enunciates a conscious and acceptable resolution of Melville's attitude towards sexuality. He affirms the reality of *eros:*

> Then for Urania, virgins everywhere,
> O pray! Example take too, and have care. (p. 221)

And in realizing that "Fate sprung Love's ambuscade" (p. 217), Melville disowns allegiance to the sterile Muse of his Victorian contemporaries. He avouches the immutable and eternal reign of Aphrodite Urania, not only the supreme Fate but also the creative force which released the powers of order in the dark bosom of endless chaos.

In a unique way "After the Pleasure Party" sheds considerable light upon a poem written to commemorate Hawthorne's death and to deplore their estrangement of eight years.[4] Actually once again in "Monody" Melville treats the subject of "cloven" man in search of his lost other self. Though apparently found in the affinity of spirit with Hawthorne, no union occurs until after the death

[4] Howard, *Herman Melville*, pp. 277–78.

of the latter. Then Melville's love reaches out towards his soul-
mate in a gesture of belated understanding:

> To have known him, to have loved him
>   After loneness long;
> And then to be estranged in life,
>   And neither in the wrong;
> And now for death to set his seal—
>   Ease me, a little ease, my song! (p. 228)

Of course, it is the creation of the poem that at last unites the two.
Their mutual shortcomings are transfingured in the flow of Melville's unashamed grief. But, ultimately, the poet delegates nature
to consecrate the nuptials of love and death. The tomb, blanketed
in snow and under the vigil of a frail mortal creature, embodies
the austere beauty of the wisdom won in selfless forgiveness:

> By wintry hills his hermit-mound
>   The sheeted snow-drifts drape,
> And houseless there the snow-bird flits
>   Beneath the fir trees' crape:
> Glazed now with ice the cloistral vine
>   That hid the shyest grape. (p. 229)

Appropriately, the evergreen, the vine, and the grape attest the
eternal return—resurrection in recurrence. For so the reader experiences the sentiments molded into the lyric. Vicariously, he grieves,
absolves, and loves. Thereby the virtues of Melville and Hawthorne live again. Thus no one, no thing, dies in vain.

An analogous vision of nature and fate is found in "The Ravaged Villa." Time, change, and dissolution reign in a setting once
devised to enrich life with the symbols of religion and art. But
now the beauty and order of a disenfranchised tradition succumb
to the forces of utilitarian progress. Pride and wealth supplant simplicity and nobility:

> In shards the sylvan vases lie,
>   Their links of dance undone,
> And brambles wither by thy brim,
>   Choked fountain of the sun!
> The spider in the laurel spins,

The weed exiles the flower:
And, flung to kiln, Apollo's bust
Makes lime for Mammon's tower. (p. 222)

The imagery of the poem bespeaks the triumph of the profane over the sacred. The "[c]hoked fountain of the sun" is a desecrated model of the *fons solis,* a temple erected for the worship of Zeus by Dionysus on the oasis of Ammon in Egypt.[5] The spirit of the year and the cyclical fertility of nature, the youthful redeemer god spread the divine knowledge of viniculture throughout Asia. The profanation of the oracle subtly dramatizes the estrangement of the Judeo-Christian culture (Mammon) from the world of nature, the nurturing mother of all life. The disunity of sensibility is figured in the fragmentation of the linked dancers on the vases whose ritual homage of Dionysus insured the revival of spring. By the same token, the defiled bust of Apollo, the god of light, reflects the displacement of the real sun by the son (Christ). But to what avail, queries Melville, in his allusion to "the tower of Mammon." The leagued forces of hypocritical materialism respect neither religion nor beauty. The art of selfishness has no kinship with the arts of lofty ideals.

Melville's description of a portrait in "The Marchioness of Brinvilliers" seems designed to contrast profane and sacred art, that is, the inspiration of a fugitive grimace as opposed to that of a religious archetype (Dionysus or Apollo):

> He toned the sprightly beam of morning
>   With twilight meek of tender eve,
> Brightness interfused with softness,
>   Light and shade did weave:
> And gave to candor equal place
> With mystery starred in open skies;
> And, floating all in sweetness, made
>   Her fathomless mild eyes. (p. 234)

As even a superficial knowledge of the historical woman discloses, Western art for the most part is concerned with representing surface emotions, not eternal truths. The painting of the Marchio-

[5] Anthon, *A Classical Dictionary,* pp. 123–24.

ness of Brinvilliers captures none of her true qualities. Though very beautiful, she was ruthless and amoral. She deserted her husband to become the mistress of another man, and then she also schemed with the former to poison her father and two brothers in order to advance her unscrupulous ambitions. The ironical difference between appearance and reality, no doubt, explains why Melville wrote the poem. To be sure, the poet realizes that the subject's Gioconda smile is the painter's symbolic hint to probe her character beyond the becoming image, and this is precisely what Melville does.

"In a Garret" envisages the creative act as the delivery of a child from the womb of the unconscious:

> Gems and jewels let them heap—
> Wax sumptuous as the Sophi:
> For me to grapple from Art's deep
> One dripping trophy. (p. 228)

The trophy of this birth, as context warns, has nothing to do with any commonplace memorial of victory. Wrested from the darkness and brought to light, the embodied inspiration is the product of the lonely struggle in a garret to bring to consciousness a gestate form. Accomplished, the artistic offspring transcends in value the most fabled earthly wealth. Indeed, it is a miraculous accomplishment worthy of honor as the birth of the Christ-child. For this is the heresy lurking in the cryptic line, "Wax sumptuous as the Sophi." Wax here is a symbol of the myrrh and frankincense that the Sophi, the Magian priests, brought as gifts to the Saviour. This turn of thought parallels the view of art developed in "After the Pleasure Party." It is a self-redemptive endeavor, which is to say that Melville prefers to harrow his own hell and to retain his own salvation, on earth not in heaven. As the much reworked "Art" discloses (pp. 506–7), Melville persists in trying to crystallize the implications of artistic zeal, especially concerned with the discrepancy between conception and execution:

> In placid hours well-pleased we dream
> Of many a brave, unbodied scheme. (p. 231)

And again he returns to the metaphor of the incarnate thought, reasserting that the process of creativity involves more than the translation of an idle reverie into formal expression. Rather the realized end is the consequence of a mysterious alchemy that reverses all the laws of nature:

> But form to lend, pulsed life create,
> What unlike things must meet and mate. (p. 231)

Nor is it simply a matter of finding ingenious relationships between ideas. Quite to the contrary, dissimilarities have to merge together and reproduce a living entity *sui generis*. As the imagery of the poem construes this nativity, it presupposes the uninhibited interplay and intermingling of thought, feeling, and intuition:

> A flame to melt—a wind to freeze;
> Sad patience—joyous energies;
> Humility—yet pride and scorn;
> Instinct and study; love and hate;
> Audacity and reverence. These must mate,
> And fuse with Jacob's mystic heart,
> To wrestle with the angel—Art. (p. 231)

As the allusion to Jacob suggests, the total experience is equivalent to a mystical sexual consummation and conception. Melville's knowledge of the relevant biblical passage, "And Jacob was left alone; and there wrestled a man with him until the breaking of day. And when he saw that he prevailed not against him, he touched the hollow of his thigh" (Gen. XXXII: 24–25), is beyond doubt. And also beyond question is his interpretation of the euphemism, "hollow of his thigh." The recurrent Old Testament equivocation for the genitals provides the poet with the sanction of *eros* in his search to understand the transformative power of artistic creation. The psychosexual resolution of the poem, especially as related to the extreme antitheses of the imagery, clearly establishes Melville's mode of sublimating the neurotic impulses of his character.

VII   Revaluations

THE MUSE of the first section of Timoleon presides over the supplementary collection of "Fruit of Travel Long Ago." Melville remains loyal to natural reality—the unmitigated fatalism of the Triple-Goddess. In short, I take exception to the date of composition usually assigned to these poems.[1] I believe they were written after his retirement from the custom-house in 1885. In tone they are out of key with observations of the *Journal* and their subsequent adaptation in *Clarel*. In the metaphor of the title they are the ripened fruits of wisdom. With a touch of cynical humor Melville derides the desperate seriousness of his trip to Europe and the Levant in 1856–57. True, some of these writings may have been undertaken directly after the trip; however, I think their final form belongs to the period of his old age.

In subject matter they maintain the focus of companion poems in the volume. Religion, art, sex, and history are again brought under scrutiny. Except for muted echoes, the *Journal* hardly illuminates the inspiration of the poems. For instance, it has been suggested that the following journal entry, "Great Britain. Turks standard. Lanterns. On the Canals. Othello's house & statue. Shylocks. L. Byron's. Foscari Palace. Fine view of G. Canal.—After dinner in Piazza," is the probable source of "Venice": [2]

> With Pantheist energy of will
> The little craftsman of the Coral Sea
> Strenuous in the blue abyss,
> Up-builds his marvellous gallery

[1] See Horsford, *Journal*, pp. 36–37, and Vincent, *Collected Poems*, p. 476, for somewhat different views.
[2] Horsford, *Journal*, p. 229, n. 6.

And long arcade,
Erections freaked with many a fringe
    Of marble garlandry,
Evincing what a worm can do.

Laborious in a shallower wave,
    Advanced in kindred art,
A prouder agent proved Pan's might
When Venice rose in reefs of palaces. (pp. 238–39)

Doubtless, Melville has in mind the city, but the poem challenges the assumptions of idle tourist curiosity. It scorns a fatuous beguilement with externals. The imagery supports this viewpoint. Though the first stanza seems to laud the divine purpose at work in nature, "Pantheist energy," actually the poet has in mind the god Pan and his phallic potency—the personification of the unceasing physical productivity of nature. Without this perspective in the poem, it is virtually impossible to comprehend the irony of the comparisons between the coral organism and man. Notice what the disparaged phallic "worm can do": out of "the blue abyss" erect a "marvellous gallery," fringed in "marble garlandry," and so anonymously carry out a vital process in the vast scheme of the universe. But then consider the aspersion cast at man: he creates "in a shallower wave," yet he believes himself "A prouder agent." And does he achieve Pan's transcendence in building "reefs of palaces?" The incongruous image implies the contrary, echoing intimations of hidden dangers and intrigues. The buildings, products of an art kindred "to Pan's might," thus envoke the moral corruption of the city. Historically, when the structures were built, the nobility, the priesthood, and the sisterhood were notoriously depraved.[3] This interpretation of the poem at least attempts to cope with the ambiguous language of the poem and with the treatment of the subject.

At any rate, "In a Bye-Canal" overtly treats the licentiousness of Venice during the nineteenth century:

Between the slats, mute summoning me,
What loveliest eyes of scintillation,
What basilisk glance of conjuration! (p. 239)

[3] See Edmund Flagg, *Venice; The City of the Sea* (New York, 1853), 1: 40–41, a travel volume with which Melville could have been familiar.

However much the double rimes of the couplet torture the sensibilities of Robert Penn Warren, they serve to focus attention on the famous romantic atmosphere of Venice, more often than its artistic glories, the chief attraction for the traveling American. The wrenched syntax and the ostentatious imagery are devised to mock the hypocrisy of the interest and to burlesque the desired assignation with a whore. Perhaps this is what Warren means in his remark that "we have here a statement of the poet's conviction that the verse which belonged to the world of respectability could not accommodate the rendering of experience undergone." [4] Paradoxically, though, Melville takes note of contemporary respectability or, at least, its foundations of inhibition. As the opening lines of the poem show, a guilty lust dominates the consciousness of the poetic voice on his canal excursion:

> A swoon of noon, a trance of tide,
> The hushed siesta brooding wide
> Like calms far off Peru;
> No floating wayfarer in sight,
> Dumb noon, and haunted like the night
> When Jael the wiled one slew. (p. 239)

The biblical allusion patently sustains the interpretation. The Israelite heroine seduced the tyrant Sisera and then slew him in his sleep. But even though he dreads some such punishment, the puritan Byron's conditioned scruples relax when his sexual fantasies promise to actualize:

> A languid impulse from the oar
> Plied by my indolent gondolier
> Tinkles against a palace hoar,
> And, hark response I hear!
> A lattice clicks; . . . . (p. 239)

Surely, "palace hoar" is meant to function as a pun and to reaffirm Melville's sentiments in "Venice." And here, without question, there is a direct echo of Othello's denunciations of Desdemona and her immoral city. Essentially, however, the poet is up to his old trick of ridiculing the obsessive association of death and sex-

[4] "Melville the Poet," *Kenyon Review*, 8 (Spring 1946), 210.

uality that he connects with the Protestant identity. Thus when he formulates the disharmonious lines so objectionable to Warren, he simply attempts to capture the comic recalcitrance of the flesh and to expose the self-deception of the romantic pose.

The temper of the next section of the poem is melodramatic. The analogies to the immediate situation are so extreme as to verge on the ludicrous. Yet Melville is not unaware of what he is doing. The effect is no more than an extension of the discordance of the double rimes:

> Fronted I have, part taken the span
> Of portents in nature and peril in man.
> I have swum—I have been
> Twixt the whale's black flukes
> and the white shark's fin;
> The enemy's desert have wandered in,
> And there have turned, have turned and scanned,
> Following me how noiselessly,
> Envy and Slander, lepers in hand.
> All this. But at the latticed eye— (p. 240)

Put in psychological terms, these lines constitute another rationalization of a morbid conscience. Symbolically, the dangers of swimming parallel the response to sexual intercourse. At least this is the only way to explain the sudden dissociation of possible disgrace, climaxed so hysterically with the reference to the waiting woman. Immediately, however, the humorous resolution of the predicament reveals Melville's complete control of theme and tone:

> "Hey! Gondolier, you sleep, my man;
> Wake up!" And, shooting by, we ran;
> The while I mused, This, surely now,
> Confutes the Naturalists, allow!
> Sirens, true sirens verily be,
> Sirens, waylayers in the sea. (p. 240)

The quick reaction of the pander-gondolier, of course, betrays the pretense of his sleeping. Now having caricatured a romantic episode in Venice, Melville turns around and addresses all those frustrated Don Juans disillusioned with the timidity of the inhibited adventurer. For the knowledgeable reader, he reserves a friendly wink, a zesty *double-entendre*—"waylayers." Added to the pun secreted in the title, it plainly demonstrates that the poet is not to be confused with the persons in the poem. He knows how to joke— with combined seriousness and levity.

In another mood Melville examines the moral-architectural dimensions of certain Italian churches. "Pisa's Leaning Tower," for example, turns the incident of a sinking foundation into a prophecy of the ultimate destiny of Christianity. First, he looks at the structure from the point of view of its designer:

> The Tower in tiers of architraves,
> Fair circle over cirque,
> A trunk of rounded colonnades,
> The maker's master-work. (p. 240)

Of necessity the last line does not have to be taken literally. It can refer both to the architect's achievement and to God's consummation of His grand scheme of salvation—the Church of Christ. Granting this, then symbolically the building, like Bannadonna's bell-tower, betrays a radical defect in its embodiment of the divine idea (the Word). It is on the verge of collapse because of the irremediable disunity in purpose; no wonder it

> Impends with all its pillared tribes,
> And, poising them, debates:
> It thinks to plunge—but hesitates;
> Shrinks back—yet fain would slide;
> Withholds itself—itself would urge;
> Hovering, shivering on the verge,
> A would-be suicide! (p. 240)

The taut vision of imminent ruin foreshadows a religious inevitability—the catastrophic extinction of Christianity. The sinking foundation takes into equal account the miscalculation in engineering and the architect's unconscious reservation about the origin of his inspiration. A similar negation undermines Bannadonna's project. While his erection of the bell-tower rehearses an act of faith, unfortunately it also represents the fulfillment of an ambition. In this conflict of aims, both the integrity of the artist's ego and of his creation are blighted. Each therefore works to weaken the other and to hasten mutual destruction. As one of Melville's journal entries indicates, his impression of the leaning tower of Pisa is colored by the short story written many years before the poem. A "Campanile like pine poised just ere snapping" [5] echoes a definite association with a passage from "The Bell-Tower": "central in a plain, stands what, at distance, seems the black mossed stump of some immeasurable pine, fallen, in forgotten days, with Anak and the Titan." [6] As Cronus fell before Zeus and Anak before the Jews, so, argues Melville, the triadic God of Christianity will also fall. The muted theme of the poem and the story crystallizes his view of art and the artist. Intuitively, the latter senses the rift in the religious sensibility of his culture long before the fact is accepted publicly. Accordingly, the perception evolves into the guiding *daimon* of his work, supplying an exhilarating but terrifying vision of the abyss. When he builds the meaning of his life on this implacable truth, he flirts with intellectual and spiritual suicide—the personal experience of Melville and many of the protagonists of his fiction and poetry.

An ambiguity of another kind permeates "Milan Cathedral." In the opening stanza Melville depicts self-sufficient nature in the service of mankind,

> Through light green haze, a rolling sea
> Over gardens where redundance flows,
> The fat old plain of Lombardy,
> The White Cathedral shows. (p. 242)

This vista is not mentioned in his *Journal;* rather the poet limits his view from the cathedral to the immediate scene: "Far below people in the turrets of open tracery look like flies caught in cobweb—The groups of angels on points of pinnacles & everywhere. Not the conception but the execution. View from sumit [*sic*]. Might well [stand] host of (heaven) upon top of Milan Cathedral." [7] The decision to add the extra prospect to the later poetic rendering

[5] Horsford, *Journal,* p. 216.
[6] *Selected Writings,* p. 355.
[7] Horsford, *Journal,* p. 239.

marks a radical shift in the interpretation of the experience. In contrast with man's close and productive relationship to the earth, the towering structure stands alone in aloof and icy grandeur, implicitly a sepulchre. This impression is sustained by the imagery; the frozen and freezing beauty aspires only towards heaven, withdrawn from the concerns of temporality. Even the tiered saints, aglow in the light, travesty the idea of an omnipresent Holy Spirit. Optical illusions of pentecostal fires, they mock the idea of a living God:

> Of Art the miracles
> Its tribes of pinnacles
> Gleam like ice-peaks snowed; and higher,
> Erect upon each airy spire
> In concourse without end,
> Statues of saints over saints ascend
> Like multitudinous forks of fire. (p. 242)

Melville's negative spiritual reaction is reaffirmed in the last stanza. Though the interrogation on the surface expresses an appreciative understanding of the creative purpose, the use of "signify" divulges his perception of a jarring discordance:

> What motive was the master-builder's here?
> Why these synodic hierarchies given,
> Sublimely ranked in marble sessions clear,
> Except to signify the host of heaven. (p. 242)

The word is an obvious substitution for "glorify," and is meant to call attention to the architect's unconscious beliefs. The cathedral (or Christianity) is alienated from nature and human nature. It does not figure a God involved in terrestrial affairs. Rather it memorializes the empty symbolism of a faith that has lost touch with the basic spiritual needs of the people.

The *Journal* offers little aid in helping to reconstruct Melville's mood when he wrote "In a Church of Padua." [8] But still a Protestant in his attitudes, he describes a confessional booth in such naturalistic detail that its function is utterly negated. As this tactic

[8] *Ibid.*, p. 26.

combines with the awkward syntax and the lone rime, it expresses his complete skepticism about its supernatural efficacy:

> In vaulted place where shadows flit,
> An upright sombre box you see:
> A door, but fast, and lattice none,
> But punctured holes minutely small
> In lateral silver panel square
> Above a kneeling-board without,
> Suggest an aim if not declare. (p. 241)

The deliberate equivocation of the last line sustains the doubt. The obvious hardly accords with the miracle of absolution. Following logically, his recreation of the private acknowledgment of transgression denies the possibility of mutual communication. The depersonalized rite is inhumanly cold, forbidding in its distances of involved feelings:

> Who bendeth here the tremulous knee
> No glimpse may get of him within,
> And he immured may hardly see
> The soul confessing there the sin;
> Nor yields the low-sieved voice a tone
> Whereby the murmurer may be known. (p. 241)

Under the circumstances the conclusion of the poem is inevitable. Melville not only denies the ultimate honesty of human nature, but he also questions the psychological likelihood of an uninhibited confession:

> Dread diving-bell! In thee inurned
> What hollows the priest must sound,
> Descending into consciences
> Where more is hid than found. (p. 241)

This does not mean, however, that he withholds pity for the guilty sinner. Rather, recalling his own agonizing spiritual reticences, he vicariously exaggerates the plight of the confessor. In any event, reversing the unpoetic tone of the first two stanzas, the poignant cry of the lyric coda avers Melville's conviction that complete self-awareness is an idle presumption of religion and philosophy. For him the psychic world is an unfathomable abyss.

Melville's impressions of Greek scenery and architecture cover
an entirely different aesthetic and psychological spectrum of art. A
studied detachment now informs his observations. As if cultivating
a pose to fit the setting, in "The Attic Landscape" he counsels a rational outlook on things:

> Tourist, spare the avid glance
>> That greedy roves the sight to see:
> Little here of "Old Romance,"
>> Or Picturesque of Tivoli. (p. 245)

Melville here invokes the villa of Hadrian in Italy to make his
point.[9] The thrilling ruins of the structure define no consistent
view of art; rather they reveal the emperor's personal taste for the
exotic, a dilettante's attempt to preserve his memories of beauty
shaped in travels through Europe and Asia.[10] The architectural remains thus induce more interest in Hadrian than in cultural history. Quite to the contrary, the Greek achievement exalts a distinct
ethos:

> No flushful tint the sense to warm—
> Pure outline pale, a linear charm.
> The clear-cut hills carved temples face,
> Respond, and share their sculptural grace. (p. 245)

Disciplined mentality prevails over pure inspiration. Mathematical
exactitude blends reason to form; creative endeavor honors only
the knowable world:

> 'Tis Art and Nature lodged together,
>> Sister by sister, cheek to cheek;
> Such Art, such Nature, and such weather
>> The All-in-All seems here a Greek. (p. 246)

Does the poet acclaim such art? The constraining "seems" in the
last line suggests a reservation on Melville's part, an emotional
protest against the impersonal unity of foreground and background. Doubtless, he reacts negatively to the diminution of

---

[9] Horsford, *Journal*, pp. 213–214.
[10] Robert Burn, *Old Rome: A Handbook to the Ruins of the City and the
Campagna* (Cambridge, 1880), pp. 237–39.

human importance. His sensibility has been shaped by values and attitudes closer to the heart than the mind.

In another prospect on the same scene Melville again responds uneasily to the beguiling serenity:

> A circumambient spell it is,
> Pellucid on these scenes that waits,
> Repose that does of Plato tell—
> Charm that his style authenticates. (p. 246)

"Spell" and "[c]harm" bespeak unconscious deprecation. The two words acknowledge the compelling attraction of the scene, but they also imply the presence of optical illusion. The apparently seductive flow of architectural line and philosophical concept, so abstractly aloof from human experience, postulates the gossamer reality of cosmic absolutes, an anathema to Melville at this stage of his career. The challenging dualities of life are theorized out of existence, leaving man contemplating his own consciousness. The poet's impersonal language and controlled emotions betray a suspicion of all this. He judges what he sees in accordance with traditional Greek standards, not with those of his individual experience. In effect, this detachment radically contrasts with the subjectivity of the Italian verse, establishing the affected posture of the two poems. At least only such an interpretation accounts for the exclusion of "Suggested by the Ruins of a Mountain-Temple in Arcadia, One Built by the Architect of the Parthenon," from "Fruit of Travel Long Ago." Sensing the difference in tone, Melville apparently prefers to maintain his uninvolved outlook on the relics of the ancient culture:

> Like stranded ice when freshets die
> These shattered marbles tumbled lie:
>   They trouble me.
>
> What solace?—Old in inexhaustion,
> Interred alive from storms of fortune,
>   The quarries be! (p. 407)

Dropping the persona of tourist appreciation, he ponders the gloomy implications of the shattered temple. Ravaged by time and circumstance, it discourages belief in the romantic notion of imperishable artistic beauty. Parthenon or pinchbeck, nothing of human creation survives temporal contingency. Only nature endures, formed and formless, silently dismissive of all efforts to differentiate her substance. And so Melville despairingly acknowledges the futility of the awe and rapture of less perceptive moments of insight.

When he actually treats the subject of the Parthenon, he retains the mood of the previous poem. However, he disguises his real feelings in clever innuendoes and sly depreciations. The Parthenon, of course, was dedicated to Athene, the *parthenos* or virgin, whose maidenhood was symbolic of the invincibility of the city; but Melville associates the temple with two of the most notorious women of classical times, Lais a priestess of Venus in Corinth [11] and Aspasia, the mistress of Pericles and the favorite target of the comic poets in their satires on the immorality of the city.[12] The subtitle of Part I of "Seen Aloft from Afar," is insidiously misleading. It offers less of a perspective on distance than an explanation of sentiments that tend to cluster around a cherished masterpiece of antiquity:

> Estranged in site,
> Aerial gleaming, warmly white,
> You look a suncloud motionless
>
> In noon of day divine;
> Your beauty charmed enhancement takes
> In Art's long after-shine. (p. 246)

As the subtitle of Part II, "Nearer Viewed," implies, he is about to expose the deficiencies of nostalgic aestheticism:

> Like Lais, fairest of her kind,
> In subtlety your form's defined—
> The cornice curved, each shaft inclined,
> While yet, to eyes that do but revel
>   And take the sweeping view,
> Erect this seems, and that a level,
>   To line and plummet true.

[11] Anthon, *A Classical Dictionary*, p. 717.
[12] *Ibid.*, pp. 216–17.

> Spinoza gazes; and in mind
> Dreams that one architect designed
> Lais—and you! (pp. 246–47)

On the one hand, the Parthenon's beauty is reduced to the poetry of fluid linearity, on the other, as in the case of Spinoza, to the influence of the indwelling God upon the inspiration of the architect. Melville, however, subtly refutes both these positions in his imagery. "Lais, the fairest of her kind," is a witty understatement for a woman who, from the age of seven, was the instrument of sexual pleasure for innumerable men of all classes. Thus, by extension, Melville argues that her corrupt and corrupting loveliness is embodied in the sensual grace of the temple, which is to say that he questions abstract, idealistic theories of classical art.

The decorative details of Part III, "The Frieze," also emphasize the erotic origins of creative endeavor. The sculptor's subjective pleasure in his task hints at unconscious sexual fulfillment. The horses, capering under a taut bit, objectify the emotional fantasies of the riders as they contemplate the teasing innocence of the girls. In effect, the entire scene celebrates and consecrates the eternal tensions of sensuality:

> What happy musings genial went
> With airiest touch the chisel lent
>   To frisk and curvet light
> Of horses gay—their riders grave—
> Contrasting so in action brave
>   With virgins meekly bright,
> Clear filing on in even tone
> With pitcher each, one after one
>   Like water-fowl in flight. (p. 247)

This visualization of the Panathenaic procession on the frieze violates the traditional conception of the community festival. The occasion is usually considered to be a solemn event, a sacrificial ritual honoring the virgin goddess, the patron saint of the city. But Melville's bias is justified by the tactic of mediacy; he looks at the shrine through the eyes of those whose temporal glory it enhances:

> When the last marble tile was laid
> The winds died down on all the seas;

> Hushed were the birds, and swooned the glade;
> Ictinus sat; Aspasia said
> "Hist!—Art's meridian, Pericles!" (p. 247)

Its architect, Ictinus, sits in quiet thought while Aspasia prattles, unwittingly blaspheming the goddess to whom the temple is dedicated. Her observation, in the light of her status as the mistress of Pericles and the underminer of his morals,[13] is an insult to Athene. The latter, the daughter of Zeus, was the protectress of the moral and social order of the city which Aspasia had disrupted. Thus we cannot accept her opinion as other than irony, Melville's proof that posterity had misconstrued the artistic aims of the Greeks. Though the tone of the poem on the surface is devoutly appreciative, the allusions to Lais and Aspasia belie its sincerity. Undeniable prostitutes, however beautiful the one and intellectually brilliant the other, they are symbols of Melville's ironic awareness that the beautiful grows out of the corruption of earthly things—the manure that fertilizes the rose. In short, he warns against the historical practice of imposing fanciful values upon the art of foreign cultures.

"The Apparition" is no less ambiguous in its representation of the spiritual import of the ruined temple, however much the first stanza appears to give credence to the apocryphal conversion of a pagan:

> Abrupt the supernatural Cross,
> Vivid in startled air,
> Smote the Emperor Constantine
> And turned his soul's allegiance there. (p. 253)

This hallucination, as a canceled stanza indicates, displays Melville's sensitive religious awareness during his sojourn in Greece. Indeed, it suggests that he has more faith in Christianity than he is willing to admit:

> With kindred power, appealing down,
> Miraculous human Fane!

[13] *Ibid.*, p. 216.

> You strike with awe the cynic heart,
>   Convert it from disdain.[14]

However, when he revises this impression in the skeptical mood of old age, he does not allow his emotions to rule his thought. Empirically, he accepts the contingent anxieties and insecurities of temporal existence:

> With other power appealing down,
>   Trophy of Adam's best!
> If cynic minds you scarce convert,
> You try them, shake them, or molest. (p. 253)

Dismissing the optical illusion, he contemplates the ineffable beauty of the Parthenon, overwhelmed by its perfection but exalted by its human inspiration. The "other power" it emanates is no longer supernatural. It is the incredible power of the imagination which, fully realized in the structure and its setting, insidiously operates to mock and minimize his own artistic aspirations. Unless he has mixed his dates, Melville in the final stanza returns to the subject of the apparition, postulating the chastening influence of such a sight on the pessimism of a philosopher:

> Diogenes, that honest heart,
>   Lived ere your date began;
> Thee had he seen, he might have swerved
> In mood nor barked so much at Man. (p. 253)

Though he appears to affirm the spiritual validity of the self-sacrifice, the qualifying "might" implies otherwise. Consistent with the revision of the second stanza, the reservation discloses Melville's lack of faith in miracles.

Evidently he resorts to such indirection in order to sustain the dupery of his creative intention. At any rate, a deletion in "Disinterment of the Hermes" supports the assumption, for in the effort to conceal his inconoclastic theme he almost totally obscures the meaning of the poem. As the archeological situation indicates, he is in a perfect position to manipulate his favorite ironical motif—the resurrection:

[14] According to the manuscript in the Houghton Library, this was the original verse.

What forms divine in adamant fair—
Carven demigod and god,
And hero-marbles rivalling these,
Bide under Latium's sod,
Or lost in sediment and drift
Alluvial which the Grecian rivers sift. (p. 252)

At the outset of the next stanza he seems to argue that the legacy of classical sculpture and architecture transcends in significance all the attempts of biblical archeologists to recover from the "arid sands" of the Holy Land tangible evidence of the existence of Christ:

To dig for these, O better far
Than raking arid sands
For gold more barren meetly theirs
Sterile, with brimming hands. (p. 252)

Even though the last two lines tail off in verbal and syntactical confusion, a canceled couplet authorizes "gold" to be read as a metaphor for the treasure of divine immortality:

The Hermes risen, reviews its span
In resurrection never proved in (by) man. (p. 513)

Literally, of course, there is nothing especially objectionable about this sentiment, at least not in the perspective of Melville's far more heretical opinions in *Timoleon*. But given his preoccupation with sexual innuendoes, another interpretation is possible. As he knows, the god Hermes subsumes the phallus. Accordingly, his witty, wicked pun burlesques the idea of an eternal rebirth.

Under the figure of Pan, Hermes is once more glorified in "The Archipelago." Voyaging through the fabled Aegean Sea, Melville is appalled by the mythico-religious sterility of the ancient playgrounds of the gods:

Sail before the morning breeze
The Sporads through the Cyclades
They look like isles of absentees—
Gone whither? (p. 249)

The allusion to the Sporads (Sporades, actually), an important chain of islands in the geography of the supernatural plots, betrays Melville's concern with the sexual implications of the dead tradition. Etymologically, they mean scattered sperm,[15] and therefore evoke the innumerable earthly shrines consecrated by the Greek gods in their amorous adventures. Unquestionably, here he aligns their antics with the various manifestations of physical phenomena as represented by the dominant school of nineteenth-century mythographers. In effect, he connects the vitality of the human psyche with the outward worship of the procreative powers of nature. And so he argues in the next stanza:

> You bless Apollo's cheering ray,
> But Delos, his own isle, today
> Not e'en a Selkirk there to pray
> > God friend me! (p. 249)

Though the sun-god Apollo still smiles on Delos where his mother Leto gave birth to him and his sister after her rape by the amorous Zeus, the island is now deserted. Nor is the reference to Selkirk (Robinson Crusoe) an accident. It expresses Melville's awareness of the deflection of human passion from the deification to the exploitation of nature, as exemplified by the archetypal capitalist. This association is validated by the ensuing comparison of an English colonizer and a redeemer deity:

> Scarce lone these groups, scarce lone and bare
> When Theseus roved a Raleigh there,
> Each isle a small Virginia fair—
> > Unravished. (p. 249)

The pun on Virginia (virginity) historically embraces the notorious rape of native female populations by European explorers and settlers, an unholy contrast with Theseus who delivered the island of Crete from the ravaging appetite of the Minotaur.

Overcome by a nostalgia for the guiltless pleasures of the Golden Age, Melville next views the islands under the aspect of their inviolable beauty and unforgettable lore of joyous life:

---

[15] Anthon, *A Classical Dictionary*, p. 1259.

> Not less through havoc fell they rue,
> They still retain in outline true
> The grace of form when earth was new
>   And primal. (p. 249)

He does not yearn for the Eden of Christianity—that depressing emotional stasis of innocence. He longs for a sinless immersion in the spontaneous expressions of human nature, beyond all caveats of good and evil, of respectability and disgrace. Typically, he construes such an existence in sexual terms:

> But beauty clear, the frame's as yet,
> Never shall make one quite forget
> Thy picture, Pan, therein once set—
>   Life's revel! (p. 249)

His image of Pan, it goes always without saying, probably entails his typical representation with a phallus of disproportionate magnitude in recognition of his superintendence of the generative forces of nature. No wonder that Melville, half laughingly, speaks about the unforgettable impression of the goat-footed God. This private delight of his old age in priapic fantasies, as in so many other instances, excites memories of his youthful adventures in the South Seas:

> 'Tis Polynesia reft of palms,
> Seaward no valley breathes her balms—
> Not such as musk thy rings of calm,
>   Marquesas! (p. 249)

Thus he finds in his own experiences the authority for belief in a paradise consonant with the impulses of common human nature. Obviously, at this point in his revery, the fact is more beguiling than any fable. But there are overtones in his interpretation of the Greek sensibility and its predilections that warrant a wholly different consideration. As opposed to the attitudes recorded in the *Journal* of the trip, the affectations of guidebook-appreciation do not color the sentiments of the poems. Melville does not gush in tourist ecstasy. What he has seen he now attempts to relate to life, not to aesthetic theory. Like his perceptions into the human element of religious art, his recognition of the paradoxes of history and historicism exercises a discipline over the subjectivity of his observations.

"Off Cape Colonna" offers a further illustration of this perspective on reality. Viewing the remains of a celebrated temple from the deck of a ship, he is enchanted by its divine grandeur:

> Aloof they crown the foreland lone,
> From aloft they loftier rise—
> Fair columns, in the aureola rolled
> From sunned Greek seas and skies.
> They wax, sublimed to fancy's view,
> A god-like group against the blue. (p. 248)

However, the relapse from objectivity lasts only for a moment. He recalls the innumerable tragedies which occurred in the turbulent waters at the base of the promontory:

> Over much like gods! Serene they saw
> The wolf-waves board the deck,
> And headlong hull of Falconer
> And many a deadlier wreck. (p. 248)

The temple so mockingly aloof from human sorrow and woe was dedicated to the goddess Athene whom Melville wryly debunks in "The Parthenon." [16] Thus once again, he questions the relationship of her alleged benevolence to the state of temporal existence, specifically her watchful surveillance over a domain under her protection. For the poet, then, the shrine is a false symbol of religious art. Its transcendent beauty mocks the contingent lot of mortal man, reducing his search for a meaningful place in the universe to an empty dream. This anti-romantic attitude is apparently designed to controvert Byron's puerile apotheosis of the cape in "Childe Harold's Pilgrimage." [17] Melville is not inclined to be patient with postures of thought and feeling.

But despite his negative reactions to the undue emphasis placed on the religious inspiration of the art in question, he still ap-

[16] Anthon, *A Classical Dictionary*, pp. 1271–72.
[17] Canto II, 86.

preciates the realized perfection of its balance and beauty—the product of the mind and the imagination working together in disciplined concord. And in "Greek Architecture" he pays tribute to this marvelous skill:

> Not magnitude, not lavishness,
> But Form—the Site;
> Not innovating wilfulness,
> But reverence for the Archetype. (p. 248)

As the first three lines clearly state, topography controls design. Therefore originality is left to express itself primarily in terms of spatial relations, for site and form have to be accommodated to the sight, even as Melville's persistent re-recreation of perspectives affirms. This very fact rules out a serious preoccupation with the glorification of any divinity except to the extent the theme is carried out in decorative details or in statues. Indeed, Melville's unidentified archetype substantiates this assumption. The model of the architecture is not a transcendental ideal. It is the impersonal knowledge of mathematics and physics (Euclidian harmonies!). In this sense every structure represents a triumph of the intellect, hardly a virtue for Melville at the time he was revising the poetry for publication.

"Greek Masonry" expresses a similar sentiment much more overtly as the poet singles out for admiration the genius of the Greeks in applying the laws of stress and strain in their building plans:

> Joints were none that mortar sealed:
> Together, scarce with line revealed,
> The blocks in symmetry congealed. (p. 248)

But however explicit the approbation, its tone and diction are full of reservations. The lone tercet sounds its sense in a vacuum of feeling, as if a robot spoke—an uninvolved voice. The visual facts are enumerated, the painstaking labor credited, the combined achievement of architect and workmen acknowledged. Then an icy spasm of revulsion suddenly rings out, "symmetry congealed." The thing has been formed. All the functions of physical laws have been served, and man has been denied any further participation in the creation. Frozen perfection reigns. Standing completely aloof from his description, Melville damns what he praises.

This attitude towards dehumanized art is rendered understandable in "Puzzlement," a poem dealing with the experiences of the same period in the poet's career. As the subtitle shows, "As To A Figure Left Solitary On A Unique Fragment of Greek Basso-Relievo," he is struck by the unconventionality of the statue:

> A crescent brow—a quiver thrown
> Behind the shoulder. A huntress, own.
> It needs be Artemis. But, nay,
> It breathes too much of Eve's sweet way,
> An Artemis is high, austere,
> Chill as her morn, a goddess mere. (p. 408)

In the invocation of Eve he instinctively defends uninhibited innocence. But, more than that, he also unobtrusively deifies woman as woman: the ineluctable impulse that led Eve to flirt with the serpent. Melville's astonishment at the unusual execution hints at his dissatisfaction with the stylized abstractions of Artemis, their neutralization of her role as the patron of the life-giving powers of nature. He clearly realizes that the mythic goddess has been sacrificed to the rational inclinations of the later Greek culture. Now confronted with her unrefined sensuality, he is utterly delighted:

> She bends, and with one backward hand
> Adjusts her buskin light,
> The sidelong face upturned—how arch!
> Sure, *somebody* meets her sight. (p. 408)

Here he is also probably thinking of the stereotyped association that he once incorporated in "The Tartarus of Maids," her fatal punishment of the hunter Actaeon who glimpsed her in the nude.[18] In any event, Melville's enchantment with the statue occasions a lengthy argument designed to prove his assumption that she is no less a temptress than Eve. Finally he discredits her connection with the Golden Age of classical art, with obvious irony

---

[18] *Selected Writings*, p. 202.

tracing the purely feminine conception of her function to moral de-
generation:

> Show'st thou the goddess, human yet—
> The austere Artemis a coquette?
> If so in sooth, some latter age
> In faith's decay begot thine art—
> Such impudence of sweet persiflage! (p. 409)

Of course, his mild rebuke is a pose. As he has already indicated in
his poetry, the Greece of Pericles hardly cultivated the restraints of
passion advocated by Artemis. As a matter of fact, Melville's bub-
bling enthusiasm in her womanhood divulges his bias for naturalistic art. It alone honors humanity.

"In the Hall of Marbles" overtly confirms Melville's equivo-
cal outlook on the artistic achievement of the Greeks. The poem
summarily disavows any empathy with idealized forms of representation. Though not included in the selection made for "Fruits
of Long Ago," its omission is not difficult to rationalize. First, it is
out of key with the tone of the other pieces, too obvious in its expressed sentiments. Second, it is a poorly executed composition, its
grating diction, meter, and rime contributing little or nothing to
the communication of meaning. Nevertheless, it serves the purpose
of documentation effectively because the subtitle, "Lines Recalled
from a Destroyed Poem," suggests that the embodied thought was
a lasting conviction. The first six lines are couched in a sequence of
interrogations which focuses on posterity's incredible rejection of an
exemplary inspiration for a less noble standard of reality:

> If genius, turned to sordid ends
> Ye count to glory lost,
> How with mankind that flouts the aims
> Time's Attic years engrossed?
> Waxes the world so rich and old?
> Richer and narrower, age's way? (pp. 388–89)

Though "sordid ends" seems to imply the prostitution of talent, it
is probably an inept phrase for the contemporary emphasis on naturalistic art. Indeed, in the light of the recollection, Melville may
still have in mind the unpopular reception of the perverse theme

of *Pierre*. Following logically, the resolution of the poem argues that the imperfections of humanity, "the clay," are the fit subject of creative endeavor; they alone apparently reflect the true course of temporal existence:

> But, primal fervors all displaced
>   Our arts but serve the clay.
> This plaint the sibyls unconsoled renew:
> Man fell from Eden, fall from Athens too. (p. 389)

The "sibyls" of this passage invite identity with the self-appointed custodians of artistic taste—the critics. Much like their fabled counterparts, they view change as catastrophe, and exalt convention as dogma. Melville disputes the authority of such cultural tyranny. So far as he is concerned, the techniques of craftsmanship express, for good or evil, the integrity of the individual artist in the diverse contexts of history.

Alternately awed and appalled by Egyptian art, he nevertheless succeeds in crystallizing its purposes. "The Great Pyramid" illustrates the process of acquiring the insight. In the first stanza he seeks to establish an analogy with an earlier experience of overwhelming grandeur:

> Your masonry—and is it man's?
> More like some Cosmic artisan's.
> Your courses as in strata rise,
> Beget you do a blind surmise
>   Like Grampians. (p. 254)

The Grampians are a wild and rugged mountain range in Scotland whose massive proportions are nature's duplication of the stark wonder of the pyramid. Almost beyond credence, both silently attest the inscrutable powers of creation. With the perception of hopelessness and helplessness they engender the unanswerable, "a blind surmise." The essence of this feeling, the only association retained in the poem of Melville's spontaneous reaction, derives from the *Journal*:

> A feeling of awe & terror came over me, Dread of the Arabs. Offering to lead me into a side-hole. The Dust. Long arched way,—then

down as in a coal shaft. Then as in mines, under the sea. The stooping & doubling. I shudder at idea of ancient Egyptians. It was in these pyramids that was conceived the idea of Jehovah. Terrible mixture of the cunning and the awful. Moses learned in all the lore of the Egyptians. The idea of Jehovah born here.—When I was at top, though it not so high—sat down on edge. Looked below—gradual nervousness & final giddiness & terror. Entrance of pyramids like shoot for coal or timber. Horrible place for assassination. As long as earth endures some vestige will remain of the pyramids. Nought but earthquake or geological revolution can obliterate them.[19]

The contrast of controlled emotion in the verse offers a certain amount of proof that the creative adaptation of the experience occurs only after a long lapse of time, an interim protracted enough to quiet his spiritual ferment. At least Melville gives most of his attention to the immensity and invulnerability of the pyramid. In the next stanza his spatial imagery re-creates the desolate and empty heights:

> Far slanting up your sweeping flank
> Arabs with Alpine goats may rank,
> And there they find a choice of passes
> Even like to dwarfs that climb the masses
> Of glaciers blank. (p. 254)

While the sure-footed goats project the notion of inaccessibility, the poet formulates the incongruous image of the last two lines in order to convey the unutterable folly of undertaking the climb. At the same time the analogy of the polar landscape increases the sense of inhuman isolation. But not only is it alien to life, it also is estranged from even the most tentative identity with anything in nature:

> Shall lichen in your crevice fit?
> Nay, sterile all and granite-knit. (p. 254)

Yet, in the most blistering of ironies, the pyramid degrades the very heavens which it pierces:

> Weather nor weather-strain ye rue,
> But aridly you cleave the blue
> As lording it. (p. 254)

[19] Horsford, *Journal*, p. 118.

The poet construes this effect in terms of the monument's superiority to destruction—its seemingly eternal presence:

> All elements unmoved you stem,
> Foursquare you stand and suffer them:
> Time's infinite you dare,
> While, for the past, 'tis you that wear
> Eld's diadem. (p. 255)

Unlike the Greek temples which honor the gods, the pyramid implicitly defies them. It remains intact, evidencing a mortal hold on immortality. As such, it is a legend unto itself, commanding the fear and reverence of its observers, almost like the shrine of the holy of holies. Though knowing it to be the tomb of the Pharaohs, Melville nevertheless is seduced into believing that it secretes some inviolable racial legacy:

> Slant from your inmost lead the caves
> And labyrinths rumored. These who braves
> And penetrates (old palmers said)
> Comes out afar on deserts dead
> And, dying, raves. (p. 255)

This climax of supernatural mystery, of course, is contrived to build up expectation of some startling revelation. Nor does the poet disappoint the reader, though in a shocking reversal of his earlier attitudes:

> Craftsmen, in dateless quarries dim,
> Stones formless into form did trim,
> Usurped on Nature's self with Art,
> And bade this dumb I AM to start,
> Imposing him. (p. 255)

The volte-face provides a clear insight into the personality of the aged Melville. He is no longer harried by the metaphysical anxieties recorded in the journal of the trip. In retrospect he perceives the megalomania underlying the erection of the pyramid. The blank mass of stone signalizes the emptiness of the achievement. What lives on in time are the fears which legend perpetuates or which human beings conceive in the darkness of their own thoughts. Thus the poet exorcizes, once and for all, the demon of the despotic God of Moses who had tormented his soul. The devastating tour de force of the ending ridicules the basis of his old despair. The Melville of "The Great Pyramid" is in firm control of the values which give his life meaning and purpose. They are not in the Greek or Egyptian past; they are in the present—in his knowledge of the exigencies of fate.

The same kind of objectivity sustains the thesis of "In the Desert," the only other Egyptian poem in the collection. Like its companion piece, its inspiration derives from an entry in his *Journal*,[20] but once again Melville appears to mock the very feelings that he recorded long ago. As before, he opens the poem on a note of almost mystical tension. The blinding radiance of the sun at its zenith, the symbolic moment of divine transcendence, excites an awe and fear far more agitating than even the biblical accounts of God's wrathful alterations of the diurnal cycle:

> Never Pharaoh's Night
> Whereof the Hebrew wizards croon,
> Did so the Theban flamens try
> As me this veritable Noon. (p. 253)

If the antithetical imagery is viewed from another standpoint, especially as mediated by Melville's use of "try," the obvious explication does not hold up. His psychological experience of day as night constitutes a denial of the sacred meaning of the visible glory of the sun (son). And so the next turn of thought affirms:

> Like blank ocean in blue calm
> Undulates the ethereal frame;
> In one flowing oriflamme
> God flings his fiery standard out. (p. 253)

The first line, flatly atonal and unpoetic, proclaims Melville's dark skepticism about miracles. The wrenched syntax of the opening phrase and the negative reciprocity of "blank" and "blue" tether the emotion, holding it in abeyance in a vacuum of silence. The pejorative quality of the simile is also enhanced by the imperfect riming of "frame" and "oriflamme." This tactic anticipates Melville's

[20] Horsford, *Ibid.*, p. 119.

conversion of the "golden flame" implicit in the etymology of the last word into a medium of death, not a blazing theophany:

> Battling with the Emirs fierce
> Napoleon a great victory won,
> Through and through his sword did pierce;
> But, bayonetted by this sun
> His gunners drop beneath the gun. (p. 254)

The historical analogy brings Melville's communion with light down to the level of ordinary experience. Anchoring his impression of the scene in factual reality, he opposes this weight of truth to the crooning (solacing) rationalizations of the Hebrew prophets. In short, if the rays of the sun are other than an impersonal aspect of the natural universe, then God is no more than a gunning savage. Fittingly, the poet resolves this problem in the last stanza, under the guise of a paean to the shining glory of God contriving a profane parody of His benevolent love:

> Holy, holy, holy Light!
> Immaterial incandescence,
> Of God the effluence of the essence,
> Shekinah intolerably bright. (p. 254)

Of course, it can be argued that the fate of Napoleon's troops reflects the vengeance of God upon the sinning soldiers; then these lines embrace Melville's pious thanks to the Almighty for His superintendence of providential justice. Such an exegesis, while respectably moral and Christian, does not accord with the grim tone of the opening of the poem, as certainly the terminal phrase, "intolerably bright," operates to neutralize the lofty oppositions of light—that is, if Melville's grandiloquence has not already emptied them of meaning. Which is to say that the mystical perception of the poem is mockingly anti-apocalyptic. Nor does the cabalistic allusion to the "Shekinah," the radiant manifestation of God, alter this interpretation. As already indicated, it is juxtaposed with an equally derogatory qualification.

Melville's "Pausilippo" envisions the significance of an Italian landscape in terms of a disillusionment similar to "In the Desert," but, paradoxically, the scene is one of enchanting beauty instead of a repellent waste of sun-stricken sands. The heavens indicted for their cruelty because the associations of place, though outwardly enchanting, remind him of unjustified human suffering parallel to the fate of Napoleon's soldiers. The irony of this response is further intensified by the etymological implications of "Pausilippo," its derivation from a Greek root meaning a release from care. Historically Melville connects the area with the Italian patriot, Silvio Pellico who, like the old man in the story, was imprisoned for his opposition to the rule of a tyrannical emperor.[21] No doubt, the name Silvio in its pastoral intimations tickled the poet's fancy as a crushing inversion of his first impression of the promontory of Pausilippo. As he then recreates the scene, he has in mind the idyllic condition of man in harmony with nature:

> A hill there is that laves its feet
> In Naples' bay and lifts its head
> In jovial season, curled with vines.
> Its name, in pristine years conferred
> By settling Greeks, imports that none
> Who take the prospect thence can pine,
> For such the charm of beauty shown
> Even sorrow's self they cheerful weened
> Surcease might find and thank good Pan. (p. 242)

The allusion to Pan, in a curious way, anticipates Melville's speculations on the defeatism which enthralls the patriot Silvio. The priapic Greek god symbolizes man's instinctive desire for a natural balance of life, divorced from social and political coercions, the ideal ostensibly of Silvio Pellico. However, the Italian after his liberation from prison becomes the insipid court poet of the Marchese di Barola, his patron. Instead of writing stirring odes of denunciation against his political persecutors he relapses into innocuous piety, devoting his life to the composition of mediocre religious poetry.[22] In the poem the young girl enacts the role of the Marchesa:

---

[21] Flagg, *Venice; the City of the Sea*, 1, 287–88.
[22] *The Encyclopaedia Britannica*, 11th edition, 21, 70–71.

A man it was less hoar with time
Than bleached through strange immurement long,
Retaining still, by doom depressed,
Dim trace of some aspiring prime.
Seated he tuned a homely harp
Watched by a girl, whose filial mien
Toward one almost a child again,
Took on a staid maternal tone.
Nor might one question that the locks
Which in smoothed natural silvery curls
Fell on the bowed one's thread-bare coat
Betrayed her ministering hand. (p. 243)

Noteworthy in this passage is Silvio's transformation into a helpless child. Consistent with this image, his plying of "a homely harp" signifies his regression into infantile reliance upon the Marchesa who reduced him to " 'walking arm in arm with a Jesuit, praying, praying!' " [23] Now he is the object of pity, not admiration:

Anon, among some ramblers drawn,
A murmur rose "Tis Silvio, Silvio!"
With inklings more in tone suppressed
Touching his story, part recalled:
Clandestine arrest abrupt by night;
The sole conjecturable cause
The yearning in a patriot ode
Construed as treason; trial none;
Prolonged captivity profound;
Vain liberation late. All this,
With pity for impoverishment
And blight forestalling age's wane. (p. 243)

The continuation of the poem, after the apparent expression of sympathy, betrays a kind of impatience with the former patriot, almost a contempt for the surrender of his self-integrity:

Hillward the quelled enthusiast turned,
Unmanned, made meek through strenuous wrong,
Preluding, faltering; then began
But only thrilled the wire—no more,
The constant maid supplying voice,

[23] Flagg, *Venice; the City of the Sea*, I, 268.

> Hinting by no ineloquent sign
> That she was but his mouth-piece mere,
> Himself too spiritless and spent. (p. 244)

Nevertheless the poet succumbs to a similar spell of defeatism, and in the next section of the poem changes his style from the prosaic matter-of-factness of objective narration to the lyrical strains of self-lamentation. In the tradition of the most sentimental of the Romantic poets, he bemoans the loss of his appreciation for natural beauty:

> Pausilippo, Pausilippo,
> Pledging easement unto pain,
> Shall your beauty even solace
> If ones' sense of beauty wane? (p. 244)

And in an extension of the nostalgia he broods womanishly over his separation from the healing powers of nature, affecting a Coleridge plunged in deepest melancholia:

> Could light airs that round ye play
> Waft heart-heaviness away
> Or memory lull to sleep,
> Then, then indeed your balm
> Might Silvio becharm,
> And life in fount would leap,
> Pausilippo! (p. 244)

Not unexpectedly, Melville suddenly reverses himself, deprecating the illusions upon which idealism feeds. In short, he returns to the perspective of the Greek and Egyptian poems:

> Did not your spell invite,
> In moods that slip between,
> A dream of years serene,
> And wake, to dash, delight—
> Evoking here in vision
> Fulfilment and fruition. (p. 244)

Melville's strategy here verges on the diabolic. Though he hints in the first section that he is not entirely satisfied with the unmanly capitulation of Silvio, the imperceptive reader may well involve himself in the overt sentimentality of the situation. This is what

Melville desires to effect. His sudden exposure of the practical deficiencies of wistful dreaming works to re-establish the authority of existential reality. Disillusionment, he declares, is the inescapable lot of man:

> Nor mine, nor meant for man!
> Did hope not frequent share
> The mirage when despair
> Overtakes the caravan,
> Me then your scene might move
> To break from sorrow's snare
> And apt your name would prove,
> Pausilippo!
>
> But I've looked upon your revel—
> It unravels not the pain:
> Pausilippo, Pausilippo,
> Named benignly if in vain. (p. 245)

These lines constitute a blanket renunciation of the philosophy of the Romantic poets, particularly of Byron in his "Childe-Harold-Prisoner-of-Chillon" ecstasies. But implicitly Melville challenges the premises of happiness which the entire school inferred from their deification of nature. He has again resuscitated the point of view of *John Marr*. He insists that man view life as it unfolds in its brute actuality:

> It ceased. In low and languid tone
> The tideless ripple lapped the passive shore;
> As listlessly the bland untroubled heaven
> Looked down as silver doled was silent given
> In pity—futile as the ore! (p. 245)

Thus Melville reaffirms the necessity of adjusting all human aspirations to the bleak limitations of the contingent universe. As he continually reiterates, there will be no relief from suffering and sorrow, not so long as chance witlessly conspires with history and nature to sabotage the idealistic hopes of man.

Despite the poet's cynical attitudes, he is not averse to hailing the happiness of the lucky few who are able to transcend the disruptions of temporality. Such is the subject that he treats in "Syra"

—the exuberant joy of a settlement of Greek refugees on an inhos-
pitable island, supposedly the unfortunate victims of a bloody ex-
pulsion from a region of their native land overrun by the Turks:

> A cone-shaped fastness on whose flanks
> With pains they pitched their eyrie camp,
> Stone huts, whereto they wary clung;
> But, reassured in end, come down—
> Multiplied through compatriots now,
> Refugees like themselves forlorn—
> And building along the water's verge
> Begin to thrive; . . . . (p. 250)

Melville's interpretation of their putative misfortune is a kind of
parody of the Fortunate Fall. Through their enforced exile they
rediscover the source and vitality of their ancient pagan ancestors.
At least so the allusions to Homer and Eve suggest:

> I saw it in its earlier day—
> Primitive, such an isled resort
> As hearthless Homer might have known
> Wandering about the Ægean here.
> Sheds ribbed with wreck-stuff faced the sea
> Where goods in transit shelter found;
> And here and there a shanty-shop
> Where Fez-caps, swords, tobacco, shawls
> Pistols, and orient finery, Eve's—
> (The spangles dimmed by hands profane)
> Like plunder on a pirate's deck
> Lay orderless in such loose way
> As to suggest things ravished or gone astray.
> (pp. 250–51)

Inverting the story of the Garden of Eden, in losing their original
homeland the Greeks stumble on another paradise. For regardless
of the outward disorder of their lives, they are inwardly content;
they find salvation in the wine of conviviality:

> Above a tented inn with fluttering flag
> A sunburnt board announced Greek wine
> In self-same text Anacreon knew,
> Dispensed by one named "Pericles."
> Got up as for the opera's scene,

> Armed strangers, various, lounged or lazed,
> Lithe fellows tall, with gold-shot eyes[,]
> Sunning themselves as leopards may. (p. 251)

Obviously, Melville assumes that they thrive on the trade of free-
booters. Be that as it may, the latter revel in the warmth of the
sun, unconcerned with divine revelations or retributions. Unload-
ing the pirate vessels, the natives likewise frolic in complete indifference to civilized morality:

> Each in his tasseled Phrygian cap,
> Blue Eastern drawers and braided vest;
> And some with features cleanly cut
> As Proserpine's upon the coin.
> Such chatterers all! like children gay
> Who make believe to work, but play. (p. 251)

The poet's invocation of Proserpine (Persephone) indicates they
live in harmony with the natural cycle of life and death. Beyond
abstractions of good and evil, they cultivate the spontaneities of
time, not the fantasies of eternity, and, almost enviously, Melville
pays homage to their carefree ways:

> I saw, and how help musing too.
> Here traffic's immature as yet:
> Forever this juvenile fun hold out
> And these light hearts? Their garb, their glee,
> Alike profuse in flowing measure,
> Alike inapt for serious work,
> Blab of grandfather Saturn's prime
> When trade was not, nor toil, nor stress,
> But life was leisure, merriment, peace,
> And lucre none and love was righteousness. (p. 252)

Hardly by coincidence, in the poetry left unpublished at the time
of his death the poet begins to advocate the wisdom of this light-
hearted truce with contingent fate. Like the Greeks on Syra, he
begins to sing the virtues of joyous participation in the transitory
pleasures of the Dionysian world. Accepting impermanence as the
fundamental and pitiless law of existence, he revels in the eternal
return—in the promise of the new beginning for man heralded by
each coming of spring. Decay, dissolution, and death no longer

143

plague his thoughts. The life-death goddess Demeter, the mother of Persephone, becomes the muse of his inspiration. Abandoning the consolations promised by a future Eden, he cultivates his happiness in accordance with the ground rhythms of nature.

The inevitable development of such an outlook is clearly signaled in the concluding poem of *Timoleon*. "L'Envoi" contains Melville's valedictory counsel to his readers. It decries the quest for all transcendental knowledge, and urges a totally human adjustment to the inevitable disruptions of ordinary existence:

> My towers at last! These rovings end,
> Their thirst is slaked in larger dearth:
> The yearning infinite recoils,
> For terrible is earth! (p. 256)

Whether these sentiments are taken as an autobiographical statement of his disillusionment over the failure of his pilgrimage to Europe and the Levant or as an objective evaluation of human destiny in terms of the subtitle, "The Return of Sire de Nesle, A. D. 16—," it is evident that Melville shares this view of the essential purposelessness of any search for ultimate truth. For to judge by his own journey, he merely confirms what he already knows: man is a historical creature, subject to all the sufferings of his finitude in the scheme of nature. Plainly, these are the deficiencies of mortality that are brutally mirrored in the external world:

> Kaf thrusts his snouted crags through fog:
> Araxes swells beyond his span,
> And knowledge poured by pilgrimage
> Overflows the banks of man. (p. 256)

Mountain and flood, relative lastingness and irresistible power, reduce human life to utter insignificance, and there are no dams of thought that can bar the flow of this bitter truth into the mind, lest it be the innate levity of a native of Syra. For the civilized, reasoning being there is only the forgetfulness of understanding love:

> But thou, my stay, thy lasting love
> One lonely good, let this but be!
> Weary to view the wide world's swarm,
> But blest to fold but thee. (p. 256)

Thus, either in the perspective of the first section of *Timoleon* or
in the retrospective view of the second, Melville renounces all attempts to resolve the meaning of life in other than a human framework. Ultimately philosophy, religion, art, and ideology are found
to be wanting. Only love, mutual physical dependence, promises an
alleviation of man's desolating inner aloneness—the terrifying
knowledge that he is orphan in the universe. Yet even this last
hope is only a hope. The voice in the last stanza pleads for this one
enduring value, but the supplication is in itself an admission of uncertainty. Not until the last years of his life does Melville finally
reconcile himself to all suffering and sorrow—and without protest.

The extreme nature of the poet's rupture with the beliefs of
his own times may be signified in the two dates which he appends
to the titles of the first and last poems in the collection. Under
"Timoleon" is "(394 B.C.)," and under "L'Envoi" is "A.D. 16—."
Neither of the two historical sources of the first piece, Bayle or
Plutarch, centers on any significant occurrence on this date. As a
matter of fact, Timoleon, whose approximate dates are 411–337
B.C. was only about seventeen years old. What then is the function
of the date if there is no important historical correlative either in
the hero's life or in the recorded annals of the period? One can
only guess that Melville is again indulging some private whimsy.
Such would be the case, at any rate, if we relate 394 B.C. to Christian history. This date or 396 B.C. is sometimes found in chapter
heading at the beginning of the Book of Malachi. It is often taken
as the approximate year of the final messianic prophecy in the Old
Testament. But it is significant in another way; it also contains Malachi's denunciation of the priesthood for its deviations from the
orthodox levitical traditions. The date therefore anticipates the
coming of Christ. On the other hand, the Book emphasizes the necessity of devotion to rigorous principles of worship in the ritualis-
tic sense. This was, of course, the ecclesiastical philosophy which
the Roman Catholic Church adopted and perpetuated successfully
among English-speaking peoples until the seventeenth century. If
we assume that Melville has in mind the Protestant Revolution
and the roots it sank in the New World, then the career of Christi-

anity for him would span the fourth century B.C. and the 16— in the title of the last poem. From this point on would ensue the breakdown of traditional Christianity, actually the loss of the meaning of the messianic figure of Malachi. Certainly no one can deny that the advent of Protestant iconoclasm has only succeeded in confusing the role of Christ in spiritual government. Not only has He been monopolistically absorbed into the dogmas of more than four hundred competing sects, but His word has come to mean less than the voices of his fanatical interpreters. Under the circumstances one can understand the dismal nihilism of "L'Envoi." It could symbolize Melville's rejection of institutional religion. The real traditions of faith, as Malachi upbraidingly observed in much the same light, were disappearing under an avalanche of innovations in dogma and creed. There was nothing left but empty gestures, forms, and usages. Melville's awareness of the loss of traditional values is manifest in *Clarel* as well as his novels. But the kinship of the poetry of his pilgrimage to the work under discussion makes it highly probable that his dates are ironical symbols of his moral disgust with the complacent hypocrisy of his Victorian contemporaries.

Of course, the surface theme of "L'Envoi" may be rigged to delude the naive reader, certainly the appropriate denomination for the members of his family circle (and some critics of today). Surely, the underlying attitudes of virtually every poem included in *Timoleon* illustrate that Melville is playing the role of a jester, and on occasions he is not averse to revealing that his portentous seriousness in the past was really no more than a grotesque comic aberration of a conditioned Puritan-Protestant conscience. Or put another way, his poetry is a confession that his emotional development did not keep pace with the growth of his intellectual and moral awareness. Unlike Hawthorne, he at last is able to effect a reconciliation with his instinctual nature without degrading his idea of the essential nobility of man.

Weeds and Wildings,
with a Rose or Two

VIII   Cyclical Time

THE MANSUSCRIPT POEMS which Melville sought to arrange under the title of "Weeds and Wildings, with A Rose or Two" in the last year of his life mark a change in poetic style but not a betrayal of the muse of *John Marr* and *Timoleon*. The focus on the disillusionments of human existence still prevails but in a deceptive variation of temper—a sardonic pastoral irony. This view, I might point out, is not shared in modern critical circles. Instead it is said that the poetry is "quiet to the point of colorlessness," being distinguished by "the homely imagery of countrified retirement and quiet domestic simplicity." [1] Or one hears that the collection discloses "evidences of a 'melting mood.' " [2] Actually the undebatable transformation of imagery and tone is the signature of poetic purpose—the artifice of assumed unsophistication. The tender sentiments and the rural subject matter of flowers, weeds, birds, and animals disguise a rollicking mockery of conventional moral and social values.

The collection trumpets Melville's radical estrangement from the systems of reference that made life purposeful for his contemporaries. He invokes an old man's sense of comedy to register his disgust with the social and moral mummery of the Victorian world. He laughingly exposes its dullness, insensitivity, and pretentiousness; its shallow materialism and grotesque piety. Focusing upon the sterile mechanization of Christianity in practice, Melville, like a jovial Kierkegaard, attacks the middle-class leveling of the individual under the tyranny of public opinion. And to accentuate his disdain for this unwholesome scourge of respectability, he disin-

---

[1] Arvin, *Herman Melville*, p. 280.
[2] Howard, *Herman Melville*, p. 337.

fects the atmosphere of this rank odor of sanctimony with a poetic chaplet of wild flowers and roses: a passionate Dionysian exhortation to deify the sexual nature of man. Thus he mockingly actualizes the repressed desires of the Victorian sensibility.

But underlying the frost of this ironic mirth is a granite core of seriousness, the conviction of Melville's old age that the poets of the time had betrayed their function. The individuals he had in mind cannot be precisely established. But certainly Tennyson, Browning, and probably Arnold were among the culprits. In any event, *Weeds and Wildings* satirizes the arid platitudinizing of the popular poets of the day, especially their sentimental and pseudo-mystical resolutions of the problems of human destiny. The discordant, prosy quality of his verse embodies an attempt to reveal the incapacity of the language of contemporary poetry to convey a valid interpretation of human experience. The gradual transfiguration of Melville's diction between the composition of *Moby-Dick* and *Billy Budd* betrays an acute awareness of this strange phenomenon of semantic disintegration. Nor should this occasion surprise. In the latter third of the century there is an overt rebellion against the sick and sickening conventions of literary expression. It is clearly evident, for instance, in the writings of Edward Lear and Lewis Carroll. Their verbal nonsense reveals the utter inanity of current habits of thought and speech. In our own times the works of Samuel Beckett argue the absolute impossibility of interpersonal communication; for the dialogue in his plays is built on the principle that each statement obliterates what is said in the previous statement. In effect, with nothing to say that one believes in, one is hard put to find words to say anything.

Feeling, on the other hand, that he has something meaningful to say, Melville is driven to improvise a vehicle for saying it. Abandoning traditional poetic practices in *Weeds and Wildings,* he devises a mode of expression whose surface form, in most instances, encourages in the reader an esthetic distance approaching instantaneous repulsion; that is, at first glance the poetry reflects an incredible mediocrity of craftsmanship. It is primarily denotative in form, what is nowadays called a poetry of direct statement. However, it lacks the precision, the conciseness, and the supple rhetoric ordinarily associated with the method. Instead it is duly and provincially concrete, a leech-gatherer's diary of banalities. Wrenched in syntax, labored in rime, broken in rhythm, affected in imagery, and unimaginative in outlook, the poetry seems contrived to carry only an insipid freight of emotion: domestic sentimentalities, all evoked in a kind of seed-catalogue setting of flowers, weeds, birds, insects, and curious wild creatures. As a consequence, one's immediate reaction is "Poor Lizzie" (Melville's wife for whom the poetry, allegedly, was written). But let me hasten to say that a closer reading of the poetry reveals that all of its ostensible defects are the result of artifice, the mask of a witty pastoral irony.

Like the language and form of *Billy Budd, Weeds and Wildings* conceals its complexity in its feigned simplicity. As the holograph manuscripts indicate, Melville carefully revised each of the poems to achieve a tone of naive literalness or of studied unsophistication. This intention, I think, is controlled by the subject matter under treatment—nature's annual rehearsal of the grim scenario of life and death, fruition and decay, regeneration and annihilation. In the Victorian world man had lost his vision of the tragic sense of life. But, unconsciously, in order to allay the insecurities and anxieties generated by the disorders of time and, by extension, history, he cultivated the illusion of optimism. And, coincidentally, this self-deception was fostered not only by historical and scientific theories but also by the consoling bromides of a fashionable Christianity. Spiritually and intellectually, then, the cumulative knowledge of the day argued that all was right with the world and that society was progressing towards secular perfection. As a pampered darling of the gods, man could now afford to sentimentalize nature, for its seasonal paradigms could also be employed to prove all the assumptions of current thought. In his poetry Melville appears to adopt a similar point of view; at least he takes the position that the Christian machinery of grace and salvation *could* resolve the desolating tensions of time.

But as the argument of *Weeds and Wildings* develops, this reservation slowly evolves into a state of complete disbelief. Even as one of the key poems, "Time's Betrayal," suggests, the basic premises of contemporary Christianity fail to serve man in moments of crisis and contingency. Without an organizing metaphysic or myth to sustain himself in the center of chaos, he is completely estranged from the universe. In this predicament he has only two alternatives: either to lapse into existential despair or to formulate a new relationship with nature. The poet or, perhaps more accurately, the mask through which he speaks, proposes the latter solution: redemption through nature, a Dionysian transcendence of the dislocations of time.

The cancellations and insertions on the title page of the original manuscripts indicate a serious effort to formulate a logical order of poetic development. At the beginning of the project, as the title "As They Fell" and several deletions suggest, Melville's uncertainty is evident.[3] However, his later changes seem to support the belief that he had found the necessary connection between the new tripartite arrangement of *Weeds and Wildings* and *A Rose or Two*. This conjuncture may also explain why certain poems on the first title page were permanently omitted. Then the preface to the collection must also be given consideration, especially since it has provided an autobiographical fulcrum for the interpretation of the poetry in some quarters.[4] Coming as an afterthought,

---

[3] See Leyda, *The Melville Log*, 2: 822, for his transcription of all the poems on the first title page.

[4] Leon Howard, for example, takes for granted the rigid correlation between the poet's personal life and his creative endeavors, *Herman Melville*, p. 336. The dedication follows:

> With you and me, Winnie, Red Clover has always been one of the dearest of the flowers of the field: an arrival—by the way—as you well ween, which implies no undelight to this ruddy young brother's demure little half-sister, White Clover. Our feeling for both sorts originates in no fanciful associations egotistic in kind. It is not, for example, because in any exceptional way we have verified in experience the aptness of that pleasant figure of speech, *Living-in-Clover*—not in this do we so take to the Ruddy One, for all that we once dwelt annually surrounded by flushed acres of it. Neither have we, jointly or severally, so frequently lighted upon that rare four-leaved variety accounted of happy augury to the finder; though, to be sure, on my part, I yearly remind you of the coincidence in my chancing on such a specimen by the wayside on the early forenoon of the fourth day of a certain bridal month, now four years more than four times ten years ago.
>
> But tell, do we not take to this flower—for flower it is, tho' with the florist hardly ranking with the florist clans—not alone that in itself it is a thing

the dedication has been taken to control the inspiration of the entire volume—a kind of floral bouquet of love. Actually it was a necessary subterfuge! Its affectations of feeling have nothing in common with the thematic patterns of the poetry. Indeed, Melville may have been compelled to add it in order to conceal his

of freshness and beauty, but also that being no delicate foster-child of the nurseryman, but a hardy little creature of out-of-doors accessable [sic] and familiar to every one, no one can monopolize its charm. Yes, we are communists here.

Sweet in the mouth of that brindled heifer whose breath you so loved to inhale, and doubtless pleasant to her nostril and eye; sweet as well to the like senses in ourselves, prized by that most practical of men, the farmer, to whom wild amaranths in a pasture, though emblems of immortality, are but weeds and anathema; finding favor even with so peevish a busybody as the bee; is it not the felicitous fortune of our favorite, to incur no creature's displeasure, but to enjoy, and without striving for it, the spontaneous good-will of all? Why is it that this little peasant of the flowers reveals in so enviable an immunity and privilege, not in equal degree shared by any of us mortals however gifted and good; that indeed is something the reason whereof may not slumber very deep. But—*In pace;* always leave a sleeper to his repose.

How often at our adopted homestead or on the hill-side—now ours no more—the farm-house, long ago shorn by the urbane barbarian succeeding us in the proprietorship—shorn of its gambrel roof and dormer windows, and when I last saw it indolently settling in serene contentment of natural decay; how often, Winnie, did I come in from my ramble, early in the bright summer mornings of old, with a handful of these cheap little cheery roses of the meek, newly purloined from the fields to consecrate them on that bit of a maple-wood-mantel—your altar, somebody called it—in the familiar room facing your beloved South! And in October most did I please myself in gathering them from the moist matted aftermath in an enriched little hollow near by, soon to be snowed upon and for consecutive months sheeted from view.

And once—you remember it—having culled them in a sunny little flurry of snow, winter's frolic skirmisher in advance, the genial warmth of your chamber melted the fleecy flakes into dew-drops rolling off from the ruddiness, "Tears of the happy," you said.

Well, and to whom but to thee, Madonna of the Trefoil, should I now dedicate these "Weeds and Wildings," thriftless children of quite another and yet later spontaneous after-growth, and bearing indications too apparent it may be, of that terminating season on which the offerer verges. But take them. And for aught suggestion of the "melting mood" that any may possibly betray, call to mind the dissolved snow-flakes on the ruddy oblation of old, and remember your "tears of the happy." (pp. 481–82) aims and dissuade a search for other than surface meaning. As his witty contradictions indicate, the poet is up to his old tricks, undermining the pretentious beliefs of his culture. This is not intended as an aspersion upon the intelligence of Elizabeth Melville. It is perhaps the delusion which the wife of every artist courts. While believing herself to be the soul-mate of his inspiration, she is only the efficient maid. Appropriately, Part I of *Weeds and Wildings* is called "The Year," and it explores the implications of man's unhappy alienation from reality (that is, from time-diseased existence). But as "Vine and Goat," a poem now lost but included in the table of contents prepared for the collection, seems to indicate, Dionysus is not dead. He merely awaits human acknowledgment that he is still annually resurrected. The desperate need for this awareness is proclaimed in the first verse of "The Year." Entitled "The Loiterer," it dramatizes man's fear that the winter of his doom has come. In the opening lines the poet pleads for a continuation of faith in the renewing vitalities of spring:

> She will come tho' she loiter, believe,
> Her pledge it assigns not the day;
> Why brood by the embers night after night,
> Sighing over their dying away— (p. 259)

Though this passage seems explicit enough, the silent question in the last two lines harbors a negation that discloses the spiritual stagnation of Melville's world. The meaning of the Christian Year is wholly forgotten. The season traditionally associated with the Resurrection and God's endlessly vigilant love excites no burning flame of hope. Apparently the poet addresses a community without any inward conviction of faith in redemption. For, as this stanza concludes, he obliquely abstracts the connotations of this pessimism:

> Well, let her delay;
> She is everywhere longed for as here;
> A favorite, freakish and young:
> Her can we gladden, then us she can cheer?
> Let us think no wrong. (p. 259)

In entreating that man "think no wrong," he hints that the opposite attitude, the one actually expressed, reflects man's reservations about divine omnipotence. And it is in this manner, clearly but deviously, that Melville questions the authority of Christianity in his culture. Here the lack of faith in the regeneration of spring symbolically parallels the lack of faith in religious salvation.

In the next stanza Melville enjoins a kind of ritual preparation for the outbreak of seasonal fecundity. Apparently he recognizes the psychological function of such ceremonies in mediating the proper emotional and moral adjustment to the dowry of spring:

> But watch and wait:
> Wait by the pasture-bars
> Or watch by the garden-gate;
> For, after coming, tho' wide she stray,
> First ever she shows on the slender way—
> Slim sheep-track threads the hill-side brown,
> Or foot-path leads to the garden down. (p. 259)

Implicitly, he argues that the coming even insures the life of the entire community of nature—human, vegetable, and animal. Melville is aware that the lack of such an outlook generates a sense of rootlessness. For next he goes on to call attention to the grip of death on the imagination of the self-interested person:

> . . . snow lingered under the fir,
> Loth to melt from embrace of the earth,
> And ashy red embers of logs
> In moonlight dozed on the hearth. (p. 260)

The snow, of course, prefigures the flow of the regenerative waters just as the moon rehearses the scenario of life, death, and rebirth in its monthly phases. But even though man is confronted with these paradigms of unchanging reality, he cowers in fear by his hearth. Neither his relationship to God nor to nature reconciles him to his finite incertitude.

When at last spring leaps forth to claim her identity, the poet hails her arrival with an exaggerated gush of sentimentality:

> By the self-same foot-path along,
> She drew to the weather-beat door
> That was sunned thro' the skeleton tree:

Nothing she said, but seemed to say—
"Old folks, aren't ye glad to see *me!*"
And tears brimmed our eyes—bless the day! (p. 260)

True, his wife probably sobbed happily at this turn of events, but a critic is obliged to maintain a more sophisticated poise. He has to concern himself seriously with the manner in which the poet has rendered the experience; the ordering of the language, the substance of the language, the metrical qualities of the language. This passage, in contrast with the tone of muted pessimism in the earlier excerpts, projects its meaning with a kind of labored prosaic candor. Scorning all subtlety, it communicates its trite pathos on a squeaky note of mechanical piety. Yet, as Melville's painstaking revisions of this poem indicate (p. 516), he strives to achieve this negative effect. The question, of course, is why? Considering the archaic "ye," the rhetorically italicized "*me,*" and the phony salutation of spring, one can only conclude that Melville is employing parody to disavow the very sentiment expressed. In short, his clumsy versification and hackneyed idiom expose the shallow spiritual awareness of his times. Man no longer has the capacity to react spontaneously to the transcendental iconography of the seasonal cycle. His rational expectations for "the blessed life" have ceased to be influenced by either Dionysian or Christian affirmations. Bewitched by the illusions of time, he surrenders his future destiny to history, trying to convince himself that self-redemption is the mark of a superior civilization.

More direct evidence of Melville's preoccupation with time and history is found in "When Forth the Shepherd Leads the Flock." Carefully preserving an order of meaning in the sequential ordering of the poems throughout the collection, the poet traces man's alienation from nature to his obsession with ephemeral materialistic values:

But alack and alas
For things of wilding feature!
Since hearsed was Pan
Ill befalls each profitless creature—
Profitless to man! (p. 261)

And quite explicitly, Melville equates this disorientation of the sensibility with instinctual atrophy, with the loss of pantheistic or Dionysian freedom. At any rate in the opening stanza, he argues that civilization itself cuts man off from the roots of his being in the universe:

> When forth the shepherd leads the flock,
> White lamb and dingy ewe,
> And there's dibbling in the garden,
> Then the world begins anew. (p. 261)

The new act of creation is sanctified by the ritual copulation of the sheep. Sexual union integrates with cosmic rhythm and therein finds its eternal validation. In effect, nature proclaims the return of pristine innocence with the commencement of every spring. Therefore it is foolish for man to seek perfection in historical time. Each rebirth of the year provides him with the opportunity to realize himself over again:

> When Buttercups make bright
> The meadows up and down,
> The Golden Age returns to fields
> If never to the town. (p. 261)

"[T]he town" in this quatrain is a synecdoche of the artificial order and security of civilization, and Melville's images of floral gold evoke the treasures of simple happiness that have been renounced by man in his infatuate pursuit of the ephemeral accumulations of time. The Golden Age in this context is a state of being—a joyful acceptance of life.

Precisely that spirit imbues the setting of the next passage. Uninhibitedly, all nature celebrates the miracle of Dionysian renewal. There were no distinctions in importance. Each growing thing is granted the freedom to fulfill itself once more:

> When stir the freshening airs
>   Forerunning showers to meads,
> And Dandelions prance,
> Then Heart-Free shares the dance—
>   A Wilding with the Weeds! (p. 261)

The disengaged wilding is the key image in this passage—Melville's epithet for the cultivated flower that has escaped from the garden to reclaim its identity with the celebrants of the Dionysian renewal.

Conversely, man is out of harmony with the democratic family of nature. He is the prisoner of linear time, desperately preoccupied with prolonging his survival in a finite world:

> Buttercup and Dandelion,
> Wildings, and the rest,
> Commoners and holiday-makers,
> Note them in one test:
>
> The farmers scout them,
> Yea, and would rout them,
> Hay is better without them—
> Tares in the grass!
> The florists pooh-pooh them. (pp. 261–62)

In fine, man inadvertently exiles himself from the garden of the present world, the only true Eden. This reverberation of meaning is set up by the title of the poem. Its New Testament echoes function to reveal his estrangement from both God and nature. In his obsessive concern with temporal utility he disavows the teachings and guidance of his Shepherd. For such are the implications inherent in "Tares in the grass." Melville travesties the familiar parable on good and evil, ridiculing the inability of Christian man to come to terms with the polarized structure of things. Because of his compulsive self-interest, he is unable to judge the worth of either time or eternity. Though the terminal stanza seems to redeem this radical disaffection from reality in the spontaneous appreciation of the young, the affirmation is only a trap for the naive reader:

> Few but children do woo them,
> Love them, reprieve them,
> Retrieve and inweave them,
> Never sighing—Alas! (p. 262)

The poet realizes that the child is not the father of the man but rather will become the conditioned product of the attitudes of his culture. The careful emphasis on play indicates that the children face a rude awakening—alas!

Reversing the disenchantment with the impersonal scheme of nature, "The Little Good Fellows" posits the perfect adaptation of lower creatures to the contingent world of time. Ironically, Melville endows his robins with a tolerance and intelligence that enables them to accept man's witless efforts to monopolize the universe:

> Make way, make way, give leave to rove
> Under your orchard as above;
> A yearly welcome if ye love!
> And all who loved us alway throve. (p. 262)

Of course, the birds' plea for love constitutes an indirect indictment of the failure of Christianity. They offer to teach man the significance of periodic regeneration, the means of adapting to the terrors of suffering and death. As the phrase "A yearly welcome" implies, they propose to define the conditions of annual as opposed to eternal fulfillment. Thus they go on to demonstrate that the interdependence of all living things is a sacred law of nature:

> Love for love. For ever we
> When some unfriended man we see
> Lifeless under forest-eaves,
> Cover him with buds and leaves;
> And charge the chipmunk, mouse, and mole—
> Molest not this poor human soul! (p. 262)

So the robins attempt to initiate man into the cult of Dionysus, promising him rebirth under their special covenant. Their burial of the dead man under "buds and leaves" signifies the transfiguration that takes place under the auspices of returning spring: out of one form of death springs another form of life in the compensatory balance of the two forces in the universe.

Repeating the central argument of "When Forth the Shepherd Leads the Flock," the robins urge man to promote the regenerative energies of nature by ritual copulation. Here Melville construes the defloration of marriage as the sacrifice (or symbolic death) that restores the circuit of life momentarily arrested by the devastation of winter:

> But toss your hats, O maids and men,
> Snow-bound long in farm-house pen:
> We chase Old Winter back to den.
> See our red waistcoats! Alive be then—
> Alive to bridal-favors when
> They blossom in your orchards every Spring,
> And cock-robin curves on a bridegroom's wing! (p. 263)

Plainly, his detailed description of the parallel ceremony is also devised to project the unity of the animate universe. Orgy on the plane of nature is correlated with marriage on the plane of human society, and both are consecrated by the blossoming orchards (surrogates of the mythic tree of life). The passion comprehended in the "red waistcoats" signals the release from frozen emotions, and "Old Winter," the scapegoat of these rites of spring, is hounded back to his cave. Thus the robins promise the renewal of all the potentialities of the primal creation, for the archetypal marriage between the sun and the earth has supplied the model for the immediate observances. This formula of temporal redemption contradicts the orthodox tenets of Christianity, and Melville subtly bolsters this intention in focusing on the red breasts of the robins. In biblical folklore the bird is often connected with the crucifixion, having stained its feathers in plucking a thorn from the brow of Christ as He hung on the cross. In short, Melville's seemingly innocuous pastoral drama blasphemously inverts the popular nineteenth-century tale.

Another of the spring poems, "The Old Fashion," celebrates the recovery of the Golden Age. Certainly the title makes this point. The time brought about is old yet new—the eternal present of each repetition of the cosmogonic act. By extension, this means the prevalence of eternal youth:

> Now youthful is Ver
> And the same, and forever,
> Year after year;
> And her bobolinks sing,

> And they vary never
> In juvenile cheer. (p. 264)

Not trusting direct statement alone, Melville illustrates the unchanging character of the season in a formula of sound. The sweet, echoic song of the bobolinks hymns the glories of a paradise never lost, of a buoyant vigor never exhausted. And even as they pour out their delight in life, they mate in conformity with the silent rhythm of earthly fertility:

> Old-fashioned is Ver
> Tho' eternally new,
> And her bobolink's young
> Keep the old fashion true:
> *Chee, Chee!* they will sing
> While the welkin is blue. (p. 264)

Thereby Melville illustrates the essential unity of life and nature, a state of bliss foreign to civilized man because he has allowed his instinctual impulses to atrophy.

The last of the spring poems, "The Lover and the Syringa Bush," traces this alienation to the effects of Christian teachings, specifically the repression of emotional spontaneity. Melville foreshadows this development of thought in the title of the poem when he couples the lover with a flowering May shrub whose name derives from the Greek *syrinx*, the musical pipe of the phallic deity Pan (and which is a carefully selected ironic gambit). Casually heaping scorn upon the ascetic bias of religion, he compares the beauty of the bush to a Christmas tree:

> Like a lit-up Christmas tree,
> Like a grotto pranked with spars,
> Like white corals in green sea,
> Like night's sky of crowded stars— (p. 265)

The simile of the grotto is devised to generate associations with the birth of Christ, even as that of the stars with the pilgrimage of the Magi. Nor is the coral extraneous to this context of interpretation. It is a conventional ornament of the infant Saviour in holy pictures, a safeguard against diabolic evil. But even while Melville invites this train of thought, he does not permit its implications to prevail in the resolution of the poem:

> To me like these you show, Syringa
> Such heightening power has love, believe,
> While here by Eden's gate I linger
> Love's tryst to keep, with truant Eve. (p. 265)

Viewed in the light of the impending erotic interlude, grotto, sea, and sky can be construed as symbols of reason (earth), instinct (underworld), and spirit (heaven)—the three conflicting human faculties of judgment and understanding that are reconciled in the act of love. According to Melville's argument, this is the mode of deliverance that the religion based on the coming of Christ has degraded into shame and guilt. Which is to say that in the self-forgetting of morally unsullied sexual intercourse there occurs a psychological rebirth. *La petite mort* is the prelude to the resurrection of a holistic self. The celebrants in the throes of mutual passion fuse time and eternity, life and death, one and all. As the closing passage implies, not until Eve is lured out of the stagnant garden of Eden does she actually realize herself in complete womanhood.

As the year makes its transition into summer, Melville sustains the radical antagonism between the Christian and Dionysian modes of existence. Again his manipulation of submerged irony transforms a naive literalism into the vehicle of mordant wit and ridicule. For example, "Butterfly Ditty" is akin in treatment and theme to Emily Dickinson's "I Taste a Liquor Never Brewed." Like her, he flippantly employs religious imagery to describe an unequivocal sensory, if not sensual, experience:

> Summer comes in like a sea,
> Wave upon wave how bright;
> Thro' the heaven of summer we'll flee
> And tipple the light! (p. 264)

His irreverent purpose is signalized in the choice of the mediating subject, the insect conventionally identified with the soul. In effect, the quaffing of the light evolves into a burlesque of the Eucharistic ceremony. Instead of inducing spiritual ecstasy, it excites irrepressible emotional elation. And why not? The world blossoms into countless paradises of overbrimming honey:

> From garden to garden,
>   Such charter have we,
> We'll rove and we'll revel,
>   And idlers we'll be!

As ordained by nature, the butterflies despoil the flowers in a drunken orgy, but in the interludes between their mating dance they pollinate the gardens and prepare for another renewal of the wheeling year. All these associations are implicit in "revel," and it may be that Melville is exploiting the etymological meaning of the word, "to rebel." At least in the final stanza he takes note of the failure of man to revolt against the psychological curse of the Fall:

> We'll rove and we'll revel,
>   Concerned but for this,—
> That Man, Eden's bad boy,
>   Partakes not the bliss. (p. 264)

The teasing iconoclasm of these sentiments simply extends Melville's earlier disparagement of the life-negating influence of Christianity. Quite obviously he argues that it is religious doctrine, not any stigma of inherited depravity, that undermines man's capacity to enjoy the temporal moment. In short, a conditioned distrust of his instincts has alienated man from himself. With abstractions of sin and hell continually at war with his instincts, he is left a prey to emotional anxieties that he mistakes for moral guilt. So he is an innately good boy laboring under the delusion that he is an incorrigible "bad boy."

In "Clover" Melville laconically comments on the ingrained asceticism of the Christian sensibility. The warm, bright colors of a summer day objectify the uncorrupted force of natural life:

> The June day dawns, the joy-winds rush,
>   Your jovial fields are dresst;
> Rosier for thee the Dawn's red flush,
>   Ruddier the Ruddock's breast. (p. 263)

Melville's progressive intensification of the red correlates with the rising pulsation of the beholder's blood as he participates in the diurnal re-creation of the cosmogonic act. Unlike the apathetic spectators of the butterfly's seasonal spree, he thrills to his sexual identity, for "the joy-winds" are the vibrations of the sensual pleasures consecrated during the bridal month of June. Of course, the trifoliate clover bolsters this play of the dialectic. In a variation on the custom of throwing rice, it too is used to express a wish for the fertile union of a wedded couple. Moreover, Melville is probably aware of its analogy with the male genitals. At any rate, this is the connotation of the allusion to the ruddocks, the "Good Fellows" of the earlier poem. The Robin Goodfellows of folklore are hobgoblins with notable priapic characteristics,[5] and in this context the color of red has to be associated with the liberation of passion. But regardless of the interpretive approach, Melville is unquestionably concerned with the celebration of instinctual freedom.

The figurative reverberations of "Madcaps" are no less outrageous. While at first glance no such purpose is in evidence, once the adult observer begins to report his thoughts, the gamboling of two children takes on subjective meaning. Beneath his delight in their antics he conceals a deep personal distress. And consistent with the mode of the late poetry, Melville projects this feeling in a subtle constellation of images:

> Through the orchard I follow
> Two children in glee.
> From an apple-tree's hollow
> They startle the bee. (p. 263)

The juxtaposition of the apple tree and the bees immediately sets up an ironical contrast with the temptation. The insects commonly personify the soul,[6] and in context they symbolize the moral innocence of the children, their present ignorance of sin or, more precisely, their lack of knowledge of the sham doctrine ("hollow") of

[5] Richard Payne Knight and Thomas Wright, *Sexual Symbolism: A History of Phallic Worship* (New York, 1957), p. 76. The reference is to Wright's *The Worship of the Generative Powers* (1866), the second part of the volume.

[6] Brewer, *Dictionary of Phrase and Fable*, p. 77.

the Fall. Since Melville always connects this event with sexuality, the "White Clover" constitutes the armor of their purity (as opposed to the red in the previous poem). By the same token, "The hedge of Red Rose" is the barrier of eroticism that in later experience they must eventually surmount:

> The White Clover throws
> Perfume in their way
> To the hedge of Red Rose;
> Between Roses and Clover
> The Strawberry grows. (p. 263)

Here the strawberry, the fruit of the straying plant according to folklore, alludes to the burden of sin and guilt that is the consequence of sexual awareness in a Puritan society. Now in the state of innocence the animal spirits of the children are in perfect harmony with the purity of their thoughts:

> It is Lily and Cherry
> Companioned by Butterflies
> Madcaps as merry! (p. 263)

No doubt having in mind "Butterfly Ditty," Melville quietly protests the restraints on impulsive behavior that experience will impose upon the two girls when they become cherry-ripe.

"The Dairyman's Child" supports the previous interpretation. Melville couches his description of a young girl in the imagery of nascent summer that captures all of the delicate beauty of emergent puberty. Allusion after allusion evokes the gradual ripening of her feminine charms:

> Soft as the morning
> When South winds blow,
> Sweet as peach-orchards
> When blossoms are seen. (p. 266)

As in "Madcaps," her innocence neutralizes sexuality; it is not an abstraction of virtue; it is a state of virginal being:

> Pure as a fresco
> Of roses and snow,
> Or an opal serene. (p. 266)

In effect, the poetic voice does not envisage her as a human but rather as an embodiment of nature. He perceives that she accepts her womanly identity under no constraints of custom or convention. Her instinctive capacity for life ("roses") is held in perfect balance by her unviolated thought ("snow"). Like the gem, she has been formed by physical processes alone.

Fittingly, Melville's last summer poem, "The Blue-Bird," exalts the Dionysian order of reality. Renouncing belief in the Christian formula of linear redemption (the timetable that moves inexorably from the Fall, through the Crucifixion, and finally to the Resurrection), he shows that life and death are but successive stages in the recurrent cycle of the year. Not at all embittered by the lawless operation of contingency, he educes concrete proof that in the scheme of nature nothing dies purposelessly. While this resolution of his thought is clear enough, the problem of interpretation pivots on reaching a logical explanation of Melville's sudden switch in tone:

> Beneath yon Larkspur's azure bells
> That sun their bees in balmy air
> In mould no more the Blue-Bird dwells
> Tho' late he found interment there.

> All stiff he lay beneath the Fir
> When shrill the March piped overhead,
> And Pity gave him sepulchre
> Within the Garden's sheltered bed.

> And soft she sighed—Too soon he came;
> On wings of hope he met the knell;
> His heavenly tint the dust shall tame;
> Ah, some misgiving had been well! (p. 265)

Obviously, the stark image of the frozen bird sharply contrasts with the trite sentiments of personified pity. Indeed, the incongruity is so extreme that it invites laughter, and, though perhaps strange to say, that is precisely the effect sought. The maudlin sentimentality of the last six lines is a parody of Christianity in practice. Melville takes note of the decline of vital religious feeling into a puerile emotionalism out of touch with naturalistic facts. In this perspective, then, the flourish of sacral imagery in the last stanza is a piece of pastoral irony:

> But, look, the clear etherial hue
> In June it makes the Larkspur's dower;
> It is the self-same welkin-blue—
> The Bird's transfigured in the Flower. (p. 265)

As Melville well knows, his use of transfiguration contradicts the process of physical change that he has described—the manuring of the flower by the decomposed body of the bluebird. No absolute transcendence has occurred. The year has simply bestowed its grace upon the earth.

Melville employs the vehicle of myth to elucidate a somewhat similar theme in "Trophies of Peace," the first of his autumnal poems. The reconciliation of the polarities of life and death is directly related to the ancient Greek mystery, the Eleusinia. Sacred to Demeter and Persephone (the great fertility goddess and her daughter), the festival took the form of an initiation and revelation that provided the celebrants with a glimpse into the intrinsic meaning of self-sacrifice. Of course, the familiar story of the rape of Persephone is the foundation of the epiphany. As figured in the deliverance of the land from the curse of barrenness visited by her angry mother, her death and resurrection rehearse the seasonal cycle of winter and spring. But beyond this rather obvious allegory, her redemption has much profounder implications (and these emerge in the poem). Her defloration or dismemberment symbolizes an act of self-renunciation that leads to a transformative regeneration, not merely as seen in the renewal of earthly fertility but more importantly in the maiden's subsequent motherhood. Now indistinguishable from Demeter, she perpetuates the continuum of life, and illustrates that nothing dies unavailingly in the Dionysian world.[7] The Eleusinian mystery, it should be obvious, is the pagan prototype of the crucifixion and atonement, and, no doubt, its chief appeal for Melville lies in the fact that Persephone's violation, a sin by Christian standards, becomes the mode of human salvation.

[7] Anthon, *The Classical Dictionary*, pp. 463–465.

Nor to be overlooked is the stress placed by the myth on physical rather than spiritual rejuvenation.

Structurally, Melville weaves all the overtones of this scenario into the imagery of his poem. For example, his description of a vast stretch of corn is a disguised exaltation of Demeter and Persephone. Both were corn spirits, the divine personifications of the fecund Eleusinian plain. Moreover, in the final stage of the religious festival a sprig of corn was solemnly elevated before the initiates in order to represent the sublime import of the daughter's ravishment.[8] Ready for harvesting, the glistening grain is the impeccable analogy of the ritual and of Persephone's dewy virginity. On the other hand, Melville's introduction of the military imagery establishes a contrasting perspective on suffering and sacrifice, that of historical contingency:

> Files on files of Prairie Maize:
> On hosts of spears the morning plays!
> Aloft the rustling streamers show:
> The floss embrowned is rich below. (p. 266)

Since the poet in the subtitle connects the scene with a remembrance of Illinois, it is probable that he has in mind the Civil War and the assassination of Lincoln. In any event, in the next stanza he invokes a loosely equivalent example of another heroic defense of a national identity:

> When Asia scarfed in silks came on
> Against the Greek and Marathon,
> Did each plume and pennon dance
> Sun-lit thus on helm and lance
> Mindless of War's sickle so? (p. 266)

At first glance the interrogatory rendering of this event resolves nothing. Yet by stressing the inanimate emblems of soldiery, "plume and pennon," Melville implies that the Persian troops are no more than robots and are wholly "Mindless" of the implications of the mutual carnage. Purely historical creatures, they have no awareness of the sacred function of death in the preservation of

[8] *Ibid.*, p. 464.

the well-being of the human community. Logically, Melville proceeds to evaluate this ignorance against the background of his controlling myth:

> For them, a tasseled dance of death:
> For these—the reapers reap them low. ·
> Reap them low, and stack the plain
> With Ceres' trophies, golden grain. (p. 266)

He depicts two opposed engagements to reality in the scenes of the scattered bodies on the battlefield and the piled corn on the prairie. The first exposes the profanation of life that underlies every effort to manipulate the course of history in order to serve the ends of egomaniacal ambition. The second reflects the ritual ordering of life that places the security and prosperity of the human community above all selfish aspirations. As "For these" implies, only such an outlook on fate can redeem man from the inevitable dislocations of time. Thus when Melville invokes Ceres (the Roman surrogate of Demeter), he renounces belief in the ability of the historical process to endow existence with any permanent meaning. She and her daughter alone are able to transfigure the sorrow and suffering of finitude.

In the final stanza Melville reaffirms this conviction, disavowing the importance of the eventual catastrophes that command the attention of historians:

> Such monuments, and only such,
> O Prairie! termless yield,
> Though trooper Mars disdainful flout
> Nor Annals fame the field. (p. 267)

There seems little doubt, too, that his apostrophe to the prairie transcends provinciality. It is a muted prayer to Demeter, the eternal custodian of the Dionysian year. As her worship on the plain of Eleusinia demonstrates, she is always present wherever life and death stage their periodic struggle, on the plain of Marathon as well as the plain of Illinois. Symbolically, she is the incarnation of perdurable time, the spirit of endless death and resurrection.

Melville again exalts her domain in "A Way-Side Weed,"

decrying historical man's inward alienation from the simple realities of nature:

> By orchards red he whisks along,
> A charioteer from villa fine;
> With passing lash o' the whip he cuts
> A way-side Weed divine. (p. 267)

Typically, his treatment of the situation is ironical. Behind the metonymic "red" he conceals his ridicule of modern Christendom's hypocrisy and self-deception. Apples are no longer reminders of the Fall and its consequences; now they are the foundation of social and economic status. And as the rider's resentful gesture reveals, the useless yield of the earth is completely dissociated from divine punishment. Of course, Melville also protests this desecration of nature on his own grounds. The herb so viciously attacked is a perennial, concrete proof of the unfailing powers of Dionysian renewal. Long after man, buggy, and villa have succumbed to the onslaughts of time, it will continue to glorify the cycle of the fading year. The crucial implications of this disengaged attitude towards the contingency of fate are dramatized in the interrogations of the concluding stanza:

> But knows he what it is he does?
> He flouts October's God
> Whose sceptre is this Way-side Weed,
> This swaying Golden Rod? (p. 267)

While Melville's terminal punctuation mark is ungrammatical, it is rhetorically logical. Even though he obviously answers the question of the first line, he knows that his contemporary readers would look upon his reasoning as either facetious or ridiculous. Yet he is deadly serious. He is shocked by the decay and degradation of symbols in the materialistic culture of his day. They have ceased to sustain the psychological life of the individual, to provide the vehicles of his adjustment to the disruptions of temporality. In the case of the goldenrod it is a vegetable surrogate of Persephone; its annual death and resurrection is a paradigm of seasonal regeneration.

Melville's preoccupation with viable symbols is indicated in the subtle antithesis of the golden flower and the villa owner's hoard of gold (wealth), the eternal and the transitory. Here Melville has in mind the pagan and Christian figuration of the flower as the redeeming sun (son).[9] Taking his cue from the religious apathy of his age, Melville disdains to pursue this association in the framework of his cultural heritage. But then his fidelity lies elsewhere—with "October's God," Dionysus Iacchos the divine child of the Eleusinian Mysteries. Worshipped primarily during the less important autumnal phase of the festival, he was dismembered and resurrected like his mother Persephone.[10] While the poet's attitude towards the sacrilege of an emblem of Dionysus Iacchos is less of indignation than of pity, it is surely obvious that he is appalled by Christendom's tragic bankruptcy of symbolism.

The loss of this inner vision is ascribed to the unfortunate glorification of abstract thought in "Field Asters" or "Michaelmas Daisies." Again the imagery functions on two planes of reference, Dionysian and Christian, in the later instance with extreme ambiguity:

> Like the stars in commons blue
> Peep their namesakes, Asters here,
> Wild ones every autumn seen—
> Seen of all, arresting few. (p. 269)

In conventional Christian iconography every star-petalled flower is an attribute of the Virgin Mary, the Sea, *Stella Maris*. Invariably she is represented in pictures as surrounded or crowned by stars, and of course attired predominantly in blue. Melville encourages an analysis of this sort in his observation on the failure of the asters to command attention. Like the goldenrod, they too are the potential vehicles of a theophany. But as the next stanza discloses, mankind has been beguiled into searching for an answer to the enigma of fate outside terrestrial boundaries:

> Seen indeed. But who their cheer
> Interpret may, or what they mean

[9] See Bayley, *The Lost Language of Symbolism*, 2: 204, for a full elucidation of the subject.
[10] Anthon, *A Classical Dictionary*, pp. 249–50.

> When so inscrutably their eyes
> Us star-gazers scrutinize. (p. 269)

Thus the manipulated clash of spatial prospects comments ironically on the tendency of both philosophical and religious speculation to overlook the simple empirical revelations of nature. In effect, "star-gazers" is converted into a pejorative epithet, a summary dismissal of all the fantasies of wish-fulfillment embodied in the conception of the heavens. For Melville, human destiny is no riddle. Its meaning is reflected in the autumnal asters which bravely await the freezing annihilation of winter. Without faith, the chill of finitude is unbearable to the putative Christian. He therefore is constantly nagged by the terrors of time and the uncertainties of eternity.

The dreadful weight of mortality is the subject of "Always with Us!," but Melville is not especially concerned with this fact. Death is a phase in the career of every living organism. And if no solace is to be found in religious faith, there is Dionysian evidence for a continuity of natural reality—the ceaseless process of flux in which creative energy is continually renewed. Melville's conviction of this truth is manifested in the social metaphor that he uses to evoke the experience of mortality:

> Betimes a wise guest
> His visit will sever.
> Yes, absence endears.
> Revisit he would,
> So remains not forever. (p. 269)

Here the robin is the transient visitor life. This explains why man is psychologically in harmony with the cycle of the seasons. His lust for life is periodically regenerated as illustrated in his enthusiasm for the returning robins:

> Well, Robin the wise one
> He went yestreen,
> Bound for the South
> Where his chums convene.
>
> Back, he'll come back
> In his new Spring vest

And the more for long absence
Be welcomed with zest. (p. 269)

The image of the "new Spring vest" conveys this emotional meaning. Like the bright red of the bird's breast, his passions flame. As
a consequence, Melville then petulantly deplores any hint of
death:

But thou, black Crow,
Inconsiderate fowl,
Wilt never away—
Take elsewhere thy cowl? (p. 270)

Unfortunately, the crow's rasping cry is the doleful knell of time.
It is the dismal counterpoint to the robins' jubilant song of life:

From the blasted hemlock's
Whitened spur;
Whatever the season,
Or Winter or Ver
Or Summer or Fall,
Croaker, forboder,
We hear thy call—
Caw! Caw! Caw! (p. 270)

"[T]he blasted" hemlock answers the question posed in the previous stanza. The Dionysian world is ruled by contingency. Fatality strikes without rime or reason. Obviously, the lightning from
the heavens is Melville's mocking judgment of the Christian belief
in a providential God. Like a similar blasphemous sentiment in his
short story, "The Lightning-Rod Man," it is his way of denying
—and perhaps here the three caws are related to Simon Peter—
that institutional religion is capable of reconciling man to his unpredictable destiny.

The final poem on autumn offers a clarification of this dilemma. On the surface, however, "The Chipmunk" appears to
have been written for a child as an explanation for the death of another member of the family. Despite the rather fatuous comparison, the opening quatrain with its italics functions to establish the
tone of treatment. Like the beauty and mildness of the fading season, transiency has to be accepted as the norm of temporal exist-

ence, and so, for all of its literalness, the simile of the iced dessert is very apt; taste is only a momentary sensation:

> *Heart of autumn!*
> *Weather meet,*
> *Like to sherbert*
> *Cool and sweet.* (p. 268)

The next turn of the poem develops this thought by analogy. Every state of feeling is liable to sudden disruption. Fortuity is blind to creatural pleasures:

> Stock-still I stand,
> And *him* I see
> Prying, peeping
> From Beech-tree;
> Crickling, crackling
> Gleefully!
> But, affrighted
> By wee sound,
> Presto! vanish—
> Whither bound? (p. 268)

As Melville resolves this issue on the human plane, the "inkling/ Touching Earth" is converted into a sign of mortality that directly reflects the laws of nature:

> So did Baby,
> Crowing mirth
> E'en as startled
> By some inkling
> Touching Earth,
> Flit (And whither?)
> From our hearth! (p. 268)

Instead of sugaring death with the sentimental (and Christian) consolation of heaven, he resorts to a dismissive interrogation. Indeed, if the parallel to the chipmunk carries any figurative authority, then the holy has likewise disappeared into a hole in the earth. But regardless of one's view here, Melville's attitudes are unequivocally naturalistic. And in this sense he exhorts man to heed the cawing of the omnipresent crow.

As the year closes in on the Christmas season, Melville's disenchantment with his inherited religious faith reaches its peak. Experience and knowledge have destroyed all of his illusions about the atonement. Nevertheless he does not disparage his old attachments and loyalties; instead he acknowledges their role in sustaining the bliss of innocence and ignorance. As a consequence in "Stockings in the Farm-House Chimney" he exults in the belief of children in the holiday:

> Happy, believe, this Christmas Eve
> Are Willie and Rob and Nellie and May—
> Happy in hope! in hope to receive
> These stockings well stuffed from Santa Claus' sleigh. (p. 270)

Taking into account the rest of the poem, one may observe that their joy is based on a total misconception of the meaning of the Saviour's birth. They do not associate the celebration of the event with man's deliverance from the curse of the Fall. Indeed, Santa Claus, a corruption of San Nicolaas, has no connection at all with Christmas. Originally, he was the patron saint of children, scholars, sailors, virgins, and thieves, a point of information not likely to escape Melville. In effect, the stanza wryly glorifies the self-deception underlying the most established custom of Christmas.

Subsequently, Melville divulges his access to such information when he traces the lineage of Santa Claus to the traditions of folklore:

> O the delight to believe in a wight
> More than mortal, with something of man,
> Whisking about, an invisible spright,
> Almoner blest of Oberon's clan. (p. 270)

This display of erudition, of course, is acidly satirical. Before Oberon was transformed into the king of the fairies and of the May orgies (*A Midsummer Night's Dream*), he was an impish hobgoblin. By the same token, the "Almoner blest," the dispenser of charity, was also once a bogy.[11] But in the light of the description, "More than mortal, with something of a man," Melville's epithet

[11] Bayley, *The Lost Language of Symbolism*, 1: 302–3.

is even still more suggestive. As a distinct echo of Christ's supernatural birth and merciful love, it evolves into a climactic vehicle of *reductio ad absurdum.* The last stanza extends this devastating play of heretical wit. The apostrophe to "Truth" is a eulogy of human credulity. For to the extent that Santa Claus figures the meaning of Christmas, he likewise develops into a surrogate of Christ:

> Stay, Truth, O stay in a long delay!
> Why should these little ones find you out?
> Let them forever with fable play,
> Evermore hang the Stocking out! (p. 270)

By extension, then, the fable in question is the redeemer myth. Its validity is taken as much on hope as the benevolence of Santa Claus. Though Melville professes to be talking about children, actually he has in mind the masses of the faithful who have apparently been able to preserve the outlook so extolled by St. Paul.

The last poem of the section on the year, "A Dutch Christmas Up the Hudson in the Time of the Patroons," is also a travesty on the holiday. Its jovial tone shows Melville's nostalgic rapport with the less austere habits of his ancestors:

> Hi, there in the barn! have done with the flail.
> Worry not the wheat, nor winnow in the gale:
> 'Tis Christmas and holiday, turkey too and ale! (p. 271)

The bluff, paternal narrator is just a bit too wordy. For to judge by the assiduous industry of the workman, idleness and diversion are not ordinarily tolerated. Moreover, considering the invitation, it is the lure of the food and drink rather than the spirit of the season that characterizes the celebration of Christmas. As other incidents unfold, the ulterior motive behind the festivities is inadvertently revealed. The occasion provides the opportunity for the narrator to set the stage for the courtship of his daughter:

> Leave off, Katrina, to tarry there and scan:
> The cream will take its time, girl, to rise in the pan.
> Meanwhile here's a knocking, and the caller it is *Van*—
> Tuenis Van der Blumacher, your merry Christmas man. (p. 271)

It goes almost without saying that the visitor is to the manor born as his surname implies. But more than that, the pun embodied in "Blumacher" crystallizes the sexual implications of the literal detail. There is no doubt that the speaker revels vicariously in the excitation of the lust of his future son-in-law; and surely his designation, "merry Christmas man," extends the association. In any event, the sensual train of his thought is fully confirmed in the next stanza:

> Leafless the grove now where birds billed the kiss:
> To-night when the fidler wipes his forehead, I wis,
> And panting from the dance come our Hans and Cousin Chris,
> Yon bush in the window will never be amiss! (p. 271)

In accordance with Melville's strategy of irony, the ceremonies unfold in the spirit of carnival. Or perhaps he has the Roman Saturnalia in mind, a festival likewise celebrated in December and distinguished by the exchange of gifts between friends.[12] One way or the other, he continues to emphasize the Dionysian mood of the impending affair. The pagan implications are also carried over in the narrator's concern with the barnyard animals, for he enjoins special treatment of them:

> But oats have ye reaped, men, for horses in stall?
> And for each heifer young and the old mother-cow
> Have ye raked down the hay from the aftermath-mow?
> The Christmas let come to the creatures one and all! (p. 271)

Bringing the argument of "The Year" full turn, Melville consecrates the old Dutchman's instinctive harmony with the seasonal rhythms. Though he believes himself to be motivated by the precepts of Christian faith, he celebrates the zodiacal rebirth of the sun rather than the birth of the redeeming Son. His every act and thought reflect his concern with perpetuating the continuity of animal and human life in the midst of winter's desolation. As the opening triplet of the poem indicates, he is a kind of primitive tribal priest:

[12] Anthon, *A Classical Dictionary*, p. 1196.

Over the ruddy hearth, lo, the green bough!
In house of sickle and home of the plough,
Arbored I sit and toast apples now! (p. 271)

Arbored in nature, he ritually takes into account the two activities
which sustain the home and community: the "sickle," a symbol of
harvesting and death, and "the plough," a symbol of planting and
life. This view of reality corresponds to the Dionysian worship of
the garden of the world, and manifests the awareness that man's
ultimate fate is bound up in the cycle of the seasons. As nature renews itself, man regenerates himself. The rebirth of the spirit of
the Year coincides with the rebirth of the hopes of society.

I have already noted that Melville does not concern himself
with moral evil. Nor does he betray any interest in the Christian
concept of immortality. All of his symbols of flowers, birds, animals, and insects mirror the inseparable marriage of life and death
in the universe, and all of them unite to urge belief in the myth of
the eternal return—time ceaselessly renewing itself. As he constantly remarks, this outlook is incompatible with Christianity. Burdened by self-consciousness and sin, the penalty of the Fall, civilized man looks upon decay and annihilation with horror and terror. Unable to reconcile himself to the polarities of existence, he
deems the order of nature a punitive act of God. Though he aspires to realize himself in time, at least as his progressivistic theories of economics, politics, and ethics assert, he ironically finds himself incapable of formulating the rationalization to explain why
Christianity insists that he will fulfill himself only at the Resurrection. Thus the garden of the world which he cultivates is spiritually barren. Inward motivations and outward acts are constantly in
conflict. As he accumulates the fruits of the world, the fruits of the
spirit die on the vine of life. Melville's "The Year" constitutes a
keen analysis of the Victorian predicament. His evocation of the
Dionysian harmony of the world stands in ironical contrast to the
chaos of the Christian world in which man believes he cannot recover the innocence once lost.

IX   The Transformations of Time

THE SECOND PART of *Weeds and Wildings,* "This, That, and the Other," focuses on time's ostensible betrayal of man. This belief springs from his inability to cope with the dilemma of historical evil, the suffering and death to which the flesh is heir. Since he cannot resolve this problem through his tepid religious faith, he falls a victim to anxiety and doubt. In the process his temporal ambitions are brought into conflict with his lingering yearning for eternity. And while he forces himself to believe that he can create a heaven on earth, he is haunted by the fear that he has been forever expelled from paradise. In other words, Melville argues that his culture fails to provide the individual with the inward integrity, either intellectual or moral, to bear the burdens of experience. As he observes at one point on this issue,

> For now intuitions
> Shall wither to codes,
> Pragmatical morals
> Shall libel the gods. (p. 383)

Therefore in "This, That, and the Other" Melville undertakes an analysis of this culture-vacuum under the metaphorical condition of the title of the first poem, "Time's Betrayal." He conceives of this trope as a paradox: either time betrays man or man betrays time. Personally he looks upon time as only the occasion for the appearance and disappearance of things. What transpires is in accord with the universal determinism that hastens the living organism on from birth to death. Conversely, his progress-oriented society refuses to accept this formula of existence and seeks to impose a higher purpose upon the flux of events. Unfortunately, this attitude contradicts the incalculable dislocations of experience and, even worse, man's psychological rapport with nature. "Time's Betrayal" enjoins the cultivation of the latter relationship as the only means of healing the prevailing schism in thought and emotion. The prologue to the poem symbolically represents the benefit of this altered outlook in the transformation of the color of a tree:

> The tapping of a mature maple for the syrup, however recklessly done, does not necessarily kill it. No; since being an aboriginal child of Nature, it is doubtless blest with a constitution enabling it to withstand a good deal of hard usage. But systematically to bleed the immature trunk, though some sugar-makers, detected in the act on ground not their own, aver that it does the sylvan younker a deal of good, can hardly contribute to the tree's amplest development or insure patriarchal long life to it. Certain it is, that in some young maples the annual tapping would seem to make precocious the autumnal ripening or change of the leaf. And such premature change would seem strikingly to enhance the splendor of the tints. (p. 273)

Or to rephrase the implications of this miracle, nature is invulnerable to the treason of man. Whatever the duration of its living forms, their demise is not unexpected nor regretted. Death (or sacrifice) always perpetuates life; time renews itself in the energies released by decay and dissolution. Such is the triumph signified in the enchanting hues of the maple. As the poem later shows, the transfiguration also has mythic overtones that embrace the personification of Dionysus as Dendrites or a tree. His annual death is the condition of the vernal rebirth that quickens the flow of the juice not only in the grape but in every living thing, an association carried over in the maple sap.

And it is this inspiriting vitality that is wittily exploited in the execution of the poem. First of all, Melville represents the tapping of the maple as a virtual crucifixion:

> Someone, whose morals need mending,
> Sallies forth like the pillaging bee;
> He waylays the syrup ascending
> In anyone's saccharine tree;
> So lacking in conscience indeed,
> So reckless what life he makes bleed,
> That to get at the juices, his staple,

> The desirable sweets of the Spring,
> He poignards a shapely young maple,
> In my second-growth coppice—its King. (p. 273)

The dismemberment offers a comic parallel to the violent, orgiastic sacrifice of Dionysus so common in the various scenarios of his shape-shifting myth. Like the ecstatic worshipers of the pagan god, the culprit acts under instinctive compulsion. Not unlike the sacramental wine and bread of the Eucharist, "The desirable sweets of the Spring" represent the instrument of salvation and rebirth. The "King" dies to redeem all the living world, animal and vegetable. And far more plausible and dramatic for the jesting poet is the evidence of transcendence explicit in his death:

> Assassin! secure in a crime never seen,
> The underwood dense, e'en his victim a screen,
> So be. But murder will out,
>   Never doubt, never doubt:
> In season the leafage will tell,
>   Turning red ere the rime
> Yet, in turning, all beauty excell
>   For a time, for a time! (pp. 273–74)

But there is still another reconciliation involved. The criminal's Dionysian fulfillment negates the ostensible breach of morality. The flaming beauty of the tree sanctifies his yearning for elementary communion with nature. Even though the stanza ends on a slightly pessimistic note, it nevertheless looks forward to a compensatory affirmation:

> Small thanks to the scamp. But in vision, to me
> A goddess mild pointing the glorified tree,
> "So they change who die early, some bards who life render:
> Keats, stabbed by the Muses, his garland's a splendor!" (p. 274)

"The glorified tree" (certainly an ironic echo of the cross) evokes the perennial beauty of Keats' garland of poesy. The "goddess mild" is the reincarnation of the divine spirit of Keats' famous ode. She is the earth-mother of the vegetation cults, the feminine consort of the sacrificed scapegoat. Like her prototype in the Eleusinian mysteries, she is the custodian of the mystery of life and death.

Whether under the aspect of Dionysus Dendrites, of Demeter and the stalk of corn, or of Keats' harvest scene, her revelation is the same. It functions to mitigate the terrors of time, transforming dismemberment, rape, despair, rage, and grief into consoling wisdom.

The "Inscription" likewise exalts Dionysian consciousness. Retrospectively, Melville perceives the implications of what might have been a mere chore of weeding—a violation of natural birthright. The victim of this spasm of energy is the "Hardtack" (p. 275), a shrub of the rose family and symbolically a vehicle of Redemption:

> A weed grew here.—Exempt from use,
>   Weeds turn no wheel, nor run;
> Radiance pure or redolence
>   Some have, but this had none. (p. 275)

These lines stress its lack of utility and its esthetic neutrality, its alienation from the human community to which it makes no tangible contribution in sustenance or sensibility. The poet here represents the attitudes of his society, but he himself is not influenced by them:

> And yet heaven gave it leave to live
>   And idle it in the sun. (p. 275)

The role of the weed is established by the sun's consecration of its sacredness. And as the prose epigraph indicates, "For a Boulder near the spot where the last Hardtack was laid low By the new proprietor of the Hill of Arrowhead" (p. 275), Melville, if he was the villain in the affair, now regrets his act. But, then, it was not until his old age that he began to realize his own relationship to Dionysian reality.

"The Avatar" continues Melville's glorification of the wild empire of the earth:

> Bloom or repute for graft or seed
> In flowers the flower-gods never heed. (p. 278)

There is no hierarchy in nature. Its forms belong to a universal process; each one is a kin of the other. This explication accords with the next turn of thought:

> The rose-god once came down and took—
> Form in a rose? Nay, but indeed
> The meeker form and humbler look
> Of Sweet-Briar, a wilding or weed. (p. 278)

The flower so apotheosized is a distant progenitor of the domestic rose, and therefore a more apt index of nature than the species produced by the hybridizing of science. Clearly, Melville is bent upon distinguishing the rose-god from the gods of institutionalized religions. The former eschews singularity, and he places no conditions on the accessibility of his grace. He ministers to everything produced and destroyed in time.

Consistent with this point of view, "Profundity and Levity" slyly mocks man's subjective distortion of the objective details of nature, and Melville sets up his strategy of treatment in the serio-comic solemnity of his prose introduction to the poem:

> An owl in his wonted day-long retirement ruffled by the meadow-lark curvetting and caroling in the morning-sun high over the pastures and woods, comments upon that rollicker, and in so doing lets out the meditation engrossing him when thus molested. But the weightiness of the wisdom ill agrees with its somewhat trilling expression; an incongruity attributable doubtless to the contagious influence of the reprehended malapert's overruling song. (p. 274)

His purpose is to burlesque the purely human outlook on the external world, and this is rendered immediately in the first stanza where he mocks the pompous pretension of the poetic voice:

> So frolic, so flighty,
> Leaving wisdom behind,
> Lark, little you ween
> Of the progress of mind. (p. 274)

From Melville's standpoint "the progress of mind" so lauded in his age has no affinity to wisdom. It is too solipsistic, and as a consequence is powerless to cope with the disillusionments of experience:

> While fantastic you're winging,
> Up-curving and singing,
> A skylarking dot in the sun;

> Under eaves here in wood
> My wits am I giving
>   To this latest theme:
> Life blinks at strong light,
> Life wanders in night like a dream—
> Is then life worth living? (p. 275)

As the imagery of light and darkness in the last three lines suggests, knowledge *per se* is a sterile possession. Out of touch with outward reality, the mind feeds on its thoughts alone; it attempts to infer a design for existence from its own frustrations. Hence thoughts of suicide are inevitable. Yet, as the prologue implies, the *raison d'être* lies without—in the spontaneous flight of the lark. But man, like the wise owl is blinded by light; he seeks truth within himself—in his own inward darkness.

A similar dissociation is the subject of "The American Aloe on Exhibition," though according to the prologue Melville ostensibly is concerned only with horticultural folklore: "It is but a floral superstition, as everybody knows, that the plant flowers only once in a century. When in any instance the flowering is for decades delayed beyond the normal period, (eight or ten years at furthest) it is owing to something retarding in the environment or soil" (p. 278). The body of the poem, on the other hand, reports the dismay of the aloe at not being distinguished from a weed. Obviously, then, this situation carries a figurative content of meaning:

> But lone at night the garland sighed
>   While moaned the aged stem:
> "At last, at last! but joy and pride
>   What part have I with them?"
>
> ["]Let be the dearth that kept me back
>   Now long from wreath decreed;
> But, Ah, ye Roses that have passed
>   Accounting me a weed! ["] (p. 279)

Not surprisingly, these lines have been interpreted autobiographically, allegedly reflecting Melville's despair over the decline of his literary reputation.[1] However, the images of time subsumed in the

---

[1] Laurence Barrett, "The Differences in Melville's Poetry," *PMLA*, 70 (September 1955), 611.

name of the flower invite a different kind of consideration. Popularly supposed to blossom at the end of a hundred years, the aloe evolves into a symbolic Tree of Life, the archetype of enduring nature. And so Melville implies at one point:

> In strange inert blank unconcern
> Of wild things at the Zoo,
> The patriarch let the sight-seers stare—
> Nor recked who came to view. (p. 279)

As a "patriarch" it represents the primordial manifestation of energy, the foundation of the green world. At any rate such an identification helps to establish a function for the roses. Affiliated with the "stem" of the aloe, they are validly equatable with the yoni. Thus the slighting of the so-called weed is equivalent to a denial of sexuality for, as the Tree of Life, it is also a phallic emblem. Thus the theme of time's betrayal is clarified in this fable of unrequited love—probably just as human as vegetable.

"The Cuban Pirate" is less veiled in its treatment of sexual ardor or, more aptly, unrestrained lust. A brief prose epigraph indicates that the title is the personification of a "West Indian" hummingbird, an insatiable addict of honey; and this fact is the topic of the first stanza:

> Buccaneer in gemmed attire—
> Ruby, amber, emerald, jet—
> Darkling, sparkling dot of fire,
> Still on plunder are you set? (p. 275)

The acts of piracy are next elucidated in the unmistakable terms of rape, and, as "Savage" implies, the bird is driven to commit his heinous crimes under the domination of an irrepressible instinctual urge:

> Summer is your sea, and there
> The flowers afloat you board and ravage,
> Yourself a thing more dazzling fair—
> Tiny, plumed, bejewelled Savage! (p. 276)

Significantly, Melville voices no condemnation. For him Dionysian orgy is outside the pale of civilized understanding. But regretfully, so he goes on to say, since the uninhibited desire reminds him of pagan bliss:

> Midget! yet in passion a fell
> Furioso, Creoles tell.
> Wing'd are you Cupid in disguise
> You flying spark of Paradise? (p. 276)

Here "Cupid" is invoked under the aspect of primal eros, of love (or lust) untainted by sin or guilt. By extension, there is an implicit reference to the Christian notion of Eden and its glorification of stagnant innocence.

Though not included in *Weeds and Wildings*, "Hearts-of-Gold," is no doubt a work of the same period of creative activity. It examines the theme of physical license on the plane of human existence. Its overt conflict of Dionysian and Christian attitudes provides a kind of gloss on "The Cuban Pirate" to the extent of disclosing Melville's persistent yearning for morally uncorrupted pleasures:

> Pity, if true,
> What the pewterer said—
> *Hearts-of-gold be few.*
> Howbeit, when snug in my bed,
> And the fire-light flickers and yellows,
> I dream of hearts-of-gold sped— (p. 394)

His italicized passage almost certainly refers to the partisans of Dionysian fatalism who read nature as a *carpe diem* text, who take for granted the ephemeral span of life. For when he invokes them by name, they all turn out to be poets as dedicated to conviviality as to their craft:

> The Falernian fellows—
> Hafiz and Horace,
> And Beranger—all
> Dexterous tumblers eluding the Fall,
> Fled? can be sped? (p. 394)

Melville's allusion to Falernian wine operates to subvert the import of the Eucharist in delivering man from the consequences of "the Fall." Or put another way, he wittily argues that the three poets achieve their immortality in song. To answer his question, though now "[f]led," they have "sped" their glory. And as worshipers of the Dionysian vine, it follows that nature will santify their triumph over time:

> But the marygold's morris
> Is danced o'er their head;
> And their memory mellows,
> Embalmed and becharmed,
> Hearts-of-gold and good fellows! (p. 394)

Not only does the morris dance of the marygold—an ancient fertility ritual—propagate their fame from year to year, but in addition it symbolically validates the sexual origin of all living things. In short, Melville restores the flower to the province of nature, severing its connection with the Virgin Mary and her son Christ (Mary's gold in the world of folklore). Thus he subverts the very basis of the Christian myth, blasphemously denying the miraculous birth of the Saviour.

Although "Iris" celebrates a memory of the Civil War, the poem also exalts the redemptive power of nature on the plane of vegetable, human, and divine reality. Melville personifies a transplanted Southern belle as the flower, and playfully assigns her the role of an envoy of peace. Like her counterpart in Greek mythology, she nurtures the universal principle of love:

> When Sherman's March was over
> And June was green and bright,
> She came among our mountains,
> A freak of new delight;
> Provokingly our banner
> Salutes with Dixie's strain—
> Little rebel from Savannah,
> Three Colonels in her train. (p. 276)

Of course, the iris is also known as a flag, and Melville weaves this association into his imagery. Much more subtly, he suggests that the flower's sword-shaped leaves render powerless the steel swords of the Northern officers. In effect, the young woman conquers hate with her appeal to common human instincts:

> Three bearded Puritan colonels:
>   But O her eyes, her mouth—
> Magnolias in their languor
>   And sorcery of the South.
> High-handed rule of beauty,
>   Are wars for man but vain?
> Behold, three disenslavers
>   Themselves embrace a chain! (p. 276)

However trite Melville's metaphors, they properly sexualize the beauty of the irresistible Iris. Looking back with half a leer at another such historical struggle with the flesh, he notes that the virile soldiers are not like their doughty forebears. They unconsciously take their cue from mother nature in aspiring for love, for only in this way can they compensate for the countless fatalities of the war, the chain in question being the continuity of the human race. Marveling at the power of defenseless woman, Melville next undertakes to probe the mystery:

> But, loveliest invader,
>   Out of Dixie did ye rove
> By sallies of your raillery
>   To rally us, or move?
> For under all your merriment
>   There lurked a minor tone;
> And of havoc we had tidings
>   And a roof-tree overthrown. (p. 277)

What he crystallizes in this meditation is the extraordinary resiliency of the female. Psychologically and physically, Iris is prepared to withstand the throes of childbirth or death, the deprivations of all unexpected calamities. Behind her mask of gaiety and wit, she conceals the innate knowledge of her sex that suffering is an unavoidable condition of existence. Unfortunately, the male never seems cognizant of this grim truth, or else he needlessly multiplies his woes in senseless combat with his fellows. But even while the poet is able to describe the virtues of Iris, he still does not understand them.

Reflecting this quandary is the sequence of questions in the next stanza. However, all of them are more or less pointless because they fail to take into consideration that the attitudes of Iris are inherent to her state of being rather than to her philosophy of life:

> Ah, nurtured in the trial—
> And ripened by the storm,
> Was your gaiety your courage,
> And levity its form?
> O'er your future's darkling waters,
> O'er your past, a frozen tide,
> Like the petrel would you skim it,
> Like the glancing skater glide? (p. 277)

The conjectures embodied in the questions disclose more about the attitude of the poetic voice than the subject. Patently, there is no desire to confront the unpredictable aspects of experience. As a consequence when death suddenly overtakes the young woman, her fate is sentimentalized:

> But the ravisher has won her
> Who the wooers three did slight;
> To his fastness he has borne her
> By the trail that leads thro' night.
> With Peace she came, the rainbow,
> And like a Bow did pass,
> The balsam-trees exhaling,
> And tear-drops in the grass. (p. 277)

Though line four casts a shadow of doubt on her immortal lot, the image of the rainbow is a conventional symbol of the salvation and the resurrection, and therefore she is represented as transcending the sorrows of time. This mawkish resolution hardly is consonant with the enveloping tone of *Weeds and Wildings*. Indeed, its inane and simplistic interpretation of death verges on parody, especially since the time setting of the poem is the Civil War, whose horrors so appalled Melville. Apparently the latter is quite conscious of the obtrusive bathos, for in the final stanza a dramatic reversal of the previous outlook occurs.

The surprising tactic is manipulated through a change in imagery. Having disposed of her fate in the tried-and-true formula of Victorian piety, Melville now restores the personified Iris to her natural setting—to the green world of paganism where life and death constitute the normal rhythm of existence. Here sorrow has no place because nothing has been lost. There is no difference between sacrifice and revel in the Dionysian view of ultimate reality:

> Now laughed the leafage over
>   Her pranks in woodland scene:
> Hath left us for the revel
>   Deep in Paradise the green?
> In truth we will believe it
>   Under pines that sigh a balm,
> Though o'er thy stones be trailing
>   Cypress-moss that drapes the palm. (p. 278)

Consistent with the way death is construed in the interrogation, the iris-woman is assimilated into the earth in a mutation of nature that looks forward to the return of the vernal cycle. Though her dissolution seems final, it is not really so. She will live again in the form of the flower, the symbol of her inward spirit. The balance of nature never changes as indicated in the union of the evergreens (life) and the cypress-moss (death). No wonder that the palm on her headstone, the icon of Christ's victory over death, is covered by a Dionysian shroud.

"A Ground Vine," the final poem of Part II, functions to attest the earthly inspiration of the creative impulse of Melville's old age, and his immediate invocation of the rose celebrates this awareness:

> Hymned down the years from ages far,
> The theme of lover, seer, and king,
> Reign endless, Rose! for fair you are,
> Nor heaven reserves a fairer thing.
> To elfin ears the bell-flowers chime
> Your beauty, Queen, your fame;
> Your titles, blown thro' Ariel's clime,
> Thronged trumpet-flowers proclaim. (p. 279)

His purpose is to make clear the complex attitudes, values, and beliefs that the flower has symbolized down through the ages. It has, without contradiction, served to embody every profane and sacred sentiment of the human heart. Nonetheless Melville's vine argues that this monopoly violates the order of universal truth because each different form of life is modified by accidents of environment.

> O Rose, we plants are all akin,
> Our roots enlock; Each strives to win
> The ampler space, the balmier air.
> But beauty, plainness, shade, and sun—
> Here share-and-share-alike is none! (p. 280)

Under the circumstances beauty is an artificial measure of quality. It distorts reality through ideality—through abstraction. Melville refuses to engage in such distinctions:

> And, ranked with grass, a flower may dwell,
> Cheerful, if never high in feather,
> With pastoral sisters thriving well
> In bloom that shares the broader weather;
> Cheerful, mayhap, in simple grace,
> A lowlier Eden mantling her face. (p. 280)

The curious image of the last line defines the basic kinship of all living things. It is a matter of degree, not of kind. Each plant springs forth under the impetus of a fertilizing pulsation of nature. Only the act of creation, ultimately, is sacred. Its Edens are graduated states of perfection.

The last stanza crystallizes the meaning of this Dionysian unity in a flash of Melville's subdued comic spirit. Figuratively, the vine forces the rose into a confrontation with the uncomfortable truth of her common origin with a less imposing plant:

> My Queen, so all along I lie,
> But creep I can, scarce win your eye.
> But, O, your garden-wall peer over,
> And, if you blush, 'twill barely be
> At owning kin with Cousin Clover
> Who winsome makes the low degree. (p. 280)

The possibility of a blush indicates that the rose is to glimpse the naked truth about herself—in short, the sexual beginning of all life. This is implied by the clover (a phallic symbol) in its opposition to the rose (a yonic symbol). Thus Melville shows that polari-

ties are the mode of reconciliation in the Dionysian world. Whatever germinates and grows is subject to this law of nature. So Melville derides Victorian prudishness and condemns the literary fare
of the day—the sentimental romance. Along with this he attacks the
realism of the commonplace which skirts naturalistic fact. In effect,
throughout this body of poetry Melville revels in elemental reality. In the case of the clover it is a symbol of earthliness and earth-
iness, even as he states in the preface to the collection: "It is a thing
of freshness and beauty, but also that being no delicate foster-child
of the nurseryman, but a hardy little creature of out-of-doors accessable [*sic*] and familiar to everyone, no one can monopolize its
charm. Yes, we are communists here." And in the resurgence of his
interest in sex, or perhaps his own early self-consciousness about it,
he cannot resist its association with his earliest months of marriage: "I yearly remind you of the coincidence in my chancing on
such a specimen by the wayside on the early forenoon of the fourth
day of a certain bridal month, now four years more than four times
ten years ago." Plainly, he thinks of the clover as a fertility symbol. For later, as if conscious of his fading virility, he dubs his wife
the "Madonna of the Trefoil." Certainly this charming piece of
irony needs no explication. In context Melville offers a ceremonial
valedictory to sexual life (quoted earlier): "Well, and to whom
but to thee, Madonna of the Trefoil, should I now dedicate these
'Weeds and Wildings,' thriftless children of quite another and yet
later spontaneous after-growth, and bearing indications too apparent it may be, of that terminating season on which the offerer
verges. But take them. And for aught suggestion of the 'melting
mood' that any may possibly betray, call to mind the dissolved
snow flakes on the ruddy oblation of old, and remember your 'tears
of the happy' " (pp. 481–82). Thus he confronts impending death
with the recognition that it is part of the natural cycle of human
destiny. In the Dionysian aspects of the world he is able to make
the design of human life intelligible.

Part III of *Weeds and Wildings*, "Rip Van Winkle's Lilac,"
is devoted entirely to a retelling of Washington Irving's popular
tale. Apart from the whimsical dedication to the latter, the effort

unfolds in the form of a combined prose and poetic narration. Except for the motif of the enchanted sleep, Melville almost totally disregards the plot of his source. As he baldly states, he is primarily concerned with the transformations of time that occur before, during, immediately following, and long after the complicating incident. But in his handling of these various situations he converts Rip Van Winkle into a comic Dionysus whose sexual impotence is accidentally redeemed by the beneficent powers of nature. His inspiration for this treatment no doubt derives from his familiarity with the contemporary folklore theory which reduced the innumerable stories of spellbound maidens, youths, saints, martyrs, and heroes to symbolic projection of the wintry sleep of nature, that is, to the abeyance of terrestrial fertilty.[2]

Melville's conception of Rip's role also reflects the outlooks of his short story "I and My Chimney," particularly in the reactions of Dame Van Winkle. At any rate, the hero's psychosexual immaturity is broached in the description of the mother complex that manifests itself at the beginning of his marriage: returning . . . at sunset from a romantic ramble among the low-whispering pines, Rip the while feelingly rehearsing to his beloved some memories of his indulgent mother now departed, she suddenly changed the subject" (pp. 283–84). Melville reveals the implications of this incident a moment later when Rip, trying to avoid work on their unfinished house artfully begins to make love to his wife:

> Setting out a little orchard for future bearing, would suit the time better, and this he engaged shortly to do. "Sweetheart," he said in conclusion, with sly magnetism, twining an arm round her jimp waist, "Sweetheart, I will take up the saw and hammer in good time." That good time proved very dilatory; in fact, it never came. (p. 284)

In the light of the euphemism, "[s]etting out a little orchard for future bearing," the "good time" in the last sentence has to be taken as a sexual pun.

[2] John Fiske, *Myth and Mythmakers* (New York, 1900), pp. 25–26. This study was first published in 1872 and by 1900 had gone through twenty-five editions.

Later Melville connects Rip's laziness with the premature loss of virility. This is made evident in the analogy drawn between the gradual deterioration of the house and Dame Van Winkle's fear of losing her youth:

> Women, more than men, disrelishing the idea of old age, are sensitive, even the humblest of them, to aught in any way unpleasantly suggestive of it. And the gray weather-stain not only gave the house the aspect of age, but worse; for in association with the palpable evidences of its recentness as an erection, it imparted a look forlornly human, even the look of one grown old before his time. (p. 285)

This symbolic equation is enforced by the bawdy puns casually embodied in "the gray weather-stain" and the "recentness as an erection." As established by immediate context, the wife is obsessed by her husband's vanishing masculinity. His "remissness" and his

> betrayed purpose [is] expressed by the uncompleted abode . . . lamented over by a huge willow . . . —a willow of the weeping variety. . . . Broken bits of rotted twigs and a litter of discolored leaves were the tears continually wept by this ancient Jeremiah upon the ever-greening roof of the house fatally arrested in course of completion. (p. 285)

No wonder, then, that she orders Rip to cut down the tree. But since he is disinclined to carry out this symbolic castration, she "herself assaulted it" (p. 286). Here the personification and the name of the tree are not to be scanted. Melville ironically invokes Jeremiah only because he disagrees with his injunction that to serve God man must remove carnal lust from the heart. And the willow, of course, has long been associated with chastity and unrequited love, and therefore is the apt symbol of Dame Van Winkle's frustration.

The phallic connotations of the willow emerge again in the fate that overtakes it during Rip's sleep: "the knotty old inhabitant had been gathered to his fathers" (p. 286). Not only does this event figure the extinction of manhood, but in addition the process of dissolution closely parallels the duration of Rip's enchantment or the suspension of his fertility. He awakens only after the decayed tree provides a lilac slip that he planted with the strength to perpetuate its species. And it is in this sense that Melville assigns him the role of a comic Dionysus. He is redeemed in his dotage by a shrub that carries out his relinquished human function on the level of natural reality.

This transformation of time, in turn, supplies Melville with the occasion for a travesty of the Christian idea of resurrection. Just a few years before Rip's return from the dead, an artist chooses the now flourishing lilac as the subject for a painting. The importance of this incident pivots on his refusal to paint a church (the earthly promise of resurrection), even though urged to do so by a local religious zealot: " 'Why,' said he, 'if you *must* idle it this way—can find nothing more useful to do, paint something respectable, or, better, something godly; paint our new tabernacle— there is it,' pointing right ahead to a rectangular ediface stark on a bare hill-side" (p. 287). The auditor, however, reacts in horror to this entreaty: "A cadaver! shuddered the artist to himself, glancing at it, and instantly averting his eyes" (p. 287). So Melville once again exemplifies the psychological and spiritual estrangement of Christianity from the temporal processes of nature. Indeed the pious critic is appalled by the Dionysian communism that produces the beauty of the shrub: " 'The Lilac? and black what-do-you-call-it —lichen, on the trunk, so old is it. It is half-rotten, and its flowers spring from the rottenness under it' " (p. 288). To this the artist responds, " 'Yes, decay is often a gardener,' " only to be greeted with, " 'What's that gibberish?' " (p. 288). Ironically, the spiritual purport of the mysterious evolution of life out of death (sacrifice) is evoked by Paul in order to illustrate the meaning of the crucifixion: "Verily, verily, I say unto you, Except a corn of wheat fall into the ground, and die, it abideth alone: but if it die, it bringeth forth much fruit" (John XII:24). This exchange allows Melville to comment on the impoverished metaphysical dimensions of fundamentalist Christianity, the literalistic interpretation of creed, sacrament, and worship. For as the artist observes in the same context, the individual sensibility atrophies under such legalistic narrowness: " 'what should we poor devils of Bohemians do . . . if Nature was in all things a precisian, each building like that church, and every man made in your image' " (p. 289).

The implications of this blasphemous statement are further elaborated in the next turn of the narrative, as the piqued zealot hastily rides off. A moment later, he reappears in the distance: "in an elevated turn of the hilly road man and horse, outlined against the vivid blue sky, obliquely crossed the Bohemian's sight, and the next moment as if swallowed by the grave disappeared in the descent" (p. 289). This spectacle constitutes the epiphany of the prose narrative: it is a manifestation of the spiritual death-in-life of Protestant sectarianism. Not content to let this parody of the vision of St. John convey its meaning elliptically, Melville blatantly introduces the pertinent text from the Book of Revelation in the artist's fanciful association: " '*And I looked and beheld a pale horse, and his name that sat on him was Death.*'—Well, I won't allegorise and be mystical, and all that, nor even say that Death dwells not under the cemetery turf, . . . no, only this much will I say that to-day I have seen him, even Death, seen him in the guise of a living man on a living horse" (p. 289). Of course, here Melville inverts the symbolic connotations of the biblical image. Instead of connecting the horse and the rider with God's wrathful punishment of disbelievers on the Day of Judgment, he ridicules the coercive psychology of prescriptive morality—the fear of death used by the fire-and-brimstone Protestant clergy to engender faith. Obviously contemptuous of this mechanical formula of heavenly salvation, he chooses to accept death as an inherent rhythm in the perennial flux of nature, as a misunderstood blessing of the processes of time—the earthly miracle that enables an exquisite lilac to spring from the moldering punk of the willow tree. And insofar as redemption is concerned, it is Rip's sexual virility that is restored in the glorious trancendence of mother nature over a mother complex.

In the poem which follows the prose tale the lilac symbolizes Rip's instinctive loyalty to perpetual youth. Though immediately unable to adjust himself to his unexpected resurrection, he once put all his trust in the silent wisdom of the green and flowering world:

> "If my cracked memory don't deceive,
> 'Twas *I* set out a Lilac fair,
> Yesterday morning, seems to me.
> Yea, sure, that it might thrive and come
> To plead for me with wife, tho' dumb.
>   . . . .
> *That* Lilac was a little slip,
> And yonder Lilac is a tree!" (p. 291)

While failing then to conciliate his wife, and her anxious engagement to time, the immense shrub now consecrates the effort: it yearly affirms his juvenescent vitality:

> Each June the owner joyance found
> In one prized tree that held its ground,
> One tenant old where all was new,—
> Rip's lilac to its youth still true.
> Despite its slant ungainly trunk
> Atwist and black like strands of junk,
> Annual yet it flowered aloft
> In juvenile pink, complexion soft. (p. 292)

In its posthumous growth into a tree, the lilac crystallizes the import of Rip's way of life. Like and unlike its biblical counterpart in the Garden of Eden (surely Melville intends the association), it is a symbol of the knowledge that is forbidden by Christianity—the knowledge of the self as an integral part of nature as opposed to a mechanical function in the apparatus of society. In short, the tree is a personification of what Rip might have been if the reigning proprieties had not forced him to seek for an escape from his disrepute. For, ultimately, his enchanted sleep represents the psychological defeat of his wishful dream of a temporal happiness uncorrupted by the nagging vexations of conventional respectability (the predicament of Melville throughout his life). Only such an interpretation can explain the eventual conversion of the lilac tree into a virtual charismatic medium:

> Truth to own
> Such reaching wafture ne'er was blown
> From common Lilac. Came about
> The neighbors, unconcerned before

> When bloomed the tree by lowly door,
> Craved now one little slip to train;
> Neighbor from neighbor begged again.
> On every hand stem shot from slip,
> Till, lo, that region now is dowered
> Like the first Paradise embowered,
> Thanks to the poor good-for-nothing Rip! (p. 293)

And so Rip metamorphoses into a Dionysian spirit, delivering the offspring of his formerly contemptuous neighbors from their conditioned enslavement to material possessions and spiritual bigotry. Here Melville implicitly contrasts his hero with the sour passerby who takes exception to the subject of the Bohemian's painting; he argues that resurrection in time is a far more fulfilling inspiration than St. John's vision of the sealed on Judgment Day. Which is to say that Rip brings Paradise to earth where it belongs and where it has been proscribed by religion.

Melville continues to press this thesis in the remainder of the poem as the man and the flower assimilate one another's identity. Yet, since nature is transcendent, the garden which his love seeded takes its name from the glorifying lilac tree:

> Some think those parts should bear his name;
> But no—the blossoms take the fame.
> Slant finger-posts by horsemen scanned
> Point the green miles—*To Lilac Land*. (p. 293)

The poet leaves little doubt that he considers Rip's instinctive planting of the original lilac a ritual act in which he asserts his faith in the unrealized possibilities of happiness for all mankind. In this perspective the terminal sentiment is ironical, for it is nature that creates the illusion of heaven:

> For there his heart flowers out confessed,
> And there you'll say,—O, hard ones, truce!
> See, where man finds in man no use,
> Boon Nature finds one—Heaven be blest! (p. 293)

Melville implies that man in the state of civilization profanes nature. In his rebellion against this attitude, Rip intuitively proclaims his fidelity to the nurturing goddess of the earth—Ceres, or Demeter whom the poet exalts in "Trophies of Peace." This outlook is supported by the revery induced in the artist by his impression of the lilac:

> In visionary flash he saw in their prime the perfect temples of Attica flushed with Apollo's rays on the hill-tops, or on the plain at eve disclosed in glimpses through the sacred groves around them. For the moment, in this paganish dream he quite lost himself. (p. 288)

The casual reference in this passage to the sacred groves subsumes the orgiastic worship of Dionysus. These are the surroundings in which his annual death and resurrection were celebrated in frenzied worship under the auspices of Demeter and her daughter. Moreover, as Dionysus Dendrites he is a tree god and an embodiment of phallic potency. This cluster of association illuminates Melville's purpose in regard to Rip's failure of virility, for his physical deficiency is a direct consequence of his inability to overcome the effects of his environment and to live in uncomplicated harmony with nature. This fact accounts for Melville's sympathetic treatment of his emasculated redeemer. Like the latter, the artist too could not overtly triumph over the sterility of his background, except to the extent that his garland of late poesy is the symbolic equivalent of Rip's *"Lilac-Land."*

X   The Sexual Rose

THE TWO-PARTS of *A Rose or Two* continue Melville's exaltation of the Dionysian spirit,[1] but the topic of linear historicism is dropped entirely. He seems mainly concerned with undermining the ascetic principles of Christianity—with subordinating the comforting gift of the Passion to the fulfilling moment of sexual passion. This intention is evident in poem after poem, as he blasphemously reverses the venereal rose instead of the Mystic Rose. So he gives sacral recognition to the transforming power of carnal love, though not in any romantic sense. As he humorously admits, the tribute has been long delayed: he "came unto [his] roses late" (p. 306). Needless to say, the fragrance of these flowers are distilled out of the experiences of *Weeds and Wildings*.

For the most part the tone of the poems evolves out of an attitude of comic self-mockery. Melville is old, and he knows it. But, in the exuberance of self-insight, he now can laugh at himself and the "arid years that filed before" (p. 310), and he can also chide his long preoccupation with the "hope of quintessential bliss" (p. 309). This state of mind is far removed from his obsession with the problem of good and evil and with his efforts to resolve it in the framework of religion and metaphysical speculation. He now is a chastened Ahab and a wiser man. Or perhaps in this phase of rec-

[1] The holographs of the various tables of contents for this part of the collection are all flawed by numerous erasures and cancellations, and seem to indicate that certain poems were either lost or deliberately destroyed. Since these manuscripts show Melville experimenting with different sequences of the titles, it is not possible to determine what his final choice would have been. However, the extant poems preserve a unity of theme which reflects the direction of his thought.

onciliation he is a satyr—a Silenus, vatic and jovial, grown into a mature understanding of Dionysian lore.

At least so one is led to believe in the poem "Amoroso." Here, in the role of a lover (or seducer?), he pens an epithalamium. Overtly the nuptial song deals with the subtleties of sexual excitation; covertly it burlesques the perpetual virginity attributed to Mary by Roman Catholic myth. In order to achieve these effects Melville secretes in its structure a series of bawdy puns. The first one is obvious but the others less so:

> Rosamond, my Rosamond
>   Of roses is the rose;
> Her bloom belongs to summer,
>   Nor less in winter glows,
> When, mossed in furs all cosey,
>   We speed it o'er the snows
> By ice-bound streams enchanted,
>   While red Arcturus, he
> A huntsman ever ruddy,
>   Sees a ruddier star by me. (p. 295)

Rosamond is, of course, literally the name of a girl. On the other hand, etymologically it means rose of the world, and in context its erotic geography is not difficult to infer. But the play on Rosamond (and perhaps Melville has in mind the Latin epigram *"Rosa Mundi, sed non Rosa Munda"*) cannot be dissociated from the Virgin Mary. In Roman Catholic iconography she is constantly symbolized as *Rosa Mundi*, for Christ is the Fruit of the Flower, the Mystic Rose. Nor does he overlook the rose's connection with martyrdom, the blood shed by the faithful in emulation of the Saviour. However, Melville's idea of self-sacrifice comprehends only virginity. And this is made fairly obvious in his euphemism on the rose of roses—of course, the maidenhead. This tactic establishes the basis of the subsumed pun in Arcturus, the lance bearer. And context suggests that Melville is deliberately resorting to homophonic punning on "rut" (sexual excitement), in "ever ruddy" and "ruddier star." If such is the case, then the phallic connotations of the passage are obvious. This interpretation also enables one to understand why the rose "glows" in winter when "mossed in furs all cosey." "[C]osey" derives from "snug" and "crevice," and "furs" is probably a pun on pubic hair, granting Melville's knowledge of *The Rape of the Lock* and Belinda's "furbelow." Thus there can scarcely be any question about Melville's focus on nuptial reality in its most blatant physical aspects.

This line of meaning continues to develop in the first four lines of the next stanza in which chastity is denoted a form of sterility:

> O Rosamond, Rose Rosamond,
> Is yonder Dian's reign?
> Look, the icicles despond
> Chill dropping from the fane! (p. 295)

The reference to the spotless virgin Dian and to "the fane" is not only a derogation of self-willed virginity but also an indirect allusion to the Virgin Mary whose sanctuary is the church. In the view of the poet the ice is not a symbol of stagnation; rather it is a teasing stimulus to amorous play:

> But Rosamond, Rose Rosamond,
> In us, a plighted pair,
> Frost makes with flame a bond—
> One purity they share. (p. 295)

The rise of sexual desire is explicit in "flame," but, of more importance, Melville designates the experience as a purifactory rite, in this flight of wit endowing the psychological response to physical love with sacred power. So the profane is transformed into the holy by a glib casuist.

In the next passage Melville, invoking Dionysian logic, argues that only the cultivation of passion can counteract the chill of winter. In short, human propagation can reverse the seasonal state of infertility:

> To feel your cheek like ice,
> While snug the furs inclose—
> This is spousal love's device
> This is Arctic Paradise,
> And wooing in the snows!

Rosamond, my Rosamond,
Rose Rosamond, Moss-Rose! (p. 295)

Significantly, Melville's puns on Rosamond, maidenhead, and coition converge in the last two lines of the poem in the succession of allusions to the girl's name. He transforms her from a human being into an archetype of fertility—the "Moss-Rose." Thematically, then, he insists that only sexual love can convert the seasonal desolation into an "Arctic Paradise."

"Hearth Roses" extends the situation of the latter work. The poetic voice now analyzes the paradoxical consequences of the consummation of marriage:

The Sugar-Maple embers in bed
Here fended in Garden of Fire,
Like the Roses yield musk,
Like the Roses are red,
Like the Roses expire. (p. 296)

Once more Melville couches the sexual meaning in a sequence of puns. As in "Time's Betrayal," the glowing tree is a euphemistic phallus.[2] In context therefore the other details of description, from the connotations of musk (testicle) to the subsiding of the blaze (passion), clearly chart the course of the sexual act. Indeed, a moment later the bridegroom tenderly consoles his despoiled bride, maintaining that true womanhood excels virginity, that sacrifice always precedes fruition:

Lamented when low;
But, excelling the flower,
Are odorous in ashes
As e'en in their glow. (p. 296)

Of course, the phrase, "odorous in ashes," delicately echoes the myth of the phoenix, suggesting that defloration (dying) is the prelude to the rebirth of a new identity. Here too is found the recurrent motif of the Persephone-Demeter story, a return to formlessness and chaos after rape, mutilation, pain, or suffering. But whatever the loss, there is compensatory gain. In this case, the sexual ravishment carries with it the promise of human fruit.

[2] *Supra.*, p. 201.

The coda of "Hearth-Roses" proffers still another comforting sentiment, the hopeful thought that both physical and sexual death culminate the same way:

> Ah, Love, when life closes,
> Dying the death of the just,
> May we vie with Hearth-Roses,
> Smelling sweet in our dust. (p. 296)

In the resolution of the situation one cannot discount Melville's silence in regard to the religious formula of death and salvation. His redemptive symbol is not Christ; it is the natural flower. The musk of the sexual rose and of life belongs to the earth, to the regenerative womb of nature. It hints at the transcendence of time implicit in the cycle of the Dionysian year.

The third poem of this group, "Under the Ground," develops the same theme, but in the framework of Victorian conventions. Employing the polaric images of the garden and the tomb, Melville defines two different attitudes towards sexuality. The garden is a symbol of the womb of nature and of woman. It contrasts with the tomb, a symbol of the finality of physical death. Of course, the garden is also a tomb if its function is denigrated. In the first quatrain this paradox is broached:

> Between a garden and old tomb
> Disused, a foot-path threads the clover;
> And there I met the gardener's boy
> Bearing some dewy chaplets over. (p. 296)

The phallic clover and the wet garlands of roses are the symbols of Dionysian orgy and sacrifice. However, in the removal of the roses from their natural setting—the attempt to extend their life artifically—the idea of chastity is introduced. The womb of life or of woman is degraded into a tomb. In essence the four lines reflect opposing views of sexual passion. On the one hand, it is sanctified by nature, on the other, devaluated by a prudish morality. The second quatrain furthers these implications in a clarifying pun:

> I marvelled, for I just had passed
> The charnel vault and shunned its gloom:

"Stay, whither wend you, laden thus?
Roses! you would not these inhume?" (p. 296)

"The charnel vault" is the key image. Literally, it is a sepulchre. However, since both charnel and carnal are derived from the same word, the Latin *carnalis*, that is, flesh, we can perceive Melville's contempt for Christianity's attitude towards sexuality. To bury the roses is to bury love. To remove sensual pleasure from the garden and condemn it to the grave is to commit a sin against life. But Melville is not really appalled since he flippantly observes that the vault is little used. Melville looks upon man as an earthbound creature who has to take his nourishment from the full breast of the eternal mother who gave Dionysus birth. In effect, he argues that ill-advised prudery corrupts instinctive pleasures. What humans enjoy spontaneously one moment they regret in the next— victims of conscience. Engendered by a morality suspicious of nature, the conflict does not permit the individual to fulfill himself in accordance with his centauric character.

The last stanza of "Under the Ground" confirms this outlook, for Melville ridicules the deceitful moral sentimentality of bourgeois marriage:

"Yea, for against the bridal hour
My Master fain would keep their bloom;
A charm in the dank o' the vault there is,
Yea, we the rose entomb." (p. 297)

Having in mind the double sexual standards of Victorian culture, Melville derides "the bridal hour" with its hypocritical emphasis on female virginity. By extension, if the entombed rose is taken as a symbol of Christ, he also disavows belief in eternal resurrection. Dank vaults possess little attraction unless they are endowed with supernatural mystery. Such may be the reaction of the gullible gardener's boy, but Melville shows his distaste for miracles. In the light of the negative diction of the stanza, the pervasive imagery of death-in-life, his disillusionment is understandable. For where the ideal of physical purity is the basic sanction of human union, mutual love has no meaning. Only the bridegroom's appetite needs to be served in conformity with the patriarchal mores of marriage. Under the circumstances the rite is perverted into self-indulgent lust. The full flowering of the emotional life of the bride commands no concern. Forever Eve, she is punished for being a woman, damned by custom and complacency.

"The Ambuscade" defends the natural impulses of sexual passion, though without the ambiguity of "Under the Ground." The poet describes the demeanor of a girl which reflects the decorums of Victorianism—its distrust of physical beauty. But, ironically, her discretion evolves into unconscious coquetry. While concealing her charm behind a snowy aloofness, she excites even more desire; instinctively, she maintains fidelity to her incipient womanhood:

> Meek crossing of the bosom's lawn
> Averted revery veil-like drawn,
> Well beseem thee, nor obtrude
> The cloister of thy virginhood.
> And yet, white nun, that seemly dress
> Of purity pale passionless,
> A May-snow is; for fleeting term,
> Custodian of love's slumbering germ—
> Nay, nurtures it, till time disclose
> How frost fed Amor's burning rose. (p. 297)

Melville's imagery dramatizes this earthy inclination. The girl's bosom is a "lawn," though here the word may also refer to a sheer cotton or linen cloth; if so, then she is artfully artless. At any rate, she teasingly invites attention. Her shyness is like the "May-snow," a paradoxical assurance of a resurgent spring. Or, psychologically, repression motivates her spotless, glacial posture. But she is not totally unaware of her plight. At least the "meek crossing" suggests that she invokes heaven for help in preserving her rigorous modesty. Melville therefore finally concludes that conventional morality cannot frustrate human nature forever. This point is underscored by the insidious sexual overtones of his religious imagery. In short, the white Christian Rose of innocence slowly metamorphoses into the Dionysian Rose of passion.

The same strategy of irony governs the structure of "The

206

New Rosicrucians." The "New" in the title announces that salvation *per crucem ad rosa* is to be redefined. It is. Redemption is offered through the cross in its phallic sense, and a tone of pagan abandon envelops the emergence of this hedonistic creed:

> To us, disciples of the Order
> Whose rose-vine twines the Cross,
> Who have drained the rose's chalice
> Never heeding gain or loss;
> For all the preacher's din
> There is no mortal sin—
> No, none to us but Malice! (p. 297)

Wickedly, Melville inverts the Eucharistic ritual. The cup of grace is drunk in the physical act of copulation. In this blasphemy he outdoes Robert Herrick from whom he undoubtedly borrows the sexual symbolism of the Dionysian vine context.[3] Unrestrainedly, he makes a frontal attack on the religious concepts of good and evil. He disclaims ecclesiastical authority in these matters along with the belief in unpardonable sins. In effect, he completely renounces not only the spiritual principles of orthodox Christianity, but also those of syncretistic movements like that of the Rosicrucians. For him, the religious obsession with evil tends to retard the growth of emotional maturity.

Less polemical than impish, he goes on to revel in his amorality. He apparently believes that he has arrived at a new understanding of love's transformative magic:

> Exempt from that, in blest recline
> We let life's billows toss;
> If sorrow come, anew we twine
> The Rose-Vine round the Cross. (p. 297)

"[B]lest recline" refers to the relaxed aftermath of sexual intercourse, a state always attainable even though rocking on the waves of adversity. The conscious recognition that grief and suffering represent the norms of human experience brings a peaceful wisdom independent of all abstract speculations on cause and effect. He adjusts to the contingencies of existence in terms of physical facts, not

[3] See "The Vine" and "On Himselfe."

spiritual truths. Thus he eschews the Christian resolution of this problem.

The same outlook is in evidence in "The Vial of Attar" in which Melville contrasts infidel fatalism with Christian hope. The point at issue is that the members of pre-Christian societies did not associate reward or punishment with death. By extension, then, ruling traditions functioned to assuage temporal despair and sorrow, not at all concerned with any eternal fate:

> Lesbia's lover when bereaved
> In pagan times of yore
> Ere the gladsome tidings ran
> Of reunion evermore,
> He wended from the pyre
> Now hopeless in return—
> Ah, the vial hot with tears
> For the ashes cold in urn! [4] (p. 298)

By contrast, of course, Christianity sentimentalizes love and death. Lacking toughness, it devises solaces for inescapable adversities that are ultimately absurd in the light of historical experience. As if totally unaware of the latter facts, Melville's poetic voice professes to find comfort in the memory of his deceased beloved one:

> But I, the Rose's lover,
> When *my* beloved goes
> Followed by the Asters
> Toward the sepulchre of snows,
> Then, solaced by the Vial
> Less grieve I for the Tomb,
> Not widowed of the fragrance
> If parted from the bloom—
> Parted from the bloom
> That was but for a day. (p. 298)

Assuming the posture of the bereaved hero of a cheap romance, he seeks to perpetuate his affection under the delusion of an unshakable fidelity to an ideal. Defying the sensory (and sensual) reality

---

[4] It is interesting to note that Lesbia was originally "woman" on the holograph.

of his Rose, he tries to subordinate existence to essence, to exalt the spirit above the flesh.

Suddenly, he experiences a revulsion of feeling, and perceives his self-deception. He recognizes that he cannot cheat love with empty words and gestures:

> Rose! I dally with thy doom:
> The solace will not stay!
> There *is* nothing like the bloom;
> And the Attar poignant minds me
> Of the bloom that's passed away. (p. 298)

Now he avers that there is nothing more sacrosanct than life in time. Love, in sum, is physical chemistry, not spiritual affinity. It is a tangible experience which one human shares with another. Its revelations and ecstasies are not susceptible to the transfigurations of eternity. Following on the heels of "The New Rosicrucians," this poem also lays the ghost of Christianity, clearing the air of what Melville deems a supernatural fraud. In this uncompromising rejection of heavenly bliss, one cannot blink the fact that he discards the greatest boon of Christianity for the transitory fulfillments of physical love. Nor is he atheistic. He worships his God in the dying and reviving cycle of the seasons—the eternal Dionysus.

In a much more offhand and jovial manner, "Rose Window" reiterates Melville's disillusionment with the redemptive promise of Christianity. The title itself perhaps conceals a hidden pun in which he revels in the feminine rose of life. For in the typical plan of the Christian Church the rose window on the western side symbolizes the womb of creation. Circular and female in form, it contrasts with the lancet-shaped east window which is high, narrow, and male. The sexual implications of this relationship are immediately manifested in the opening stanza; the spiritual rose of Christ is ironically juxtaposed with the sexual rose of the Canticles in its literal representation of a nuptial ritual:

> The preacher took from *Solomon's Song*
> Four words for text with mystery rife—
> *The Rose of Sharon,*—figuring Him
> The Resurrection and the Life;

And, pointing many an urn in view,
How honied a homily he drew. (p. 299) [5]

Like Henry Adams in *Mont Saint-Michel* and *Chartre*, Melville has made too close a study of religious symbols to accept only univocal interpretations, especially since so much of Christian iconography is borrowed from the older pagan cultures. Of course, the minister is entitled to elaborate his allegory of the marriage of the Saviour with the Church, but, in Melville's eyes, there is no prerogative for his trite and tedious repetition of theological platitudes: "honied" truth.

However sleepy the auditor of the sermon, the poet himself is eagerly alert to the possibilities of travesty in the situation. Given the opportunity to exploit the relation of resurrection to the Sacrament of Communion, he portrays the negative impact of its mystery upon the soul of man. It functions as a spiritual sedative instead of a quickener of the spirit:

There in the slumberous afternoon,
Through minster gray, in lullaby rolled
The brimmed metheglin charged with swoon.
Drowsy, my decorous hands I fold
Till sleep overtakes with dream for boon. (p. 299)

Behind the obvious satirical literalities, Melville also conceals a cluster of outrageous blasphemies. The "metheglin" is both a comic surrogate of the wine of the Eucharistic ceremony and the preacher's soporific sermon. The strong wine made from honey subverts the parallel drawn between The Song of Solomon and the mystical marriage of Christ to the Church. Since ancient times, metheglin has been used as an aphrodisiac, and, as a matter of fact, the term honeymoon derives from the custom of drinking it for a month (moon) to insure conception. In short, Melville asserts his belief that The Song of Solomon is a ritual celebration of the beauty of sexual love.

[5] Melville's annotation on the Canticles follows my interpretation: "The original verses are full of nature and truth" (William Braswell, *Melville's Religious Thought* [Durham, N.C.: Duke University Press], p. 11). He also refers to uncalled-for interpolations in this context.

The same vein of iconoclasm emerges in the next stanza. Quite obviously, the dream burlesques the Annunciation. Melville's Rose attests the finality of death, not resurrection through "*The Rose of Sharon*":

> I saw an Angel with a Rose
> Come out of Morning's garden-gate,
> And lamp-like hold the Rose aloft,
> He entered a sepulchral Strait.
> I followed. And I saw the Rose
> Shed dappled down upon the dead;
> The shrouds and mort-cloths all were lit
> To plaids and chequered tartans red. (p. 299)

The "strait gate" to salvation (Matt. VII:13–14) ceases to have meaning; there are no choices on the road to extinction. The ceremonial character of the valedictory gesture by the angel separates human destiny completely from the heavenly order of existence. The rose of life is a gift of the cyclical movement of nature, "Morning's garden-gate." It has no affinity with eternity. The sacramental offering in the sepulchre consecrates Melville's fealty to Dionysian reality—his unprotesting acceptance of cosmic flux and dissolution.

The imagery of the last stanza is carefully chosen to express this attitude. Paradoxically, it is the dream that awakens the delinquent worshiper's mind to his grim fate. Gazing at the western window, he now is blind to its associations with the Virgin Mary. Instead he there envisages a union of Iris (the goddess of the rainbow) and Aurora (the goddess of dawn). This combination is highly significant. Iris is sometimes called the mother of Love, and Aurora is often represented as a nymph, garlanded in flowers, who scatters roses to signify the fertility of the earth: [6]

> I woke, the great Rose-Window high,
> A mullioned wheel in gable set,
> Suffused with rich and soft in dye
> Where Iris and Aurora met;
> Aslant in sheaf of rays it threw

[6] Anthon, *A Classical Dictionary*, pp. 242, 685.

> From all its foliate round of panes
> Transfiguring light on dingy stains,
> While danced the motes in dusty pew. (p. 299)

Moreover, as the messenger of the gods, Iris figuratively proclaims the dawn of pagan truth. The sterility of the dogmas of Christianity are exposed by the pure rays of the benevolent sun. In eclipsing the artificial beauty of the window, nature dismisses man's efforts to image a deity greater than herself. In retrospect this poem returns us to the symbolic implications of "Amoroso." Once more the *Rosa Mundi* is identified with the rose of life in its primordial connection with human love and birth.

Employing a similar technique of inversion, Melville's "From Beads for a Rosary" [7] subverts the orthodox roles of the Virgin Mary. Or perhaps with smiling rancor, the poet simply restores her to the pantheon to which all of her antecedents can be traced —the innumerable fertility goddesses of antiquity. In any event, in what we may presume to call the first surviving quatrain ("The Accepted Time") the initial prayer on the beads takes the form of an exhortation:

> Adore the Roses; nor delay
> Until the rose-fane fall,
> Or ever their censers cease to sway:
> "To-day!" the rose-priests call. (p. 300)

This summons to love controverts belief in Christian eternity. It sanctifies the present moment. And Melville, in the image of censer, affirms this philosophy of life. Inverting its religious significance, Melville equates the scented bloom of the rose with woman and sexual pleasure. Ordinarily liturgical incensing takes note of the everlasting vigilance of Christ in protecting the individual against the temptations of the flesh. Here, of course, the opposite form of conduct is glorified in the *carpe diem* imperative. To wit,

---

[7] Vincent has no real authority for renumbering the stanzas of this poem. The first one was cancelled out, and the others were left numbered two, three, and four. Hence, logically, it ought to be considered an incomplete work. It is this fact that leads me to retitle the poem as it is found on one of the tables of contents. This seems to make more sense than Vincent's simplification.

nothing can mitigate the relentless cruelties of time except the fleeting forgetfulness of carefree dalliance.

The next stanza develops another dimension of the apostasy from conventional morality. As the subtitle "Without Price" implies, Melville sets out to weigh the tangible importance of the redemptive role of Christ as embodied in such allusions as "one pearl of great price" and "the price of blood" (Matt. XIII:46; XXVII:6). Patently, Melville places little credence in the future salvation promised by the crucifixion. For him it is the willing sacrifice of virginity that constitutes the priceless gift of mutual self-fulfillment:

> Have the Roses. Needs no pelf
>   The blooms to buy,
> Nor any rose-bed to thyself
>   Thy skill to try:
> But live up to the Rose's light
> Thy meat shall turn to roses red,
>   Thy bread to roses white. (p. 300)

Dissociating himself from the dogma that a scapegoat can buy ("pelf") eternal happiness for all mankind or that self-mortification can lend a prick to conscience (the test in the thorny "rose-bed"), Melville offers his own conception of the meaning of transubstantiation. His use of the vulgarism "meat" indicates that "Roses red" represent the ardor of the act of love and that the "bread" turned "roses white" is the offspring of the union. In short, this is the Dionysian solution to perpetuating life. The final quatrain of the poem ("Grain by Grain") displays the despairing awareness that time and death continually menace love. Thus Melville justifies the urgency of taking the pleasures of the day:

> Grain by grain the Desert drifts
> Against the Garden-Land:
> Hedge well thy Roses, head the stealth
> Of ever-creeping Land. (p. 300)

The garden in this context is the tabooed bower of sexuality, and, beyond the literal lands of time, the desert shadows forth the dismal emotional fate of all betrayers of the Rose.

An identical rejection of Christianity occurs in "The Devotion of the Flowers to their Lady." Allegedly written by a troubadour turned monk, the poem professes to affirm belief in immortality—that is, in the redemption of the rose through the Rose of Sharon (Christ). Melville's handling of the dramatic situation reveals his acquaintance with the symbolism of Dante's *Paradise*. Implicitly, his earthly rose also metamorphoses into the image of Paradise, of the Virgin Mary and her spiritual love, of the Flower of God and the Divine Grace of the Son. However, the tone of execution tends to negate the overt assertions of unshakable faith in salvation. The unidentified persona of the poem, a spokesman for the common garden flowers, invokes the eternal rose so whiningly and self-pityingly that all the expressed sentiments are reduced to a parody of faith. This effect is likewise conveyed rhetorically in a sequence of interrogations which divulge the lurking doubt behind the posture of piety:

> O Queen, we are loyal: shall sad ones forget?
>   We are natives of Eden—
> Sharing its memory with you, and your handmaidens yet.
>
> You bravely dissemble with looks that beguile
>   Musing mortals to murmur
> Reproachful "So festal, O Flower, we but weary the while?
>
> What nothing has happened? no event to make wan,
>   Begetting things hateful—
> Old age, decay, and the sorrows, devourers of man?" (p. 301)

The mode of dialectic in the three tercets is typically Melvillian, for the attitudes of the persona disclose that belief in the penalty of the Fall is not a conviction but a habit of thought, a product of religious conditioning. An instinctive desire to enjoy life underlies the almost envious admonitions. Or put in the framework of the parody, what we have here is an illustration of the failure of Christianity to provide the sustaining principles to cope with the contingent anxieties and sufferings of temporal existence. Almost criminally, man has been taught to hate his own mortal flesh, to violate his own human nature.

The querulous but unconscious protest against this fate is also voiced in the next segment of the poem. And once more the persona betrays a disaffection from Christian dogma, and unwittingly directs attention to its alienation from the immediate problems of existence in time:

> They marvel and marvel how came you so bright,
>   Whence the splendor, the joyance—
> Florid revel of joyance, the Cypress in sight!
>
> Scarce *you* would poor Adam upbraid that his fall
>   Like a land-slide by waters
> Rolled an out-spreading impulse disordering all;
>
> That the Angel indignant, with eyes that foreran
>   The betrayed generations,
> Cast out the flowers wherewith Eve decked her nuptials with man.
>
> Ah, exile is exile, tho' spiced be the sod,
>   In Shushan we languish—
> Languish with the secret desire for the garden of God. (pp. 301–02)

Ironically, of course, the first tercet exalts the erotic rose ("Florid revel") above the mystic Rose of Paradise. The ecstasies of sexual love more effectively mitigate the fear of death ("the Cypress") than the consolations of heavenly bliss. Moreover, the very admission of such a possibility casts further doubt upon the actual authority of the opposite Christian doctrines. The italicizing of the *"you"* along with the rather grudging admiration evinced by the audacity of the rose clearly indicates that the persona would also like to disavow concern with the penal consequences of the Fall. Thus the sentiment in the last tercet emerges as a blatant rationalization of impotent volition. The prevailing languor results from the repression of the instinctual impulses, not from the unsatisfied longing for union with the divine.

Consistent with this interpretation, the final stanza of the poem is enveloped in a mood of velleity that conceals a virtual death-wish. The conflict between the flesh and the spirit defies resolution. At least so the imagery of sterility—"pallor is passion," "muse nor forget," "pale priestly hand"—in the contradictory setting of the rebirth of day suggests:

> But all of us yet—
> We the Lilies whose palor is passion,

We the Pansies that muse nor forget—
In harbinger airs how we freshen,
When, clad in the amice of gray silver-hemmed
    Meek coming in twilight and dew,
The Day-Spring, with pale priestly hand and begemmed,
    Touches, and coronates you:—
Breathing, O Daughter of far descent,
Banished, yet blessed in banishment,
    Whereto is appointed a term;
Flower, voucher of Paradise, visible pledge,
    Rose, attesting it spite of the Worm. (p. 302)

If this description is meant to parallel Dante's vision of the eternal Rose that derives its life and light from the divine sun,

and if the lowest row gathers to itself
    so much light, how great is the width
    of this rose in its outermost petals! (Par. XXX, 115–17)

then its parodic function is unequivocally established by Melville. The ineffable luminescence of God is an illusion. It does not reconcile the living to their emotional death. It is not in "spite of the Worm" that the rose glows as it blows. Rather it is because "of the Worm." There seems little doubt that here Melville is wryly evoking a phallic image, the voucher of life that the poetic voice of the poem refuses to recognize. Indeed, if we are to take Melville's epigraph seriously, then we can understand why the alleged author of "The Devotion" entered a monastery while still in his prime manhood: he was terrified by the diabolic negations of his religion.

Another irreverent parody unfolds in "The Rose Farmer" which makes up the entire second part of *A Rose or Two*. The poem deals with the conversion of the poetic voice into a devotee of the blossom instead of the attar of the rose. "Come unto [his] roses late" (p. 303), that is having finally decided to take a stand on the temporal or the eternal pursuit of happiness, he seeks the advice of a "gentleman-rose-farmer" (p. 305), Melville's euphemism for a connoisseur of maidenheads. The moral and emotional crisis evolves when he inherits "a farm in fee/Forever consecrate to roses" (p. 304), which is located on the outskirts of Damascus. Here the geographical setting is of crucial importance since it pro-

vides the main clue to the real subject of Melville's parody. Historically, of course, Paul also experienced his remarkable conversion
outside of Damascus when the risen and glorified Christ (the symbolic Mystic Rose) appeared before him in a blinding manifestation
of heavenly light and said: "I am Jesus whom thou persecutest: *it is*
hard for thee to kick against the pricks" (Acts IX:5). Because of
Paul's persistent condemnation of the pleasures of the flesh after
this event, "For to be carnally minded *is* death" (Rom. VIII:6),
Melville fiendishly resolves to interpret "pricks" as a vulgar colloquialism (no doubt, taking his cue from Shakespeare). At any rate,
the opening stanza sets up the strategy of his burlesque *Roman de
la Rose:*

> *Coming through the rye:*
> Thereof the rural poet whistles;
> But who the flute will try
> At *scrambling through the thistles!*
> Nor less upon some roseate way
> Emerge the prickly passage may. (p. 303)

Melville poses the difficulty of preserving a romantic attitude towards temporal love in the face of the threat of eternal punishment. His two italicized verses operate to establish this conflict.
The one is a quotation from Robert Burns's lyric about a seduction;
the other is an elliptical reference to the curse ("thistles") pro-
nounced against Adam for his sexual sin (the cause of the Fall), inherited by man, and expiated by Christ (the "roseate way" so pas-
sionately expounded by Paul). But lurking behind the seriousness of
this proposition is a coruscating levity. The source of Burns's poem
is the old song "The Bob-tailed Lass." Like "The Rose Farmer,"
the epithet is a euphemism, in this case for an indecent woman with
a lively yoni, enough to make a poet play his figurative lute. On the
other hand, no pious Christian is apt to try the "prickly passage"
(coition) of the indecent rose without fear for his soul.

The next stanza considers the problem of guiltless sexuality
from the standpoint of old age, and once more Melville blandly
employs his foul double-talk. Ostensibly, however, he assumes the
pose of righteous conventionality:

> But we who after ragged scrambles
> Through fate's blessed thorns and brambles
> Come unto our roses late—
> Aright to manage the estate,
> This indeed it well may task us
> Quite inexperienced as we be
> In aught but thickets that unmasque us
> Of man's ennobling drapery. (p. 303)

The first two verses envisage life under the aspect of the rose as a symbol of sin and sorrow, imperfect man struggling to reconcile himself to his earthly lot and in the process emulating the suffering Christ on the cross, the "blessed thorns and brambles." This outlook culminates in the admission that mankind is incapable of any lofty form of terrestrial self-realization. This outward expression of piety, it develops, becomes pure mummery when explicated in the idiom of the profane rose. Actually Melville exalts sensual experience; the "scrambles" (a variant of scambles, amorous activity) conducted among the "blessed thorns and brambles," the condemned garden of love, preclude the possibility of a moral ("Aright") preparation for spiritual deliverance. Knowing "aught but thickets" (the Shakespearean "O" in its symbolic topographic guise), man is impelled to disdain the rewards of salvation. In short, there is no point in robbing Peter to pay Paul.

In the following verse paragraph we find a confirmation of this philosophy. Now rich in roses, the persona takes the position that such a fortune cannot be renounced; after all, in his own fashion he is a proponent of the "sweet content of Christian cheer" (p. 304), to be sure, slightly inverted. This perversity dictates his mock disparagement of wealth and, by extension, of Paul's insistent iterations that the poor are God's children: "As sorrowful, yet always rejoicing; as poor yet making many rich; as having nothing, and yet making many rich; as having nothing, and *yet* possessing all things" (2 Cor. VI:10). Certainly the tone and logic of his argument take the form of a *reductio ad absurdum:*

> Indigence is a plain estate:
> Riches imply the complicate.
> What peevish pestering wants surprise,

What bothering ambitions rise!
Then, too, Fate loans a lot luxurious
At such hard cent-per-cent usurious!
Mammon, never meek as Moses,
Gouty, mattressed on moss-roses,
A crumpled rose-leaf makes him furious.
Allow, as one's purveyor here
Of sweet content of Christian cheer,
"Vile Pelf" we overestimate.
Howbeit, a rose-farm nigh Damascus
Would Dives change at even rate
For Lazarus' snow-farm in Alaskus? (pp. 303–4)

Melville's pun on "scent-per-scent" indicates that only a fool would scant the temporal pleasures of his symbolic rose garden. Inventing his own parable to sweeten the sop of his gleeful moral imposture, he nonsensically affirms what he denies, having already answered the question that he asks.

The next segment of the poem is devoted to a description of his inherited estate, and Melville has only one purpose in mind—to establish the sexual symbolism of the garden. Faintly echoing Coleridge's "Kubla Khan" (and possibly Melville's interpretation of the cryptic masterpiece), the various details clearly evoke the tabooed bower of bliss:

A brave bequest, a farm in fee
Forever consecrate to roses,
And laved by streams that sacred are,
Pharpar and twin-born Abana,
Which last the pleasure-ground incloses,
At least winds half-way roundabout—
That garden to caress, no doubt. (p. 304)

Subsequently, in the persona's interview with the rose-farmer, he is inducted into the responsibilities of maintaining a harem of rosy virgins. He quickly learns that they have to be deflowered regularly under the auspices of Aurora, the goddess of fertility notorious for her numerous seductions:

"Ay, pluck a rose in dew Auroral,
For buttonette to please the sight,—
The dawn's bloom and the bloom but floral,

> Why, what a race with them in flight!
> Quick, too, the redolence it stales.
> And yet you have the brief delight,
> And yet the next morn's bud avails;
> And on in sequence." (pp. 307–8)

These fatalistic sentiments, needless to say, take for granted that the law of life is based on the principle of perpetual sacrifice. The bud of morn and maid cannot stay, else their roses will not flower and complete the cycle of nature. Thus the implicit argument of the rose-farmer is that time alone is the domain of existential fulfillment, that the at-one-ment of life and death is a more sustaining truth than the atonement of the Mystic Rose. To dramatize the necessity of accepting this notion of reality, Melville's persona reports the reaction of the roses in the garden to this piece of advice:

> What agitation! every rose
> Bridling aloft the passionate head!
> But *what* it was that angered here,—
> Just *why* the high resentment shown,
> Pray ask of her who'll hint it clear—
> A Mormon's first-wife making moan. (p. 308)

Beyond the obvious sexual innuendoes, supported in context by the phrase, "roses husbanded by him" (p. 308), there is also the intimation that Christianity has stifled such emotional spontaneity and, as a consequence, has destroyed the foundations of normal human happiness. In any event, only such an explanation harmonizes with the rose-farmer's introduction of a biblical tale—another of Melville's parodies of the revealed word of God:

> "This evanescence is the charm!
> And most it wins the spirits that be
> Celestial, Sir. It comes to me
> It was this fleeting charm in show
> That lured the sons of God below,
> Tired out with perpetuity
> Of heaven's own seventh heaven aglow;
> Not Eve's fair daughters, Sir; nay, nay,
> Less fugitive in charm are they:
> It was the rose." (pp. 308–9)

The "evanescence" in question applies to the maidenhead, and the infatuation of "the sons of God" with the fugitive flower comprises the crucial facet of Melville's poetic causistry. His puckish logic is based on the fact that the progeny of this unholy union is of heroic mold:

> And it came to pass . . . .
> That the sons of God saw the daughters of men that they *were* fair; and they took them wives of all which they chose.
> And the Lord said, My Spirit shall not always strive with man, for that he also is flesh: yet his days shall be a hundred and twenty years.
> There were giants in the earth in those days; and also after that, when the sons of God came in unto the daughters of men, and they bare *children* to them, the same *became* mighty men which *were* of old, men of renown. (Gen. VI:1–4)

Yet in the following verse there is contradiction. God decides to punish man for his evil deeds (?), and the outcome is the Flood. This inconsistency in cause and effect supplies Melville with biblical authority for his coronation of the sexual rose, and by the same token confutes Paul's degradation of the flesh. Sophistry or not, this comic wrenching of an apparently misplaced myth is no more absurd than some of the doctrinal formulations of denominational Christianity during Melville's day.

The rose-farmer's assessment of spiritual absolution emerges in his discussion of a Parsee—as in *Moby-Dick,* the personification of the superego's coercive moralism. Like a fanatical penitent, the latter forsakes the joys of the immediate world:

> "Yon Parsee lours
> Headsman and Blue Beard of the Flowers.
> In virgin flush of efflorescence
> When buds their bosoms just disclose,
> To get a mummified quintessence
> He scimiters the living rose!" (p. 307)

The combined image of "Headsman" (public executioner) and "Blue Beard" (a misogynous and misogamous murderer) is devised to expose the sadism and masochism that lurk behind pious rigorism. The moral disguise conceals a pathological hatred of sexual woman, and in the final analysis is a displacement for censored egotistic (erotic and violent) impulses at work in the unconscious. Analogously, these observations can be applied to Paul who, before his conversion, was a diabolical persecutor of Christians. If Melville here anticipates Freud, he is not the first creative artist to uncover the secrets of the dark underworld of the instincts.

Fittingly, the poem climaxes with the poetic voice marveling at the serene wisdom of the rose farmer, at the soothing effect of flowered knowledge:

> Discreet, in second thought's immersion
> I wended from this prosperous Persian
> Who, verily, seemed in life rewarded
> For sapient prudence not amiss,
> Nor transcendental essence hoarded
> In hope of quintessential bliss:
> No, never with painstaking throes
> Essays to crystallize the rose. (p. 309)

Noteworthy in this treatment of ordering philosophy of life is the absence of torturing doubts. None of the ambivalent moral attitudes of Melville's fiction obtrude. He revels in the freedom his aging flesh has found. At least enough so to end up with a bawdy guffaw: "The flower of a subject is enough" (p. 310).

"L'Envoi" of "The Rose-Farmer" crystallizes this jovial insight. Melville still laughs at himself, but he does not retreat an inch from his position that, as an old man who has assimilated the experiences of life, he can exercise the prerogative of an elder to communicate the knowledge to curious ears:

> Rosy dawns the morning Syrian,
>   Youthful as in years of Noah:
>   Why then aging at three-score?
> Do moths infest your mantle Tyrian?
>   Shake it out where sun-beams pour!
> Time, Amigo, does but masque us— (p. 310)

Mockingly, he again invokes scriptural truth to justify his youthful ebullience. The "years of Noah" allude to the patriarch's begetting three sons at the age of five hundred. No wonder, then, that he entreats exposure to the fertilizing rays of the sun; they are the source of Dionysian renewal. Of course, the epiphany of the "damsels of Damascus" parodies Paul's vision, and brings the argument of the poem full circle:

> Boys in gray wigs, young at core.
> Look, what damsels of Damascus,
> Roses, lure the Pharpar's shore! (p. 310)

Ultimately, however, he is forced to admit that for him regeneration is a psychological phenomenon that brings belated self-understanding:

> Sigh not—Age, dull tranquilizer,
> And arid years that filed before,
> For flowers unfit us. Nay, be wiser:
> Wiser in relish, if sedate
> Come gray-beards to their roses late. (p. 310)

This reconciliation to the past and the present indicates that Melville has resolved all his religious and emotional conflicts. As he ponders all the circumstances of his life, he seems to conclude that he was a victim of temperament, not of fate. Nor does he regret what occurred, perhaps because it produced the late roses of his poetry.

Marquis de Grandvin

XI   The Wine of Life

THE LAST OF Melville's verse projects, *Marquis de Grandvin,* is a
retrospective undertaking. It contains two poems, "At the Hostelry," and "Naples in the Time of Bomba." Both of them employ
details of impressions recorded in the *Journal* of his trip to Europe
and the Near East,[1] but now they are assimilated into a view of
historical experience colored by a hedonistic philosophy of wine
and roses. As the proposed title of the collection indicates, its composition takes the form of a tribute to a symbolic Dionysus, a port-
manteau figure who is at once the Marquis de Grandvin, Jack Gentian, and the poet himself. A cancelled title, "Parthenope/An Afternoon in Old Naples:/In the Time of Bomba/with/A Salutato-
ry/Touching/New Italy and Old Romance/&c/Painters and the
Picturesque/and so forth/more or less versified by Herman Melville from the/original suggestions of the noble/The Marquis de
Grandvin," and a quotation from a group of prose sketches devoted to characterizing the latter conceive him as the self of a
wishful fantasy. This suggests what Melville might have been if
he had not become immersed in the insoluble metaphysical and
theological problem of good and evil.[2] An observation from another sketch clearly points up the change in question: "The wisdom
they [the disciples of de Grandvin] by contact give out is not celi-

---

[1] Horsford, *Journal,* pp. 178 n 8; 180 nn 6, 7; 184 n 6; 187 n 4; 254 n 5.
[2] One is tempted to consider all of the complementary prose writings in the
de Grandvin manuscripts as instances of Melville's own self-glorification; for
there is no doubt that he, in a renewal of his frequent visits to the gatherings at Evert Duyckinck's home, Howard, *Herman Melville,* p. 329, had
regained much of the old verbal gusto which the latter had once denominated
" 'an orgie of indecency and blasphemy,' " Perry Miller, *The Raven and the
Whale* (New York, 1956), p. 334.

bate and sterile like Solomon's,[3] but wedded to enjoyment, and hence productive." Autobiography also enters the two poems from another direction. Melville's past provides him with a historical analogy to his speculations on the meaning of life then and now. Garibaldi's efforts to secure Italy's political emancipation some thirty years earlier parallels his own search for spiritual deliverance. Finally able to abstract the implications of the occurrences, he brings them into ironical juxtaposition with the symbols of wine in "At the Hostelry" and of the rose in "Naples in the Time of Bomba." Thus he shows that events involving the human race have no real import in the scheme of cyclical nature.

The prose introduction of "At the Hostelry" clearly assigns a special function to the past. According to the poetic voice Marquis de Grandvin, the topics of history are invoked "with an ulterior design" (p. 313). Aware of the current obsession with historical progress based on the belief in Darwinism,[4] Melville selects Garibaldi's career to test the validity of the conception. The first part of the poem appears to be an unrestrained glorification of Garibaldi's achievements. It hails the inevitable advent of a political, economic, and social Utopia. But when Marquis de Grandvin draws upon the arguments of linear historicism to prove this, his amusement is self-evident:

> The Spirit o' the Age he'll take a hand.
> He means to dust each bric-a-brac city,
> Pluck the feathers from all banditti;
> The Pope he'll hat, and, yea or nay ye,
> Rejuvenate e'en old Pompeii!
> Concede, accomplished aims unite
> With many a promise hopeful and as bright. (p. 316)

"The Spirit o' the Age" embraces the universal illusion of the moment that man stands on the threshold of cultural perfection. Not only the playful imagery but also the imperative mood of

---

[3] Quotation from unpublished manuscript.
[4] Melville's poem, "The New Ancient of Days," subtitled "The Man of the Cave of Engihoul," is a hilarious treatment of this subject as well as a mocking subversion of the Christian myth (p. 374).

"[c]oncede" disclaim the seriousness of the poetic voice. Nonetheless he petitions his auditors in the inn to give their attention to his presentation:

> Candid eyes in open faces
> Clear, not keen, no narrowing line:
> Hither turn your favoring graces
> Now the cloth is drawn for wine. (p. 313)

This act of dedication seems to be a parodic imitation of the Offertory, the first part of the Eucharistic rite. At least the oblation turns out to be far more sincere than that of the Catholic clergy which, contrary to its advocacy of human brotherhood, obstructed the unification of Italy up until the time Garibaldi undermined its power. In short, more was accomplished under his leadership than Christ's. Of course, the Marquis de Grandvin is in this instance a Dionysian priest, a spokesman for the earthly truth:

> From that red Taurus plunging on
> With lowered horns and forehead dun,
> Shall matadores save Bomba's son?
> He fled. And her Redeemer's banners
> Glad Naples greeted with strown flowers
> Hurrah and secular hosannas
> That fidgety made all tyrant powers. (p. 314)

Hence his tribute operates to ridicule the failure of the Saviour's messiahship to effect a reformation of history. Unlike the latter who came but once and who will return only on Judgment Day when the linear timetable of salvation has run its course, Garibaldi as Taurus figures the perennial manifestation of the human redeemer. Like the potency of the zodiacal bull, his emancipative spirit will forever excite emulation. Thus Garibaldi's career illustrates the law of resurrection in recurrence on the plane of history. He plays out his heroic and patriotic role in time like his counterparts in other ages and civilizations. A more blatant dismissal of Christ is also implicit in the allusion to Taurus whose constellation has immemorially been associated with the Tau cross, a phallic symbol. Figuratively, then, Garibaldi's physical energy is more efficacious than the spiritual power of Christianity. This blasphemy is extended in the way the liberator is welcomed, with "secular hosannas" and "strown flowers." These practices subsume the rites of pagan orgy, a restoration of instinctual freedom within the framework of nature. In effect, the entire scene celebrates a release of those creative vigors which have universally consecrated another lease on life for primitive man. The Golden Age for an interlude returns with Garibaldi.

This natural freedom is next contrasted with the shameful political machinations of the ambitious priesthood:

> Italia, how cut up, divided
> Nigh paralyzed, by cowls misguided;
> Locked as in Chancery's numbing hand,
> Fattening the predatory band
> Of shyster-princes, whose ill sway
> Still kept her a calamitous land. (p. 315)

These intrigues evince more concern with secular than spiritual affairs, and reveal that the Church attempts to direct the course of human events in contradiction of the divine plan of eschatology. Melville, however, insists that such endeavors do not change the piecemeal continuum of temporality:

> Ye halls of history, arched by time,
> Founded in fate, enlarged by crime,
> Now shines like phosphorus scratched in dark
> 'Gainst your grimed walls the luminous mark
> Of one who in no paladin age
> Was knightly—him who lends a page
> Now signal in time's recent story
> Where scarce in vogue are "Plutarch's Men,"
> And jobbers deal in popular glory.— (p. 314)

Fate, irrational causality, combines with frantic human activity to produce the architecture of events. Essentially designless, this house of life is occasionally brightened by the flame of idealism, but only for a moment. Here the allusion to Plutarch falls into this pattern of logic. His biographies follow no ordered chronology; they record the passions and pursuits of individuals which, for a brief moment, rippled in the current of time, only to melt away into oblivion.[5] Arnold J. Toynbee, in his view of Plutarch's philosophy of history, allies it with the grim phrase, "Death the Leveler." [6] Melville looks upon Garibaldi's exploits in much the same light. The latter is entitled to "a page" in the "story" of time, to a passing role in the plotless drama of human ambition. Like Plutarch's heroes, he died as do the permanent significance of his deeds. Over them hangs the formula of fate which defines nature—life and death:

> In best of worlds if all's not bright,
> Allow, the shadow's chased by light,
> Though rest for neither yet may be.
> And beauty's charm, where Nature reigns,
> Nor crimes nor codes may quite subdue. (p. 313)

Echoing Voltaire's *Candide*, the phrase, "best of worlds," ironically annuls any hope of eternity. Now is the only heaven man may know. Light and dark chase one another on the diurnal hinge, as one phase of history follows another in alternating patterns of good and evil. In effect, Melville merely repeats that what has happened once will happen again. No event is unique unto itself. Thus "The Spirit o' the Age," whatever its illusions about human potentialities, is but a fever of desire and aspiration that lends a hectic tint to the dreams of man.

The second part of the poem shifts to a discussion of the techniques of the "picturesque." Rendered in the form of imaginary conversations among the shades of various European painters, the undertaking purports to clarify "one of the manifold aspects of life and nature which under various forms all artists strive to transmit to canvas" (p. 317). However, considering the festive atmosphere of the gathering, the reader has to stay alert to the usual Melvillian trickery:

> Thus for a while. Anon ensues
> All round their horizon, ruddying it,
> Such Lights Auroral, mirth and wit—
> Thy flashes, O Falernian Muse! (p. 321)

[5] Anthon, *A Classical Dictionary*, p. 1099.
[6] *Greek Historical Thought* (Mentor Book; New York, 1953), p. 112.

The poetic voice's invocation of the muse of the fiery Falernian wine acknowledges the instinctive inspiration of the most vital creative endeavors—the imagination ruled by Dionysian passion. This conception of art runs counter to the standards of popular taste during the nineteenth century, the vogue of the picturesque based on sentimentality and genteel respectability:

> Ay. But the *Picturesque*, I wonder—
> The *Picturesque* and *Old Romance!*
> May these conform and share advance
> With Italy and the world's career? (p. 317)

As the interrogation suggests, the way of the middle-class world dictates the fashions of pictorial representation. The conformity and progress in question ironically take note of the corruption of artistic values. Even as the glazing glory of Garibaldi fades quickly from the scenes of history, so too does an appreciation of excellence in craftsmanship. Under the impact of the Industrial Revolution, materialism and mediocrity conspire to strife individual self-integrity:

> "Adieu, rosettes and point-de-vise!"
> All garnish strenuous time refuse;
> In peacocks' tails put out the eyes!
> Utility reigns—Ah, well-a-way!—
> And bustles along in Bentham's shoes.
> For the Picturesque—suffice, suffice
> The picture that fetches a picturesque price! (p. 317)

The Benthamite taste here ridiculed stresses the conversion of beauty into the greatest good for the greatest number. Such a criterion leads to the devaluation of originality and to the debasement of technique. Subject matter and treatment are controlled by the market, and reputations are determined by the prostitution of talent.

Marquis de Grandvin's attitudes reflect Melville's contempt for the cheapening of the traditions of painting by the social and economic pressures of the complacent middle class. Therefore all the opinions expressed by the company of painters are directed at a criticism of the Victorian notion of the picturesque. The various spokesmen are not bound by the conventions of respectability in any age. They are devotees of the "cheerful wine," of a life that is free, joyous, proud, and rich in its promise of experience. As a consequence they revel in any topic, however gross, that excites wit and laughter. Translated to "the Inn of Inns" by the benevolent magic of poetic artifice, they form a sainthood of immoralists. Melville's handling of this motif is, of course, influenced by FitzGerald's *Omar Khayyam* with its sensuous fatalism, its ridicule of asceticism and renunciation, and its bewildering mystical materialism. Indeed, it is the latter paradox that often finds expression in "At the Hostelry," no doubt because of the opportunity provided to burlesque Christianity:

> On themes that under orchards old
> The chapleted Greek would frank unfold,
> And Socrates, a spirit divine,
> Not alien held to cheerful wine,
> That reassurer of the soul—
> On these they chat.
>
> But more whom they,
> Even at the Inn of Inns do meet—
> The Inn with greens above the door:
> There the mahogany's waxed how bright,
> And, under chins such napkins white. (p. 334)

"Chapleted" introduces the theme of Dionysian orgy, and the "greens above the door" place the inn in a domain of nature where man is in harmony with himself. And holding forth as virtual master of ceremonies in this irreverent fantasy is that notorious Dutchman Jan Steen: "sapient spendthrift in shabby raiment, smoking his tavern-pipe and whiffing out his unconventional philosophy" (p. 328). Exchanging merry jests with him are a number of roisterers whom history has immortalized for their dissolute lives as well as their painting: Fra Lippo Lippi who, if not a defrocked priest, was always susceptible to the temptations of the flesh; Frans Hals who, though much of his personal life is lost in the shadows of time, left behind a reputation for drunken and disorderly behavior; Adriaen Brouwer who borrowed Hals' taste for debauchery and shortened his own life considerably. In affinity with the latter four, even though dissociated from them in personal habits, is still another group of protagonists of the full life. In this company is Veronese, that incomparable historian of Venetian pomp and ceremony; Peter Paul Rubens, courtier, diplomat, scholar, superlative colorist, and gorgeous naturalist; and Anthony Van Dyck, painter-in-ordinary to Charles I of England, portraitist extraordinary, and social de Grandvin. Melville also gives equal status to another category of artists, those whose devotion to naturalistic art brought painting down to the level of ordinary human visualization. Among these are the energetic Spaniard Ribera, the little Spaniard who jealously and splenetically followed his own muse; Gerald Dou who meticulously cultivated genre painting; and Tintoretto who brought to the canvas the design of colossal proportions in his extravagant absorption in sheer physicality. Artists of lesser and greater fame also participate in the dialogues or receive mention, but Melville's aim, it seems, is primarily to extol those men who closely observed life and nature before they put the brush to the canvas.

In any event, Jan Steen propounds the aspects of the picturesque to be sought,

> "In nature point, in life, in art
> Where the essential thing appears.
> First settle that," (p. 318)

and Ribera is called upon to supply pertinent examples from his own works. He chooses the *Flaying of St. Bartholomew* and *Laurence on the Gridiron*, claiming they are "done as well/As old Giotto's *Damned in Hell*" (p. 318). Frater Lippi greets this statement with an ironic jeer, and cites Guido's *Herod's Massacre* as a far better illustration of the treatment. Apart from manner, all of the paintings center on religious subjects, projecting a vision of reality consonant with a belief in Christian eschatology, in the eternal resolution of human fate as based on the dogmas of Roman Catholicism; and all of them express faith in the power of the Saviour to deliver man from temporal sorrow and suffering. But to the extent that the paintings represent the arbitrary discriminations of the poet, the reader is compelled to apprise them in the light of Marquis de Grandvin's philosophy of life. However devotional and emotional, they are gruesome and morbid in content, contemptuous of the joys of the here and now. From Herod's massacre, the prelude to the birth of Christ, to the damnation of unrepentant sinners, the picturesque is depicted in the mode of the grotesque—Melville's sardonic evaluation of supernatural history.

In the next turn of dialogue Swanevelt, a landscape painter, links da Vinci's *Medusa* with the picturesque. A cunning ironical tactic, the choice is manipulated to show that the most dramatic sacred subjects produce more or less the same emotional response as the most fantastic pagan themes:

> "Like beauty strange with horror allied,—
> As shown in great Leonardo's head
> Of snaky Medusa,—so as well
> Grace and the Picturesque may dwell
> With Terror. Vain here to divide." (p. 319)

The mordancy of this comparison is heightened by the coupling of "Grace" and the picturesque with "Terror." The equation of divine favor and a compositional technique of deformity and irregularity argues that dogma is a contrivance devised to warp thought. In fine, there is no difference between God and the Medusa. Since Melville invariably uses this monster of the underworld to symbolize unconscious anxieties and fears, then the machinery of salvation is a diabolical invention of the priesthood that operates to coerce and frighten the gullible. The fear of the Medusa therefore becomes indistinguishable from the fear of hell. In other words, theology is a dialectic of phantasmagoria, and the concept of divine grace functions to degrade earthly human integrity and dignity.

Thus Swanevelt's next contention that nature provides man with inward contentment takes the form of a substitute for religious bliss:

> "The Picturesque has many a side.
> For me, I take to Nature's scene
> Some scene select, set off serene

> With any tranquil thing you please—
> A crumbling tower, a shepherd piping.
> My master, sure, with this agrees,"
> He turned appeal on Claude here lighting.
> But he, the mildest tempered swain
> And eke discreetest, too, may be,
> That ever came out from Lorraine
> To lose himself in Arcady[.] (p. 319)

However, knowledge of Swanevelt's slavish imitations of Claude
—landscapes transfigured into shimmering illusions of distance and
peopled with figures from mythological and biblical sources—reduces his notion of the picturesque to a vapid and nostalgic retreat
from reality. He attempts to escape from life into a pastoral day-
dream. This sentimental version of man's relationship to nature
contradicts Marquis de Grandvin's amiable fatalism. In the same
context of narration there is also a derogatory representation of
Claude's picturesque illusions:

> (Sweet there to be lost, as some have been,
> And find oneself in losing e'en)
> To Claude no pastime, none, nor gain
> Wavering in theory's wildering maze;
> Better he likes, though sunny he,
> To haunt the Arcadian woods in haze,
> Intent shy charms to win or ensnare,
> Beauty his Daphne, he the pursuer there. (p. 320)

Indeed, the sentimentality of the parenthetical insertion voices
Melville's self-mocking comment on his own idyllic predilections.
As he discovered after his South Sea experiences, Christian morality does not permit innocent pleasures. Once a Daphne is raped or
seduced, even by a god, she is forever besmirched, notwithstanding
the cultivation of a poetic self-deception like Claude's. Not until
physical existence is accepted on the terms of nature does guiltless
peace come—the rose wisdom of Melville's old age.

It is this awareness that pervades the next section of the poem,
a whimsical digression by Marquis de Grandvin. "With all the
ease of a Prince of the Blood" (p. 320), he launches into jubilant
praise of the mortals who have immortalized the joys of temporality:

> "*Ma foi!* The immortals never die;
> They are not so weak, they are not so craven;
> They keep time's sea, and skip the haven.—" (p. 320)

As the image of "time's sea" (the urgencies of the moment) reveals, de Grandvin urges total involvement in experience: the haven of heaven is the retreat of the betrayers of natural man—the cowardly saints. Then, flippantly, he describes the communication supper of this imaginary elite:

> " 'Twas all in off-hand easy way—
> *Pour passer le temps,* as loungers say.
> In upper chamber did we sit
> The dolts below never dreaming it.
> The cloth was drawn—we left alone,
> No solemn lackeys looking on.
> In wine's meridian, halcyon noon,
> Beatitude excludes elation." (p. 321)

Surely the "upper chamber" of this scene is a profane parallel to the "upper room" of Christ's passover meal (Luke XXII:12). With this innuendo we are encouraged to read "lackeys" as a metaphor for the celebrants of the Eucharist. No Host is elevated in the immediate ritual; rather Marquis de Grandvin, the host, toasts the bliss of the serene comforts of time—the Dionysian gift of life.

The next canto again picks up the topic of the picturesque with some introductory byplay between Frans Hals and Van Dyck. True to his philandering principles, the former rejects mundane success for the transient moment of good fellowship shared over a glass of wine:

> " 'Tis gay," said Hals, . . .
> "And witty should be. O the cup,
> Wit rises in exhalation up!"
> And sympathetic viewed the scene.
> Then, turning, with yet livelier mien,
> "More candid than kings, less coy than the Graces,
> The pleasantness, Van, of these festival faces!—" (p. 322)

Of course, Melville's reference to "The Graces" is a pun on the royalty painted by Van Dyck, the class of society he attempted to cultivate most of his career and mostly with disillusionment. Confronted with Hals' sly needling, he remains discreetly silent. Therefore, Tintoretto, the last of the great Venetian painters of the sixteenth century, intrudes to offer his opinion on the designated topic of the dialogue:

> "This *Picturesque* is scarce my care.
> But note it now in Nature's work—
> A thatched hut settling, rotting trees
> Mossed over. Some decay must lurk:
> In florid things but small its share.
> You'll find it in Rome's squalid Ghetto,
> In Algiers at the lazaretto,
> In many a grimy slimy lair." (p. 323)

The opening sentiment offhandedly leads us into the underlying meaning of this passage, that is, if one gives credence to Vasari's disapproval of Tintoretto because he made a joke of art (and Melville knew the famous *Lives*). In short, his care is religious art only because he is given the chance to display his virtuosity in techniques of composition. Moreover, lurking behind his illustrations of the picturesque are obvious jibes at Christianity and divine providence. The "squalid Ghetto" evokes the intolerance of God's earthly institutions, even as does "the lazaretto" (a cynical pun on Lazarus) the lot of the beggared and diseased millions of His world—"blessed be *ye* poor" (Luke VI:20).

However, the brandy-blossomed Brouwer is not revolted by this ugly glimpse of reality; it provides an excuse for carousing, if any is necessary. Like a satyr in "[h]is wine-stained vesture" (p. 323), he therefore begins to ridicule Carlo Dolce for his egregious sentimentality. Dolce's characteristic figures, soft and pearly features bathed in tears with heads raised ecstatically towards the heavens, are implicitly contrasted with the squalid ghetto and the lazaretto:

> "*Grime* mark and *slime!*—Squirm not, *Sweet Charles.*"
> Slyly, in tone mellifluous
> Addressing Carlo Dolce thus,
> Fidgety in shy fellowship,
> Fastidious even to finger-tip,
> And dainty prim; "In Art the stye

Is quite inodorous. Here am I:
I don't paint *smells*, no no, no no,
No more than Huysum here, whose touch
In pinks and tulips takes us so;
But haunts that reek may harbor much;
Hey, Teniers? Give us boors at inns,
Mud floor—dark settles—jugs—old bins,
Under rafters foul with fume that blinks
From logs too soggy much to blaze
Which yet diffuse an umberish haze
That beautifies the grime, methinks." (p. 323)

So this debauched devotee of the grape, whose pictures of drunken and brutalized louts are transfigured into beauty by his brilliant coloring, expresses a love for man at his bestial worst. Though himself endowed with genius, he does not disavow his kinship with them. Throughout his life he emulates them, ever a devout worshiper of Dionysus. By proxy, then, Marquis de Grandvin (and Melville) apotheosizes the power of vinous communion to deliver man from the suffering and anxiety of temporal existence.

The next dialogue originates under the impetus of Willem Van der Velde, the greatest marine painter of the Dutch school. Dreaming of his country's outstanding naval victories, he conjures up the shades of two of its most famous admirals, De Ruyter and Van Tromp. No digression from the main stream of thematic development results from the intrusion of these masters of the sail. Rather their experiences refute the validity of the theories of linear historicism supposedly objectified in the feats of Garibaldi, that is, deterministic political, social and economic progress—"The Spirit o' the Age." Van Tromp's remembrances permit no other conclusion:

Reminiscent he sat. Some lion-heart old,
Austerely aside, on latter days cast,
So muses on glories engulfed in the Past,
And laurelled ones stranded or overrolled
By eventful Time. (p. 324)

Time gorges itself upon the greatest human achievements. All is for naught. Event after event nullify one another's effect in accord-

ance with the formula of life and death. In a similar vein of reminiscence Admiral DeRuyter confirms this inexorable truth. The sailors in the secret deeps of the sea can hope only that nature redeems
their sacrifices. Such is the implication of the allusion to Pan, a surrogate of Dionysus:

> "On Zealand's strand
> I saw the morn's rays slant 'twixt the bones
> Of the oaken *Dunderberg* broken up;
> Saw her ribbed shadow on the sand.
> Ay—picturesque! But naught atones
> For heroic navies, Pan's own ribs and knees,
> But a story now that storied made the seas!" (p. 325)

Realistically, De Ruyter concedes that the heroic virtues of individuals pass into oblivion. On the other hand, he recognizes that
pantheistic energies control the phenomenon of *anakuklosis,* the
eternal return. The deeds of the brave undergo ceaseless resurrection in corresponding human dreams and actions.

But such serious meditations are alien to the mood of those jovial guests whom death cannot terrify, the twin-souled lovers of
life's gorgeous splendors, Peter Paul Rubens and Paolo Veronese.
Slightly piqued by Dou's praise of the commonplace, the former
urges the latter to convert his canvas of a kitchen into an allegori-
cal representation of love, no doubt remembering the inspiration of
the sixteen-year old maiden who was his model in his old age:

> "Ay, hollow beats all Arabesque!
> But Phillis? Make her Venus, man,
> Peachy and plump; and for the pheasant,
> No fowl but will prove acquiescent
> Promoted into Venus' swan;
> Then in suffused warm rosy weather
> Sublime them in sun-cloud together." (p. 326)

Veronese's quick approval of this change is met with Dou's sarcastic
rejoinder:

> "O, we Dutch,
> Signor, know Venice, like her much.
> Our unction thence we got, some say,
> Tho' scarce our subjects, nor your touch." (p. 327)

This thrust is aimed at Veronese's portrayals of the sumptuous pageantry of Venetian life. His use of "unction" underscores the simulated piety of the Venetians who, as Roman Catholics, were held in contempt by the Protestant Dutch. Dou's "subjects" refer to the characteristic feature of Dutch art—its fidelity to life. Of course, Veronese's pagan exuberance has much in common with Melville's own penchant for ribaldry—how could the latter forget the *Marriage at Cana* and the wrath of the Inquisition at the license taken with the sacred subject.[7] Nonetheless, the poet sides with the Dutchman in this discrimination—a prejudice less of his ancestral antecedents than of his love of ordinary human existence.

Moreover, Melville admits of no compromise of this principle, as evidenced again in the banter between Veronese and Jan Steen. Undaunted by Dou's sharp wit or by Ribera's scorn of royalty, the irrepressible Italian persists in building castles in the air —verbal imitations of his paintings. In the spirit of Comus, the drunken God of festive mirth, he proceeds to conjure up a vision of Venetian passion and intrigue:

> "but see, on ample round
> Of marble table silver-bound
> Prince Comus, in mosaic, crowned;
> *Vin d'oro* there in crystal flutes—
> Shapely as those, good host of mine,
> You summoned ere our *Sillery* fine
> We popped to Bacchus in salutes;"—
>
> . . . .
>
> "Midmost, a Maltese knight of honor
> Toasting and clasping his Bella Donna;
> One arm round waist with pressure soft,
> Returned in throbbed transporting rhyme;
> A hand with minaret-glass aloft,
> Pinnacle of the jovial prime!" (pp. 328–29)

Of course, the allusion to Comus has a personal meaning for Melville, who despises the Puritan Milton and his theological machinery. No divine grace will stem the tide of this temptation. De-

---

[7] Some authorities attach this story to another canvas, but accuracy in this matter is less important than the association with heresy.

fender of Christianity or not, the Maltese knight will seduce or be seduced by "his Bella Donna" (look at the pun on this phrase with its rubric of capitals—beauty and poison). And the imagery bears this out. The "minaret-glass" converges with "Pinnacle of the jovial prime" (phallic desire) to symbolize the sexual fall in the making. Unimpressed or uncomprehending, Steen protests this religio-aristocratic buffoonery. For him there is no difference between a priest and a prostitute:

> "Come, a brave sketch, no mincing one!
> And yet, adzooks, to this I hold,
> Be it a cloth of frieze or cloth of gold,
> All's picturesque beneath the sun;
> I mean, all's picture; death and life
> Pictures and pendants, nor at strife—
> No, never to hearts that muse thereon.
> For me, 'tis life, plain life, I limn—
> Not satin-glossed and flossy-fine
> (Our Turburg's forte, good for him).
> No, but the life that's *wine and brine,*
> The mingled brew; the thing as spanned
> By Jan who kept the Leyden tavern
> And every rollicker fellowly scanned—
> And, under his vineyard, lo, a cavern!
> But jolly is Jan, and never in picture
> Sins against sinners by Pharisee stricture.
> Jan o' the Inn, 'tis he, for ruth,
> Dashes with fun art's canvas of truth." (pp. 329–30)

Here Steen is the mouthpiece of the stage manager of these dialogues—Marquis de Grandvin. With his wisdom keyed to natural reality, he exalts both life and death. For him the two are not "at strife." They are the two poles of cosmic equilibrium: pleasure and pain, good and evil, "*wine* and *brine*." The cup of life decants a "mingled brew," bitter and sweet. And transcendence awaits man but in "a cavern," the tomb and womb of earth where he merges once again with clay, just as De Ruyter's Pan makes of "heroic navies, [his] own ribs and knees" (p. 325). Steen does not moralize; he describes humanity in the state of Dionysian communism where sin and salvation are meaningless abstractions.

"At the Hostelry" terminates with Marquis de Grandvin's valedictory to his guests, who now relapse into a silence befitting their status of shadows. As his fantasy recedes, he reverts again to the subject of Garibaldi and the progressivistic delusions fostered by political and scientific revolutions:

> Shall coming time enhance
> Through favoring influence, or abate
> Character picturesquely great—
> That rumored age whose scouts advance?
> And costume too they touch upon:
> The Cid, his net-work shirt of mail,
> And Garibaldi's woolen one:
> In higher art would each avail
> So just expression nobly grace—
> Declare the hero in the face? (p. 334)

The interrogatory rhetoric expresses his skepticism about historical determinism, especially the developing effects of the Utopian dream. He foresees the decline of creative individualism—the rise of the featureless middle class and its obsession with conformity. Such a world would hardly tolerate the picturesque originality of his company of painters, each of whom pursued the path of his genius, not the dictates of convention. In this sense the innovations of art constitute the only bulwark against the pressures of external progress, that is, the despotism of quantity.

The sequel of the poem clearly expounds these sentiments, but now the narration is turned over to Jack Gentian, the aspiring disciple of Marquis de Grandvin. No less sarcastically, he restates the problem at issue:

> That rumored Age, whose scouts advance,
> Musters it one chivalric lance?
> Or shall it foster or abate
> Qualities picturesquely great? (p. 336)

The virtues he has in mind are both personal and professional, the artist and his art, and he also is obviously concerned with the restrictions that an atmosphere of optimism is apt to place on the subjects of treatment:

Well now, in days the gods decree,
Toward which the levellers scything move
(The Sibyl's page consult, and see)
Could this our Cid a hero prove?
What meet emprise? What plumed career?
No challenges from crimes flagitious
When all is uniform in cheer;

. . . .

In dumps and mumps, how far from menace,
Tippling some claret about deal board
Like Voltaire's kings at inn in Venice.
In fine, the dragons penned or slain,
What for St. George would then remain! (p. 336)

Melville's parenthetical expression is the guide to the tonal key of
this excerpt. Earlier he exploited the irony of the forged Sibylline
Books and their prophesy of the messianic sacrifice of Christ to
show that the Church Fathers were not averse to promoting a comforting illusion. Here Jack Gentian invokes the same analogy, but
it is applied to the current bromide of inevitable progress towards
perfection, the nineteenth-century secular substitution for religious
salvation. The reference to Voltaire's *Candide* embraces his rejection of all the consolations offered by determinists of all sorts to
mitigate the terrors of immediate experience. In this *reductio ad
absurdum* of optimism he alludes to Saint George in order to reveal how the tendencies of contemporary thought are eliminating
the need for any dependence upon the supernatural. If man alone
cures the rampant evils of temporality, then he is on the way to de-
posing God.

This interpretation of moral history inspires Jack Gentian's
parody of the future social, economic, and political Eden. The dramatic vehicle is a dialogue between two clubmen, the one old and
cynical, the other young and naive. The former speaks first:

"Assume, and say
The Red Shirt Champion's natal day
Is yet to fall in promised time,
Millennium of the busy bee;
How would he fare in such a Prime?
By Jove, Sir, not so bravely, see!

> Never he'd quit his trading trips,
> Perchance, would fag in trade at desk,
> Or, slopped in slimy slippery sludge,
> Lifelong on Staten Island drudge,
> Melting his tallow, Sir, dipping his *dips*,
> Scarce savoring much of the Picturesque!" (p. 337)

Here Melville's own experience intrudes—the twenty odd years of humdrum employment as an obscure customs inspector, checking the purchases of passengers and the cargoes of ships. Even as the energies of his genius were exhausted by this routine function of bureaucratic efficiency, so too would the emancipative vigor of a Garibaldi atrophy in servitude to the millennial economic apparatus that is in the process of displacing the prophetic empire of Christ on earth. Taking exception to this pessimistic outlook, the young man interrupts:

> "Pardon, but tallow none nor trade
> When, thro' this Iron Age's reign
> The Golden one comes in again;
> That's on the card." (p. 337)

His punning glorification of the industrial revolution, a sign of supposed intellectual enlightenment, really betrays the traditionless character of progress. Though completely uprooted from the past, he persists in interpreting his destiny in the metaphors of a cultural myth based upon cyclical time. When finally he resorts to the jargon of fortunetelling to justify his optimism, he discloses the futility of his dream of a Golden Age. Nor does the old man overlook this confusion of thought. Quickly picking up the figure of the playing card, he puns on the suit connected with ill luck:

> "She plays the spade!
> Delving days, Sir, heave in sight—
> Digging days, Sir; and, sweet youth,
> They'll set on edge the sugary tooth;
> A treadmill—Paradise they plight." (p. 337)

Carrying over the connotations of spades to delving and digging, he consigns his auditor to a symbolic grave of living death, to a wearisome round of enslavement to the machine of progress, the

implacable enemy of romantic fools. Then, ironically, the portman-
teau poetic voice intrudes to address a mock prayer to the spirit of
the times, beseeching absolution from the boredom of engineered
attitudes and values:

> Angel o' the Age! advance, God speed.
> Harvest us all good grain in seed;
> But sprinkle, do, some drops of grace
> Nor polish us into commonplace. (p. 338)

As the picturesque of the old masters has faded from these imaginary converations, so has all understanding of man's relationship to
nature. Nothing is left for anyone in love with fallible mankind except the wine of knowledge fermented from bitter experience. And
Melville drinks this draught with humor and relish.

XII The Dionysian Rose and History

INCARNATE IN THE ROSE, the wine-god consecrates his annual covenant with man in "Naples in the Time of Bomba." The revelation
converts the poet into an apostle of Bacchus or Dionysus. For the
greater part of his life obsessed by the linear movement of time,
Melville attains this self-insight only after he is able to interpret
the Neapolitan defiance of historical eventualities in its proper
light.[1] This occasion, as we have seen, is also celebrated in "At the
Hostelry" in conjunction with his examination of the significance
of Garibaldi's liberation of Italy. In denoting the picturesque—the
creative relationship of man with nature—superior to the momentary convulsions of history, Melville at last finds himself ready to
assimilate his experiences of thirty years before into the wisdom of
old age.

As the manuscript of "Naples in the Time of Bomba" indicates, he envisioned twelve structural divisions, a design coherent
with his apotheosis of the wine-god who, of course, is the Spirit of
the Year, the dying and reviving force of nature. Unfortunately,
as most students know the poem in printed form, it has been arbi-
trarily reduced to nine parts.[2] Yet the division of twelve determines Melville's strategy of irony, a plan of verbal maneuvering
which leads to the deposition of Christ from His role of Redeemer
and the ascendance of Dionysus. To add further spice to this comic
inversion, Melville connects the number with the apostles of Christ

[1] See Horsford, *Journal*, *passim*, for details of the subjective conflict that
deadened his intuitive perceptions.
[2] Granting the illegibility of certain sections, I still feel that the reader un-
acquainted with Melville's structural purpose will be deprived of a crucial
directive of interpretation. Seeking to make the poem intelligible, Vincent
can be excused for this lapse in editing.

who are His inspired voices. In effect, he contrasts the revelations of nature with their apocalyptic pronouncements.

This purpose is immediately evinced in the prose introduction to the first part of the poem, for Melville openly renounces the Heavenly City of St. John the Divine for the temporal joy of the worldly city of Naples: "Jack Gentian drives out, and is unexpectedly made the object of a spontaneous demonstration more to be prized by an appreciative recipient than the freedom of the city of New Jerusalem presented in a diamond box by a deputation from the Crown Council of Seraphim" (p. 339). The substance of this hyperbole is drawn from the following passage in Revelation, "And I, John, saw the holy city, new Jerusalem, coming down from God out of heaven, prepared as a bride adorned for her husband" (XXI:2), and is devised to show how Melville's Jack (John) awakens to the realization that paradise has to be regained on earth:

> Behind a span whose cheery pace
> Accorded well with gala trim—
> Each harness, in arch triumphal reared,
> With festive ribbons fluttering gay;
> In Bomba's Naples sallying forth
> In season when the vinyards mellow,
> Suddenly turning a corner round—
> Ha, happy to meet you, Punchinello! (p. 339)

All living things participate in the rites of jubilation that celebrate the ripening of the Dionysian grape. As for man, he ceases to be a historical being. Instead he enacts that role which brings him into empathy with the unfolding drama of the seasons. Such a perception underlies Jack Gentian's reaction to the appearance of Punchinello, the burlesque impersonator of the wine-god. Thus when the clown performs not "far from shrine in niche of wall" (p. 339), he is not impelled to do so by religious belief:

> His rug or bed
> In midmost way a tumbler spread,
> A posturing mountebank withall;
> Who, though his stage was out of doors,
> *Brought down the house* in jolly applause. (p. 339)

Rather he revels in the sheer intoxication of life, in the release from the repressive decorums of church morality. Jack Gentian's response to this exhibition takes a similar direction, though he is at first astonished by the reception of the onlookers, illogically attributing their sense of fellowship to social propriety. Unused to demonstrations of spontaneous feelings, he seeks a rational explanation for the behavior. This response is typical of the self-conscious Puritan who has been taught to distrust emotions:

> Catching an impulse from their air,
> To feet I spring, my beaver doff
> And broadcast wave a blithe salute.
> In genial way how humorsome
> What pleased responses of surprise;
> From o'er the Alps, and so polite!
> They clap their hands in frank acclaim
> Matrons in door-ways nod and smile
> From balcony roguish girls laugh out
> Or kiss their fingers, rain their nosegays down. (pp. 340–41)

Showered by affection and flowers, he begins to view the experience in terms of an initiation into the cult of the wine-god. The merry-makers actualize in his thought the instinctual freedom that he has failed to exercise:

> No, nor young Bacchus through glad Asia borne,
> Pelted with grapes, exulted so
> As I in hackney-landeau here
> Jolting and jouncing thro' the waves
> Of confluent commoners who in glee
> Good natured past before my prow. (p. 341)

This self-deification springs from the awakening of primal emotions. The modern surrogates of the worshipping satyrs and maenads bring him into harmony with his inward nature and rejuvenate his true identity, the being of flesh and blood too long warped by the restraints and reticences of civilization.

In thus reliving the experiences of his alter ego, Melville conjures up the past with all of its inward conflicts in order to recapture those ineffable moments of union with the churning heart of nature. The endeavor reverses the movement of time in the sequence of past, present, and future. For in bringing order to the chaos of the past, he creates a new self with its infinite possibilities of holistic fulfillment. He dies completely to the old divided Melville, exorcising in the poetic act all the poisons of doubt and unhope that had so long burdened his consciousness and conscience. We can observe the subjective struggle between linear and cyclical time in the next phase of the retrospective narration. Separated from the festive climate of Bacchus, Jack Gentian reassumes his own cultural identity and proceeds to ponder the historical predicament of Naples, the tyranny of Bomba:

> Flattered along by following cheers
> We sped; I musing here in mind,
> Beshrew me, needs be overdrawn
> Those shocking stories bruited wide,
> In England which I left but late,
> Touching dire tyranny in Naples. (p. 341)

He calls down curses upon himself because events supposedly are out of key with immediate reality. He still thinks that life is produced and shaped by human activity, by external forces. In effect, he remains bound by the intellectual conditioning of "The Spirit o' the Age." He does not realize that the freedom of the Neapolitans is an instinctive possession, not a willed attitude of frivolity:

> True freedom is to be care-free!
> And care-free seem the people here
> A truce indeed they seem to keep
> Gay truce to care and all her brood. (p. 342)

Obviously, Melville seeks to reconcile his misunderstood experiences of the past to the mellow wisdom crystallized in "At the Hostelry" and *Weeds and Wildings*. Therefore next he undertakes to relate the growth of Jack Gentian's self-understanding to the comprehension of the true meaning of ephemeral political despotism. Perceiving that the Neapolitans are not cowed by a show of military strength, he concludes that they are armored against fear by their fidelity to the joys of life, regardless of the enveloping circumstances:

In serious sort my way I hold,
Till revery, taking candor's tone
With optimistic influence plead:
Sad, bad, confess; but solace bides!
For much has Nature done, methinks,
In offset here with kindlier aim.
If bayonets flash, what vineyards glow!
Of all these hells of wrath and wrong
How little feels the losel light
Who, thrown upon the odorous sod
In this indulgent clime of charm
Scarce knows a thought or feels a care
Except to take his careless pleasure:
A fig for Bomba! life is fair
Squandered in superabundant leisure! (p. 344)

Jack Gentian's intuitions are sounder than all of his logical speculations. Though inclined to dualistic judgments, he manages to curb the impulse and to acknowledge that the procreative light of the sun cannot be blotted out by its own reflections, that no interlude of callous slaughter can impede the everlasting resurgence of life. In the midst of death Dionysian nature always girds herself for another birth and another beginning. According to one nineteenth-century mythographer, it is the secret of the wine-god's irresistible appeal for instinctual man: "The vine was not the only, but the most perfect, expression of this earth-life; and as the new force that appeared in the grape resulted from the combined effects of earth-moisture and sun-heat, it waxed more and more potent from spring to vintage; but since it shared in the general torpor of winter, we may think of the growth, fruitage, and decay of the vine as expressing the life of Nature in what might be called 'the rejoicing and the sorrowing of vegetation.' " [3] Biographically, it was only under the benign sun of the Neapolitan skies that Melville, for a fleeting moment thirty years earlier, overcame his dread of the frightening antinomies of existence. Hence from the vantage point in which he wrote the poem he, necessarily, had to recapture the brief interlude of communion with nature that became the source of the inward balance in his old age. He had to return to the inspi-

[3] S. A. Scull, *Greek Mythology Systematized* (Phila., 1880), pp. 199–200.

ration of the fertile, female earth that gave birth to Dionysus and his cult of worshipers.

Almost immediately following this resolution of cosmic contradictions, a revery by Jack Gentian recalls Melville's blind involvement in the portents and signs of history:

> Ah, could one but realities rout
> A holiday-world it were, no doubt.
> But Naples, sure she lacks not cheer,
> Religion, it is jubilee here—
> Feast follows festa thro' the year;
> And then such Nature all about!
> No surly moor of forge and mill,
> She charms us glum barbarians still,
> Fleeing from frost, bad bread, or duns,
> Despotic *Biz*, and devils blue. (p. 345)

These observations disclose the uncertainty that plagued Melville throughout his trip. Never quite able to trust his own intuitions, he allowed the incidental turmoil of the world to blight his innocent pleasures. Here, for instance, his alter ego debates the respective reality of nature, religion, and secular obligations, yet Gentian has already indicated his subjective preference. When he finally does assert his self-integrity, it is virtually a gesture of bravado:

> They win this clime of more than spice,
> These myrtled shores, to wait the boat
> That ferries (so the pilots say),
> Yes, ferries to the isles afloat,
> The floating isles of Paradise
> In God's Ægean far away!
> O, scarce in trivial tenor all,
> Much less to mock man's mortal sigh,
> Those syllables proverbial fall,
> *Naples, see Naples, and—then die!* (p. 345)

Indeed, concealed behind this fantasy of escape is a death wish, a desire to resolve his emotional and spiritual despair by any expedient. The plaintive longing for a perfect world contradicts his immediate experience. As the Neapolitans prove, happiness and joy can co-exist with historical anguish, the deprivations of Bomba's military dictatorship.

has another wand in mind as her caressing fingers indicate. She is an emissary from the garden of love:

> And rounding by the bay
> Nigh Edens parked along the verge,
> Brief halt was made amid the press;
> And, instantaneous thereupon,
> A buoyant nymph on odorous wing
> Alighting on the landeau-step,
> Half-hovering like a humming-bird,
> A flower pinned to my lapelle,
> Letting a thrill from finger brush
> (Sure, unaware) the sensitive chin;
> Yes, badged me in a twinkling bright
> With O a red and royal rose;
> A rose just flowering from the bud. (pp. 347–48)

Since this incident occurs immediately after Jack Gentian's exposure to the martial din of Bomba's mercenary troops, it seems evident that Melville wishes to call attention to the hero's obsession with historical time (so reliving in humorous self-ridicule his own angular past). For how quickly seriousness fades when the little baggage touches his "purse," a pun on scrotum familiar to every student of Shakespeare:

> my landeau rocked,
> The ribbons streamed; while, ruddy now,
> Flushed with the rose's reflex bloom
> I dwelt no more on things amiss:
> Come, take thine ease; lean back, my soul;
> The world let spin; what signifies?
> Look, she, the flower-girl—what recks she
> Of Bomba's sortie? what indeed!
> Fine sortie of her own, the witch,
> But now she made upon my purse,
> And even a craftier sally too! (p. 348)

The dramatic pattern of this scene hardly requires any further explication. Witch or bitch, the flower-girl raises his spirits, and from this moment on the rose figures the way of deliverance from repression and guilt, from shame and blame.

As the prose epigraph to the next section of the poem indicates, Melville's narrator begins to realize that he faces a crisis in personal existence: "Giving way to thoughts less cheerful than archaic, he is checked by a sportive sally from the Rose. But is anew troubled, catching sight of an object attesting a Power even more nitrous and menacing than the Bomb-King himself. In short, another and greater crowned artilleryman, a capricious denominator, impossible to dethrone, and reigning by right incontestably divine. Pondering which discouraging fact, once more our genial friend is twitted by the festive Mentor" (p. 348). He has to subscribe to either the belief that life is an unalterable product of history or that history is an accidental condition of life. Still affected by the exhilarating encounter with the girl, he is impelled to meditate on her surrogate, the rose, in order to probe the foundations of his uncertain self-identity. Paradoxically, with all of his attempts to analyze the experience logically, he cannot separate thought from emotion, that is, the objective from the subjective world. Though his feelings are pleasantly titillated, he is afraid to trust their integrity:

> What blandishment in clime, or else
> What subtler influence, my rose,
> From thee exhaled, thou Lydian one,
> Seductive here could flatter me
> Even in emotion not unfelt
> While fleeting from that warmish pair! (p. 349)

This state of ambivalence frustrates the resolution of the conflict projected in the images of heat, and therefore he turns to the past for understanding. But Vergil's legendary tomb on the promontory of Pausilippo bespeaks the impermanence of the glories of history and of epical triumphs. Eventual paradises are forever threatened by the anarchic forces of contingency, in this case the hellish fires of Vesuvius:

> I mused on Vergil, here inurned
> On Pausilippo, legend tells—
> Here on the slope that pledges ease to pain,
> For him a pledge assuredly true
> If here indeed his ashes be—

Rome's laureat in Rome's palmy time;

. . . .

What Mohawk of a mountain 'lours!
A scalp-lock of Tartarian smoke. (p. 349)

This vision of reality mocks the ability of man to transcend his finitude. Death and annihilation stand in attendance on life. As the
Tartarian allusion further implies, man, symbolically, is a prisoner
of nature. He cannot escape the fate that she decrees for living
things.

Perceiving this fact, Jack Gentian dismisses the ultimate significance of historical events:

> The Siren's seat for pleasurists lies
> Betwixt two threatening bombardiers
> Their mortars loaded, linstocks lit—
> Vesuvius yonder—Bomba here.
> Events may Bomba's batteries spike:
> But how with thee, sulphurous Hill
> Whose vent far hellward reaches down! (pp. 349–50)

Yet, strangely enough, he still degrades the intrinsic value of physical bliss, of the Dionysian joys that alternate with the sorrow of
unfolding Time. Almost sadistically, he enthrones diabolic circumstance as the sovereign god of the universe. After this splenetic
outburst, he seems to move towards a more reconciliatory outlook
on the human plight when confronted by the contradictory motifs
of life and death that pagan sculptors saw fit to memorialize:

> Ah, funeral urns of time antique
> Inwrought with flowers in gala play,
> Whose form and bacchanal dance in freak,
> Even as of pagan time ye speak
> Type ye what Naples is alway?
> Yes, round these curved volcanic shores,
> Vined urn of ashes, bed on bed,
> Abandonment as thoughtless pours
> As when the revelling pagan led. (p. 350)

However, intellectually he yearns for a formula to explain the
sights, even if it is a theory of pessimism. This is characteristic of
historical consciousness. It wants order in disorder, purpose in pur-

poselessness. Uncomplicated *joie de vivre* has no appeal for the determinist who mistakes the bloom of the Rose for the thorns:

> And here again I droopt the brow,
> And, lo, again I saw the Rose,
> The red red ruddy and royal Rose!
> Expanded more from bud but late
> Sensuous it lured, and took the tone
> Of some light taunting Cyprian gay
> In shadow deep of college-wall
> Starting some museful youth afoot—
> "Mooning in mind? Ah, lack-a-day!" (p. 350)

Overwhelmed by depression, Jack Gentian looks at the flower through the crossed-eyes of an atheist who still clings to the Christian belief in original sin. As a consequence, he has no recourse except to hate the natural process that gave him life without happiness. Thus the Rose metamorphoses into a seductive Cyprian, a prostitute who has corrupted the ideal of love. Ironically, the original Cyprians were priestesses in the temple of Aphrodite, the archetypal goddess of love who personified the feminine principle in nature and who was the mother of Eros, the cosmogonic power of unity in the world. Her degradation by Jack Gentian illustrates his emotional disorientation, his fear of sexuality. "Mooning in mind," which is to say indulging in loony fancies, he betrays his failure, "Ah, lack-a-day," to come to terms with Dionysian time.

The epigraph to the succeeding phase of narration stresses this fact, for he "falls into an untimely fit of historic reminiscences. For which dereliction, the Rose . . . touchingly upbraids him" (p. 350). The use of "untimely" subtly functions to depreciate his desire to find an absolute pattern of destiny in external events. This compulsion, it must not be forgotten, represents the psychological displacement of faith by reason, of Christianity by scientism, of God by man, in the nineteenth century. But this quest for certitude is hopeless in a contingent universe, as the symbolic import of the song and the juggling act indicate:

> "The balls, hey! the balls,
> Cascatella of balls—
> Baseless arches I toss up in air!

Spinning we go,—
Now over, now under;
High Jack is Jack low,
And never a blunder!
Come hither—go thither:
But wherefor nowhither?
I lose them—I win them,
From hand to hand spin them,
Reject them, and seize them
And toss them, and tease them,
And keep them forever in air,
All to serve but a freak of my glee!" (p. 351)

Here is depicted the causeless, capricious play of circumstance in a universe presided over by a self-absorbed jester-god. Or analogously, so man is disported by the perpetual activity of nature. Whether he chooses to or not, he participates in this endless game. Wisdom obtains when he realizes that this is his role in life—to play the game of the moment:

"Sport ye thus with your spoonies, ye fair,
For your mirth? nor even forbear
To juggle with Nestors your thralls?
Do ye keep them in play with your smiling and frowning,
Your flirting, your fooling, abasing and crowning,
And dance them as I do these balls?" (pp. 351–52)

To the extent the juggling reflects the ceaseless act of creation, the procreative dynamics of the eternal feminine, man is irresistibly attracted to woman, hence the euphemistic description of sexual dalliance, of frolicking seduction and coition. In effect, this song ironically comments on Jack Gentian's failure to take the day of pleasure and joy. Melville proceeds to emphasize the bawdry in the impressions of his hero, especially bent upon disclosing his unconscious lust:

. . . like Mercury dropped from heaven,
Precipitate there a tumbler flew,
Alighting on winged feet; then sang,
Dancing at whiles, and beating time,
Clicking his nimble heels together
In hornpipe of the gamesome kid. (p. 352)

259

Mercury as Hermes, of course, is a trickster god, symbolically the personification of the phallus, "a disobedient and self-willed thing it is," as Plato remarks in Timæus (91B), "like an animal that will not listen to reason." Yet, by the same token, the messenger of the gods is an intermediary between the upper and lower worlds (reason and instinct), a guide or psychopompos who is the bearer of momentous revelations. So Jack Gentian perceives him in his orgiastic goat dance, but his problem is to recognize that the demonstration is meant to reconcile him to Dionysian naturalism. The subsequent song unfolds as a paean to the wine-press, and its celebration of both vinous and sensual intoxication posits the worship of the goddess of love. However, there is more than pure eroticism involved. The performance likewise consecrates the universal principle of fertility that sustains nature and the human community. This benevolent feudalism cannot survive in the atmosphere of the kind of individualism that Jack Gentian cultivates. Though his plight is pitiable, it is the product of self-conceit and self-pity. On the other hand, the goat-song encourages ritual forgetfulness, a union with the wine-god which succeeds in "[d]rowning thinking" and egoity (p. 353):

"Over mines, by vines
That take hot flavor
From Vesuvius—
Hark, in vintage
Sounds the tabor!

"In brimstone-colored
Tights or breeches
There the Wag-fiend
Dancing teaches;

"High in wine-press
Hoop elastic
Pigeon-wings cut
In rite fantastic;

"While the black grape
Spiriting, gushing,
Into red wine!
Foameth rushing!

> "Which wine drinking,
> Drowning thinking,
> Every night-fall,
> Heard in Strada,
> Kiss the doves
> And coos the adder!" (pp. 352–53)

Structurally the dithyramb objectifies a tension between Christian and Dionysian imagery. The wine is, symbolically and literally, a produce of hell-fire, the grapes growing on the hot slopes of a volcano. The dance of the trickster devil is unquestionably sexual, and his vintage is an aphrodisiac. But all the Wag-fiend's attributes are those of Dionysus, a shift in identity manipulated by the Church to denigrate the pagan ecstasies of the flesh. Aware of this fact, Melville in turn converts the pigeons (Aphrodite's birds) into lascivious surrogates of the Holy Spirit who sanctify the bleeding grape in their mating act. Thus they naturalize the wine that excites the lust of lovers on the streets of Naples.

Jack Gentian, however, will not surrender his personal identification to the anonymity of Dionysian revelry. He still seeks to construe human destiny in historical terms. As a consequence he lapses into a meditation on the blood-stained past of Naples. Stubbornly, he refuses to profit from his exposure to the mysteries of psychological and physical rejuvenation. But rebelling against this tendency, the rose, the symbol of instinctual knowledge, protests:

> But intervening here, my Flower,
> Opening yet more in bloom the less,
> Maturing toward the wane,—low breathed,
> Again? and quite forgotten me?
> You wear an Order, me, the Rose,
> To whom the favoring fates allot
> A term that shall not bloom outlast;
> No future's mine, nor mine a past.
> Yet I'm the Rose, the flower of flowers.
> Ah, let time's present time suffice,
> No Past pertains to Paradise. (pp. 354–55)

Not only does the Rose assert the primacy of the moment, but in addition she repudiates the logic of linear time. For her there is no future because when she blows, paradoxically she achieves the past. Otherwise she is content with her different states of being, not with illusions of becoming—the burden of the historico-religious sensibility of Jack Gentian. Nonetheless the Rose's expostulation does induce him to clarify his thinking on the subject:

> Time present. Well, in present time
> It chanced a lilting note I heard,
> A fruit girl's. . . . (p. 355)

Obviously, this is not a mere verbal quibble. He is fascinated by a distinction that he cannot articulate. "Time present" refers to time in the sense of duration, something measurable, extensible, and continuable. So it emerges in his equation of time and history. For him the chronicle of Naples is a succession of political (and moral) crimes. In this perspective time is profane, estranged from divine influence. The "present time" of the fruit girl is mythic; her song is inspired by ritual precedent, the tradition of seasonal festivals. Thus her experience of time is sacred since it is in harmony with one of the cyclical manifestations of the Spirit of the Year, Dionysus. Unconsciously, Jack Gentian abhors the profane time of history, but, intellectually, he is a product of his cultural conditioning and therefore assumes that progress is an inherent dynamic in the structure and development of human society. What he does not discern is that in all of his judgments on Neapolitan affairs he ultimately is confronted with his own rootless subjectivity. Conversely, the tumbler, the peri, and now the fruit-girl are not especially overwrought by the immediate political situation simply because they look upon daily existence as a cyclical rehearsal of the suffering and joy, the sorrow and hope, the death and resurrection of the immortal wine-god. Thus the fruit-girl sings not of herself but of her role as the eternal woman, the sacrificial virgin:

> "Love-apples, love-apples!
> All dew, honey-dew,
> From orchards of Cyprus—
> Blood-oranges too!
>
> "Will you buy? prithee, try!
> They grew facing south;

See, mutely they languish
To melt in your mouth!

" 'Tis now, take them now
In the hey-day of flush,
While the crisis is on,
And the juices can gush!

"Love-apples, love-apples,
All dew, honey-dew,
From orchards of Cyprus—
Blood-oranges, too!" (p. 355)

The love-apples, of course, are pomegranates, the symbols of fertility sacred to Persephone and Dionysus (her son in the Eleusinian
mysteries). Grown on the island of Cyprus, they also figure the
power of Aphrodite. Along with the blood-oranges, they attest the
pain and pleasure of sexual union, of death (defloration) and resurrection (fruition). In fine, the girl's song affirms the revelations
of nature on the biocosmic plane of existence as she pleads with
man to spur on the flow of universal creation. Her warning that
"the crisis is on" stipulates the need for a ritual sanctification of
fertility if he is to survive the impending winter. As "the hey-day
of flush" specifies, the urgency of the moment must be met, else
the despot Bomba will establish the domination of profane time.

As before, Jack Gentian allows the historical past to darken
his perceptions into the present, and fails to heed the message of
the flower-girl:

Warbling and proffering them she went,
And passed, and left me as erewhile,
For the dun annals would not down. (p. 356)

On this occasion he considers the attempt of a patriotic Neapolitan
fisherman to overthrow the rule of the Spanish in 1647. The fisherman apparently succeeds, but then his own people betray him. Patently, Jack Gentian's melodramatic representation of the affair discloses his inability to comprehend its logic:

The darling of the mob; nine days
Their great Apollo; then, in pomp
Of Pandemonium's red parade,

His curled head Gorgoned on the pike,
And jerked aloft for God to see. (p. 356)

The allusion to Pandemonium captures Gentian in the act of not
only converting Satan and his followers into the sovereign powers
of the universe but also venting his scorn of Milton's theodicy. By
the same token, he begins to ridicule himself for his unwillingness
to recognize that the monsters of the deep all reside in human unconsciousness—the instincts turned into devouring Gorgons under
the tyranny of fear and cowardice. He realizes that his disillusionment has sprung from an intellectual and moral confusion over the
meaning of freedom:

A portent, Yes, and typed the years
Red after-years, and whirl of error
When Freedom linkt with Furies raved
In Carmagnole and cannibal hymn,
Mad song and dance before the ark
From France imported with *The Terror!*
To match the poison, mock the clime,
Hell's cornucopia crammed with crime!
Scarce cheerful here the revery ran. (p. 357)

Surveying the later French Revolution in the same perspective, he
cynically concludes that there is no such thing as freedom divorced
from an empathy with nature and her gods. This epiphany emanci-
pates Jack Gentian from his infatuation with linear historicism. Almost in a rage of self-insight, he implicitly contrasts the vengeful
murders of the fanatical mobs with the self-sacrificing gestures of
the two Persephones encountered on his journey around Naples.
Both of them displayed their inward possession of freedom in vol-
unteering to die (to engage in the ritual sexual intercourse man-
dated by Dionysus). So they attested the doctrine of redemptive
love that subsumes his annual death and resurrection. This awareness is crystallized in Jack Gentian's phrase, "Hell's cornucopia."
The oxymoron constitutes a sacral pronouncement of his submission
to the will of nature. The pagan symbol of the fruitful earth does
not bear the profane harvests of history. No wonder, then, that his
Dionysian monitor remains silent:

Nor did my Rose now intervene,
Full opening out in dust and sun
Which hurried along that given term,
She said would never bloom outlast. (p. 357)

The "dust and sun" legitimate the one marriage of life and death that the wise man cherishes above and beyond the bloodshed of human strife.

As a direct extension of Jack Gentian's epiphany, the next turn of the poem presents a ritual abolition of history. A Levantine gamin pours out an extemporaneous song that dispatches Bomba and his might to the limbo of triviality. An epigraph again serves as the rubric of interpretation: "He encounters a prepossessing little tatterdemalion Triton, shell in hand, dewy in luminous spray of a rainbowed fountain. [He] . . . entertains his street-audience accordingly with certain improvisations partaking alike of the sentiment and devil-may-care incident to the Neapolitan" (p. 357). The boy voices the inarticulate knowledge of the deepest instincts. His shell, the *concha veneris* of the foam-born Aphrodite, bespeaks the supreme power of sexual love that unites, sustains, and perpetuates the green world of Dionysus.

Jack Gentian's sketch of his mundane antecedents does not degrade either his sacred role or his vatic message. Ubiquitous, he manifests the irrepressible vitality of the nature-god whose redemptive activities have been forced underground by the ignorance of an artificial civilization. He still communicates with the bulk of humanity, a psychopompos who adjusts his tongue and his thought to its now corrupted emotional impulses:

A weed of life, a sea-weed he
From the Levant adventuring out;
A cruiser light, like all his clan
Who, in repletion's lust for more,
And penury's strife for daily bread,
As licensed by compassionate heaven
To privateer it on their wits,
The Mid Sea rove from quay to quay,
At home with Turban, Fez, or Hat;
Ready in French, Italian, Greek—

265

Linguists at large; alert to serve
As chance interpreters or guides;
Suave in address, with winning ways—
Arch imps of Pandarus, a few;
Others with improvising gift
Of vowelled rhyme in antic sort,
Or passionate, spirited by their sun
That ripens them in early teens;
And some with small brown fingers slim
Busier than the jackdaw's bill.

But *he*, what gravity is his!
Precociously sedate indeed
In beauty sensuously serene.
White-draped, and ranked aloft in choir
A treble clear in rolling laud
Meet would he look on Easter morn. (p. 358)

Confidence man, pimp, and pickpocket, he teaches contempt for all
the moral and social proprieties that frustrate spontaneity and freedom. Immoralist and trickster, like the phallus that he incarnates,
he exalts the sinlessness and innocence of primitive eros. Not a
trained robot in a choir loft, his psalm of praise for human salvation is informed by the pure beauty of the endlessly renewed year.

Consistent with Jack Gentian's description, the disfranchised
priest of Dionysus recites his proscribed liturgy directly under the
inspiration of the eternal love goddess:

, . . . in posture grave,
With sidelong leaning head intent,
The shell's lips to his listening ear. (p. 360)

Translating Aphrodite's occult revelations into a message befitting
the crisis of Naples, he advocates a rebellion against Bomba.
Though he professes to speak in the name of Parthenope, a siren,
actually he endows her with all the attributes of Aphrodite. It is
difficult to determine the purpose behind Melville's shape-shifting
here. However, as the mythic founder of the city, she personifies
its extraordinary earthly fertility. In this sense the despot is her an-
tagonist because he thwarts the worship of her abundant fruits.
The allusion to metheglin, an aphrodisiac, hints that her people re-

sort to drink in order to assuage their fears. Instead it should arouse them to sacrifices for the freedom to utilize the honey of love:

> "Metheglin befuddles this freak o' the sea,
> Humming, low humming—in brain a bee!
>
> "Hymns it of Naples her myriads warming?
> Involute hive in fever of swarming.
>
> "What Hades of sighs in irruption suppressed,
> Suffused with huzzahs that buzz in arrest!
>
> "Neapolitans, ay, 'tis the soul of the shell
> Intoning your Naples, Parthenope's bell.
>
> "O couch of the Siren renowned thro' the sea
> That enervates Salerno, seduces Baiæ;
>
> "I attend you, I hear; but how to resolve
> The complex of conflux your murmurs involve!" (p. 360)

Confronted with this paralysis of will power, the young priest of erotic bliss indicates his determination to find a solution for their predicament.

Thereupon he counsels his auditors to seek strength in the juice of the grapes, that is, to exercise their prerogative to live or die by their own choice:

> "*Grapes, ripe grapes!*
> In cheer evading;
>
> "Lazarus' plaint
> All vines upbraiding;
>
> "*Crick-crick-crack*
> Of fusillading!" (p. 361)

So he encourages them to scorn Christian resignation to the disruptions of history. He asserts that life in time with all its sufferings and deprivations transcends the eternal bliss of an impotent Lazarus. As Melville manipulates this dialectic, it is obvious that he is mocking the vicarious atonement of Christ and upholding man's integrity to face death without dread. Guns, therefore, invite comparison with the innocuous sound of grasshoppers. Together these in-

sinuations function to undermine all the linear formulas of historical and spiritual destiny. Since death awaits all things, man has to
fulfill himself in the province of nature. This truth is confirmed
when Jack Gentian glances at his Rose and observes its fate:

> Then first it was I chanced to note
> Some rose-leaves fluttering off in air,
> While on my lap lay wilted ones.
> Ah, Rose, that should not bloom outlast—
> Now leaf by leaf art leaving me? (p. 364)

This incident anticipates the boy's final judgment on the outcome
of Bomba's temporal rule. Nothing that the upstart king can do
will survive the annihilation of the Dionysian world:

> "Lo, the King's men
> They go marching!
> O, the instep
> Haughty arching!—
> *Live the King!*
>
> "What's the grin for—
> Queer grimacing?
> Who, yon grenadiers
> Outfacing,
> Here dare sing
> Ironically—
> *Live the King?*" (p. 364)

Song by song, the divinely inspired priest of the immortal gods of
nature has ritualistically dramatized the abolition of the profane
time of history.

The last section of the poem, the twelfth in the manuscript,
ostensibly exalts the mystic Rose of Christianity and the authority
of sacramental time. The procession of the Host through the
streets (the medium of the Sacrament of Extreme Unction) apparently is far more efficacious in bringing the semi-insurgent popula-
tion to their knees than the military power of Bomba. Temporality
ceases to have meaning in the perspective of eternity:

> A hush falls; and the people drop
> Stilly and instantaneous all
> As plumps the apple ripe from twig

And cushions motionless in sod.
My charioteer reins short—transfixed;
The very mountebanks, they kneel;
And idlers, all along and far,
Bow over as the *host* moves on—
Bow over, and for time remain
Like to Pompeiian masquers caught
With fluttering garb in act of flight,
For ages glued in deadly drift. (p. 366)

This outward expression of awe and devotion, however, shocks rather than amazes Jack Gentian. At least Melville's allusion to the catastrophe of Pompeii suggests the sudden advent of a curse, not a blessing. Whereas the same observers earlier shared the exhilaration of the pagan rebel, now they cower in fear:

Yet scarce as men who mirth await—
More like crowds that wait eclipse,
So gravely sobering seems to fall
Those light lilt chimes now floating near. (p. 366)

The reaction, wholly out of harmony with the absolution and peace of the Viaticum to be administered, ironically parallels their response to Bomba's soldiers:

"No more larking,
No more laughing,
No more chattering
Nay, nor chaffing—
    All is *glum!*" (p. 362)

The emotional and moral disparagement of the Catholic rites of passage reflects Melville's blanket rejection of the supernatural machinery of salvation. As Jack Gentian reports the effects of the procession, it operates to pervert an adjustment to the inescapable dislocations of human existence. By contrast with the consoling implications of Dionysian ritual, it intensifies the terrors of time. But not so for Jack Gentian. He heeds only the final epiphany of the Rose:

But, look, the Rose, brave Rose, is where?
Last petals falling, and its soul
Of musk dissolved in empty air! (p. 367)

Vicariously, then, Melville has resolved the enigma of human destiny. In the apotheosis of the rose and the wine he has achieved a reconciliation with nature. In the cycle of dissolution and metamorphosis symbolized in the dying and reviving Dionysus he has found the solace for all sorrows.

Nor can there be any doubt that Melville's creative activity in his old age served to exorcise all the disillusionments of his young adulthood. It enabled him to impose the order of art upon the chaos of experience. For, as he looks back upon the finished work, he sees its wholeness and unity, a well wrought urn in which the essence of truth is incarnate:

> And here this draught at hazard drawn,
> Like squares of fresco newly dashed,
> Cools, hardens, nor will more receive,
> Scarce even the touch that mends a slip:
> The plaster sets; quietus—bide. (p. 367)

Thus, without a qualm, he comes to terms with life; he now awaits only death. Therefore he looks back upon Garibaldi's deliverance of Naples as a glorious event in time doomed to fade and to blow like the beauty of the Rose:

> But Garibaldi—Naples' host
> Uncovers to her deliverer's ghost.
> While down time's aisle, mid clarions clear
> Pale glory walks by valor's bier. (p. 367)

And in a final gesture of self-mockery he humorously chides himself for his sentimental preoccupation with the past:

> Pale "Glory-walks-by-Valor's bier."
> Now why a catafalque in close?
> No relish I that stupid cheer
> Ringing down the curtain on the Rose. (p. 368)

Thus he inters his historical obsessions in the tomb with "The Spirit o' the Age," the contemporary illusion of inevitable progress. At this point "The Spirit of the Year," incarnate in the wine and the rose, is enough to ease the travail of old age.

Selected Bibliography

ALL THE MELVILLE scholars and critics listed below have, in one way or another, influenced my thinking in the course of writing this book.

ARVIN, NEWTON. *Herman Melville.* New York: William Sloane, 1950.

BAIRD, JAMES R. *Ishmael: A Study of the Symbolic Mode in Primitivism.* Baltimore: Johns Hopkins University Press, 1956.

BARRETT, LAURENCE. "The Differences in Melville's Poetry." PMLA, LXX (Sept. 1955), 606–623.

BEZANSON, WALTER E. "Melville's Reading of Arnold's Poetry." PMLA, LXIX (June 1954), 365–391.

————, ed. *Clarel: A Poem, and Pilgrimage in the Holy Land.* New York: Hendricks House, 1960.

BRASWELL, WILLIAM. *Melville's Religious Thought.* Durham, N. C.: Duke University Press, 1943.

BRIDGMAN, RICHARD. "Melville's Roses." *Texas Studies in Literature and Language,* VIII (Summer 1966), 235–244.

BROOKS, VAN WYCK. *The Times of Melville and Whitman.* New York: Dutton, 1947.

COHEN, HENNIG, ed. *The Battle-Pieces of Herman Melville.* New York: Thomas Yoseloff, 1963.

————, ed. *Selected Poems of Herman Melville.* New York: Doubleday, 1964.

DAVIS, MERREL R. and WILLIAM H. GILMAN, eds. *The Letters of Herman Melville.* New Haven: Yale University Press, 1960.

FIESS, EDWARD. "Melville as Reader and Student of Byron." *American Literature,* XXIV (May 1952), 186–194.

FOGLE, RICHARD HARTER. "The Themes of Melville's Later Poetry." *Tulane Studies in English,* XI (1961), 65–86.

HAYFORD, HARRISON and MERTON M. SEALTS, JR., eds. *Billy Budd.* Chicago: University of Chicago Press, 1962.

HORSFORD, HOWARD C., ed. *Herman Melville: Journal of a Visit to Europe and the Levant.* Princeton: Princeton University Press, 1955.

HOWARD, LEON. *Herman Melville: A Biography.* Berkeley: University of California Press, 1951.

LEYDA, JAY. *The Melville Log: A Documentary Life of Herman Melville,* 1819–1891. New York: Harcourt, Brace, 1951. 2 vols.

MATTHIESSEN, F. O. *American Renaissance: Art and Expression in the Age of Emerson and Whitman.* New York: Oxford University Press, 1941.

METCALF, ELEANOR MELVILLE. *Herman Melville: Cycle and Epicycle.* Cambridge: Harvard University Press, 1953.

————. *Herman Melville: Journal of a Visit to London and the Continent,* 1848–1850. Cambridge: Harvard University Press, 1948.

MILLER, PERRY. *The Raven and the Whale.* New York: Harcourt, Brace, 1956.

MURRAY, HENRY A. "Personality and Creative Imagination." *English Institute Essays,* 1942. New York: Columbia University Press, 1942. Pp. 139–162.

POMMER, HENRY F. *Milton and Melville.* Pittsburgh: University of Pittsburgh Press, 1950.

POULET, GEORGE. *Studies in Human Time,* trans. Elliott Coleman. Baltimore: Johns Hopkins Press, 1956. Pp. 337–341.

SEALTS, MERTON M., JR. *Melville's Reading.* Madison: University of Wisconsin Press, 1967.

SHULMAN, ROBERT. "Melville's 'Timoleon': From Plutarch to the Early Stages of *Billy Budd.*" *Comparative Literature,* XVII (Fall 1967), 351–361.

SUTTON, WALTER. "Melville's 'Pleasure Party' and the Art of Concealment." *Philological Quarterly,* XXX (July 1951), 316–327.

THOMPSON, LAWRANCE. *Melville's Quarrel with God.* Princeton: Princeton University Press, 1952.

THORP, WILLARD, ed. *Herman Melville: Representative Selections.* New York: American Book Company, 1938.

VINCENT, HOWARD P., ed. *Collected Poems of Herman Melville.* Chicago: Packard and Company, Hendricks House, 1947.

WARREN, ROBERT PENN. "Melville the Poet." *The Kenyon Review,* VIII (Spring 1946), 208–223.

WEAVER, RAYMOND. *Herman Melville, Mariner and Mystic.* New York: George H. Doran, 1921.

Index

THE FOLLOWING INDEX contains references to Melville's individual poems, as well as to his short stories (in boldface), and his novels (in boldface italics).

273